Interreligious Resilience

Also Available from Bloomsbury:

All Religion Is Inter-Religion
Edited by Kambiz GhaneaBassiri and Paul Robertson

Contemporary Muslim-Christian Encounters
Edited by Paul Hedges

Ritual Participation and Interreligious Dialogue
Edited by Marianne Moyaert and Joris Geldhof

Interreligious Resilience

Interreligious Leadership for a Pluralistic World

By
Michael S. Hogue and Dean Phillip Bell

BLOOMSBURY ACADEMIC
LONDON • NEW YORK • OXFORD • NEW DELHI • SYDNEY

BLOOMSBURY ACADEMIC
Bloomsbury Publishing Plc
50 Bedford Square, London, WC1B 3DP, UK
1385 Broadway, New York, NY 10018, USA
29 Earlsfort Terrace, Dublin 2, Ireland

BLOOMSBURY, BLOOMSBURY ACADEMIC and the Diana logo are trademarks of
Bloomsbury Publishing Plc

First published in Great Britain 2022
This paperback edition published 2024

Copyright © Michael S. Hogue and Dean Phillip Bell, 2022, 2024

Michael S. Hogue and Dean Phillip Bell have asserted their rights under the Copyright,
Designs and Patents Act, 1988, to be identified as Authors of this work.

For legal purposes the Acknowledgments on pp. vi–viii constitute an extension
of this copyright page.

Cover design: Tjasa Krivec
Cover image: Green reeds at the water with sun shining (© Rike_/Getty Images)

All rights reserved. No part of this publication may be reproduced or transmitted
in any form or by any means, electronic or mechanical, including photocopying,
recording, or any information storage or retrieval system, without prior
permission in writing from the publishers.

Bloomsbury Publishing Plc does not have any control over, or responsibility for, any third-
party websites referred to or in this book. All internet addresses given in this book were
correct at the time of going to press. The author and publisher regret any inconvenience
caused if addresses have changed or sites have ceased to exist, but can accept no
responsibility for any such changes.

A catalogue record for this book is available from the British Library.

Library of Congress Control Number: 2021952919

ISBN: HB: 978-1-3502-1366-1
PB: 978-1-3502-1370-8
ePDF: 978-1-3502-1367-8
eBook: 978-1-3502-1368-5

Typeset by Deanta Global Publishing Services, Chennai, India

To find out more about our authors and books visit www.bloomsbury.com
and sign up for our newsletters.

Contents

Acknowledgments	vi
Introduction: Interreligious Resilience, Why It Matters, and How We Got Here	1

Part 1 Building a Model of Interreligious Resilience

1	Interreligious History and Models: Addressing Religious Supremacy and Religious Pluralism	19
2	Interreligious Contexts: Globalization, Postsecularism, Acceleration, and Polarization	44
3	Interreligious Leadership: Challenges and Opportunities	74
4	Interreligious Resilience	108

Part 2 Practical Application

5	The VITA Pathway of Interreligious Resilience	143
6	Case Studies: From Theory to Practice and From Practice to Theory	151

Notes	203
Bibliography	219
Index	226

Acknowledgments

According to a famous passage from the tractate *Taanit* (23a) of the Babylonian Talmud,

> One day, he [Honi] was walking along the road when he saw a certain man planting a carob tree. Honi said to him: This tree, after how many years will it bear fruit? The man said to him: It will not produce fruit until seventy years have passed. Honi said to him: Is it obvious to you that you will live seventy years, that you expect to benefit from this tree? The man said: I myself found a world of carab trees. Just as my ancestors planted for me, I too am planting for my descendants.

We hope profoundly that the planting we have done in this book will bear fruit and be of value now and in the future. At the same time, we are quite aware that we have benefitted from those who toiled and planted before us—from the scholars whose work we have cited and engaged to the many people who have helped us to think about and interrogate our own thinking about the issues we raise in this book and far beyond. We are grateful to our many thoughtful students in our courses at Meadville Lombard Theological School and Spertus Institute for Jewish Learning and Leadership and in many other workshop sessions we conducted over the past several years, who willingly entertained our musings and helped us to refine our ideas. We are also delighted here to recognize the very helpful feedback (and occasional challenges) from our colleagues Hal Lewis, Russ Rogers, Sharon Welch, and Keren Fraiman (who, among other things, encouraged us to develop the VITA framework we present in the book as we began to teach aspects of this book in a variety of pandemic-era programs). We are also especially grateful to Bloomsbury's Lalle Pursglove, who early on saw the promise of this project and encouraged us throughout.

Of course, we are indebted to our home institutions, which supported our work and provided us a wonderful environment for thinking and collaboration. Thanks to the Wabash Center for Teaching and Learning in Theology and Religion for a grant to develop and co-teach a course on Interreligious Leadership in the early stages of this project. Special thanks to the Arthur Vining Davis Foundation for a generous grant to support extended research, writing, and workshops, as well as course curricula development. And thanks also to Columbia University Press for permission to integrate selected material from Mike's *American Immanence: Democracy for an Uncertain World* (2018) into Chapter 4 of this book.

Dean thanks Sharon Silverman, Spertus Board Chair, and Peter Bensinger, Jr., Immediate Past Chair, for their exemplary leadership and especially for their partnership, intellectual curiosity, and encouragement and support of all aspects of this, and so many other, projects. He thanks Keren Fraiman for her partnership and the intellectual challenges and nourishment that she has provided in every aspect of his work on this project and beyond. She has helped him to think differently, reflect deeply, understand and hold multiple narratives and truths, and always made him think about the goals, effectiveness, and meaning of his teaching and work. Dean thanks Mike for his partnership on this and other projects. Mike is a deep thinker who brings conceptual clarity to every discussion and who inspires Dean with his insights, thoughtful teaching, ability to turn a phrase to make a significant point, and also for his love of family and community and his remarkable friendship. Finally, Dean thanks his family, as always, for their love and support. Juli has been a sounding board and thoughtful interlocutor with whom Dean has rehearsed many of the themes in this volume, even as she has supported him and the entire family with her creative spirit and all that she does. His children—Malkaya, Chanan, Roni, and Yair—have each, in their own ways, opened him to seeing the beauty in the diversity of perspectives and the importance of understanding and engaging with others, central themes in this book and in many of his other projects and explorations.

Mike thanks his colleagues from Meadville Lombard Theological School, especially the inspiring and resilient leadership of Lee Barker, Elias Ortega, Pamela Lightsey, and Cindi Redman. He also thanks his faculty colleagues Elyse Ambrose, Mark Hicks, Nicole Kirk, and Julie Taylor for shaping a community of learning and teaching committed to forming religious leaders for a more just, compassionate, and equitable world. He also would like to thank Meadville's outstanding librarians, John Leeker and Sarah Levine, who have always offered unfailingly expert advice on research matters and have always responded quickly to research requests. Most of all, Mike would like to thank his family. Deepest thanks to Sara, who has always accompanied him through the ups and downs of the writing process, reminding him to trust the process and to keep the larger picture in mind—she has always been his wisest, most understanding, and encouraging counsel. His children—Kincade, Mikaela, and Kamryn—have been some of his greatest teachers, in addition to keeping him laughing and providing him with many creative distractions from work! And finally, Mike would like to thank Dean, whose invigorating collaboration and leadership, scholarship, initiative, curiosity, and friendship have made work on this project, as well as others, such a life-enriching experience through the years.

Introduction

Interreligious Resilience, Why It Matters, and How We Got Here

This book is not about religion. Readers will not learn in this book about the varieties of Buddhism or Islam or any other religious tradition. It is not a book that aims to increase readers' religious literacy. There are plenty of excellent books that do that work. Instead, this book is about interreligious resilience and will be useful to religious and community leaders committed to working more effectively among diversely religious people within and beyond their own faith traditions and communities.

Resilience is often defined as the capacity to cope with disruption or endure change and return to a previous equilibrium or status quo. We believe that there is a deeper, more complex resilience that is characterized by an ability to learn, grow, and lead through vulnerability, disturbances, disruptions, and uncertainty. This more complex form of resilience when applied to interreligious work is what we term interreligious resilience, which can be cultivated and applied through a set of practices that we refer to as VITA—Vulnerability, Intentionality, Trust, and Awareness—key elements to developing deeper and more effective interreligious leadership. While there is a vast literature on effective leadership, which offers many important insights into how to cultivate and practice good leadership, in this book we contend that the lessons learned from a study of interreligious engagement and the application of resilience to the field of interreligious work generally advance leadership in new and helpful ways for today and for the future. What is more, through our own work we know that the approach to interreligious resilience and interreligious leadership that we develop and advocate in this book has broad and useful application in other areas of leadership as well.

Interreligious resilience is an integrative, systemic, and multidimensional approach to interreligious leadership. Other approaches to interreligious leadership focus on the virtues and ideal characteristics and skills of individual leaders, on principles of interreligious dialog and collaboration, or on the religious, theological, or spiritual aspects of interreligious engagement. Although these are all important, and arguably indispensable, aspects of interreligious leadership, all interreligious engagements, whether between individual persons or collaborations among diverse communities, are embedded in and influenced by complex layers of social, historical, and cultural dynamics.

As an integrative, systemic, and multidimensional approach to interreligious leadership, interreligious resilience is a pathway (a way of life, VITA) that can help interreligious leaders to navigate this complexity more effectively. Rather than focusing on either the theological and spiritual or the social and historical, or either the interpersonal and dialogical or the communal and organizational or societal, interreligious resilience offers a new suite of interpretive questions and practices relevant to all these important aspects of interreligious leadership. When integrated into a pathway for interreligious leadership, interreligious resilience enables strategic thinking and engagement across multiple levels or dimensions of interreligious encounter—personal, organizational, communal, and societal. Interreligious resilience is thus an interreligious leadership pathway calibrated to the peculiar differences, difficulties, and dynamics of contemporary religious life and leadership in a multireligious world.

* * *

So, this is a sketch of what this book is about. But who are we? We are good friends who enjoy working together and have learned a great deal from one another, both personally and professionally. But we are otherwise very different. Dean is an early modern European historian and a Jewish studies scholar. Mike is a philosopher of religion and theologian who works primarily with traditions in American philosophy and theology. This means that what Mike thinks of as ancient history, Dean describes as current events; and when Dean does his medievalist thing, Mike wonders what the contemporary moral, theological, or political point is. Nor do we share very many religious commitments. Dean is a Modern Orthodox Jew who keeps kosher, honors the sabbath, and wears a yarmulke (as well as a suit and tie); Mike teaches at a Unitarian Universalist theological school and observes the sabbath by interrogating it, wears a baseball hat, and is most comfortable in shorts and sandals. Although Dean is witty and has a great sense of humor, as a Modern Orthodox Jew he is quite serious about his religious life; although Mike is not particularly witty, his religious life is more playfully suspicious than serious. When it comes to music, Dean likes Black Sabbath (he honors the sabbath!), and Mike likes indie folk. We both drink coffee like fiends, but Dean likes his mellowed out with cream and Mike likes his straight up. So, given our many differences, how in the world is it that we have come to be collaborators on a project such as this?

Let us start by saying we are not interfaith activists, nor are we ordained religious professionals. Given that we are neither of these things, a discerning reader may wonder what expertise or authority we have with respect to the topic of this book! In addition to this, you may also notice that we just used the term "interfaith" whereas up to this point we have been using the term "interreligious." We think this is an important distinction that helps to explain where we are coming from. In making this distinction, we are not levelling a critique of the interfaith movement, which we think is very important and which many of our students, friends, and colleagues are gifted for. Not all religious people understand their religious lives and commitments through the concept of "faith," which has primarily Western and theistic roots, and tends, especially in our US American context, to have an individualistic and a belief-oriented focus. "Interreligious" is meant to encompass a wider diversity of religious options.[1] The "inter-" in "interreligious" refers to the many types and levels of interactions between and among diversely religious people. In this sense, interreligious is different from "multireligious," which is a term that for us simply describes the social fact of religious diversity. We live in a multireligious world, which is to say a world in which there are not only different religions but also different ways of being religious. Whereas "multireligious" describes this social fact, "interreligious," as we are using the term, refers to interactions among diverse religious actors intentionally engaging one another across their different ways of being religious. At times, we may use the term "intrareligious" to discuss differences internal to traditions, because we strongly believe that these differences are often as significant and difficult to navigate as differences between traditions.

If we are "not this, not that" (neti neti), neither interfaith activists nor ordained religious leaders, then who and what are we, and what qualifies us to write a book such as this? In terms of our vocational identities, we are educator-scholars committed to teaching, researching, and writing about religion in ways that increase human understanding and contribute to a world that is more humane, equitable, and compassionate. But these values in themselves do not provide us with the expertise to write this book. Instead, our expertise comes through a combination of institutional, professional, and personal experiences as well as shared theoretical pursuits. We are leaders and teachers in educational institutions that train religious professionals, ministers, rabbis, chaplains, religious educators, interfaith community organizers, faith-based social justice activists, and more. This means that a good portion of our teaching is "formational," to use a favored abstraction among theological educators. Formation refers to a type of education that is not simply about the depositing of knowledge or the acquisition of skills. It is about shaping dispositions, cultivating habits, and nurturing modes of understanding that religious and community leaders need in an ever-changing, culturally and religiously diverse, and morally complex world.

Our students and institutional contexts are religiously diverse. Although most of Mike's students are Unitarian Universalist, if you know anything about Unitarian Universalism, you will know that he teaches in a tradition that, especially in its US American form, is theologically and culturally diverse. Most of his students are religiously hyphenated. Although Unitarianism and Universalism have deep theological lineages in Christianity, and although these lineages morphed over time into Protestant Christian denominations, most Unitarian Universalists today do not think of Unitarian Universalism as a Christian denomination. Instead, they think of Unitarian Universalism as an inclusive liberal religious movement with Christian historical roots that provides a communal context in which they can explore and integrate diverse theological, spiritual, ethical, and devotional practices. It is an experiment in inter-theological and inter-spiritual communal learning and worship. All this is to say that Mike's institutional context is culturally, theologically, and spiritually diverse, precisely because it is primarily Unitarian Universalist. He also knows that although Unitarian Universalists tend to think of themselves as special cases, this internal theological and spiritual diversity is not that unusual—all traditions are constituted by internal diversity. Although most of Dean's students are Jewish, his institutional context is nondenominational and offers courses to students from other traditions as well. He teaches Reform, Reconstructionist, Orthodox, Conservative, and Humanistic Jews, among others. Our staff and faculty colleagues are diversely religious as well. We teach and work every day with spiritual-but-not-religious (SBNRs), agnostics, atheists, "nones," and all variety of Unitarian Universalists and Jews. While most of our students are US American, we teach students from many other nations as well, including Chile, Hungary, Japan, India, South Africa, Nigeria, Kenya, and Israel. And in addition to all that we have learned through our interreligious engagements with our students and colleagues, we have also learned a great deal through chavruta with one another.

In terms of our religious commitments and identities, Mike has been deeply formed by his years of work among Unitarian Universalists, currently is a member of a Methodist church, for many years was involved with an Episcopal church, and was raised as a "pastor's kid" in the United Church of Christ. He sometimes describes himself as culturally Protestant with an Anglo-Catholic liturgical aesthetic and Unitarian Universalist ethic. In short, he is a religious hybrid, and happily owns it because he thinks the same is true of most religious people, more or less! In other words, and foreshadowing a later discussion of his philosophical commitments, Mike understands that religious difference is internally constitutive of his religious identity, as well as a reality in his relation to religious others.

Like his religious identity, Mike's scholarship has always been conjunctive. He describes his work as socially engaged theology, which is to say theology concerned with modern ethical and political issues, especially life in a time of intersecting social and ecological crises. His previous books have compared different theological approaches to environmental responsibility, examined diverse ways of integrating naturalistic and religious worldviews, and explored the intersection of political theology and climate justice. He situates himself as a scholar within the naturalist, process, and pragmatist traditions in American philosophy and theology. Given the ambivalent place of God within these traditions, he sometimes refers to them as the left-wing of American radical theology. He is also profoundly informed by the basic impulses of liberation theology, which is to say that, for him, theology is less about systematizing and justifying beliefs than it is about the holy work of imagining and realizing a more socially, economically, and environmentally just world. The relevance of his scholarly orientation to this book project is that it means he is especially inclined toward the philosophical and theological aspects of interreligious engagement and leadership and is committed to the importance of this work not only for spiritual but also for ethical and political reasons. Ethical and political responses to complex global problems, such as the climate emergency, require wisdom, experience, insight, and expertise from diverse religious, cultural, and disciplinary perspectives. But learning and collaborating across diversity requires an empathic intercultural imagination—the capacity to listen actively and learn deeply from different points of view across diverse cultural contexts. Interreligious engagement is a powerful means for building this type of imagination.

Dean has always been interested in the social history of ideas and his approach to religion, personally and professionally, has focused on how ideas and practice intersect and how their contexts shape both. In work on Jewish and Christian relations and on Jewish communal structures in late medieval and early modern Germany he has been struck by the symbioses as much as by the conflicts. In a real sense, however, neither can really be understood in isolation. Despite long-standing notions of "lachrymose" history, which has asserted that Jewish history was about great scholars on one hand (usually taken in a predominantly Jewish setting, with less regard to the influences and instigations of the broader world) and persecution of Jews on the other (which has typically assumed that the primary form of interaction Jews had with the "external" world was one of animosity), Dean has participated in pioneering efforts to see more nuance and to recognize the impact that broader social and historical trends have had on Jewish experiences. Even in the age of the ghetto, Jews never lived completely separate existences, Dean has discovered. Mutual influence—in all the places that Jews have lived throughout history, including during the rabbinic period and, even before there was Rabbinic Judaism, when ancient Israelites inhabited the Ancient Near East—affected the communities and cultures in which Jews lived and Jews themselves drew from these influences, adopting some prevailing norms in religious rites as well as social and communal structures, and contesting and reacting to others in the quest to define and shape their own lives and societies.

From this standpoint, Dean's work, consciously or not, has always been about interreligious engagement and, to the extent that he has focused on community and leadership, about interreligious leadership. Before he knew about the concepts of resilience and vulnerability, Dean would have likely pointed to many aspects of the Jewish history he studied and found latent in them these very ideas. Dean's own religious life is similarly infused with commitment both to tradition and active discussion and questioning. From his perspective, religious life provides structure and meaning, along with moral and ethical guidelines, and opportunities to think about how to grow as an individual and apply aspects of Judaism to address and solve contemporary and emerging issues within and beyond the Jewish community—what he likes to refer to as "applied Jewish learning." Interreligious resilience, with its emphasis on engaging vulnerability and openness, thinking in larger systems, understanding one's own tradition while opening oneself to the perspectives of others and the ongoing quest to make meaning and positively impact the world aligns perfectly with how he sees his religious observance and his work in applied Jewish learning.

And yet there is more to the story of our collaboration that helps to explain the difference that we believe makes a difference in our approach to interreligious engagement. It all goes back to the primal elements of coffee and conversation. But there is no "ex nihilo" in the creation of this collaboration—it is plural and relational all the way down. On his way up the elevator one day, Dean had a brief conversation about his interest in environmental history with one of Mike's colleagues and friends, Sharon Welch. Sharon, who has a gift for connecting people and ideas, told Dean that he should meet Mike, since Mike also works in the religion and the environment area. So, after an initial email exchange, we met for coffee. Mike told Dean about the importance of resilience and vulnerability theory in the book he was writing on political theology and the climate. At the time, Dean was working on a book that interpreted medieval Christian and Jewish responses to the plague, about half a millennium prior to the time period in which Mike was working.

Although these might seem like quite different projects, both were concerned with the impact of massive environmental and social disruptions on the ways religious people make meaning, build and sustain religious community, and relate to one another across their differences. Through discussion, it became clear to Dean that the concepts of resilience and vulnerability could be very useful in his work. Thus, while Mike's book integrated theories of resilience and vulnerability into a theology of democratic pluralism for twenty-first-century planetary and political disruptions, Dean's book used them as hermeneutic categories to illuminate the ways early modern European Jewish and Christian (and to some extent Islamic as well) communities interpreted their texts and traditions and interacted with one another as they responded to the traumas of mass illness and death. In short, both books used the concepts of resilience and vulnerability to make sense of how religious communities work together and against one another in times of crisis.

This brief origin story about our interreligious collaboration allows us to underscore the idea that in addition to functioning as tools that can facilitate more effective interreligious leadership, the concepts of resilience and vulnerability themselves can function as vehicles for such engagement. In other words, they have value as comparative and interpretive categories across religious traditions. Resilience and vulnerability have analogs across religious traditions and exploring these can illuminate new ways of inhabiting our own religious traditions, new ways to learn about and from others, and new approaches to interreligious leadership.

To explain why we think interreligious resilience is relevant to these concerns it is important for us also to discuss the practical bearing of some of our broader philosophical and pedagogical commitments, and in particular, aspects of process philosophy and postmodern thought. Probably the most important source for modern process philosophy is the work of Alfred North Whitehead (1861–1947). The language of Whitehead is notoriously difficult and there is no need in this context to elaborate his philosophy in much detail.[2] What is relevant in this context is to say that for Whitehead, what is fundamentally real, from the quantum to the cosmic, from plants to persons, are relational events. To say this is to say that the identities of individual things are internally constituted through their relation to the differences of other things: to be is to be in relation to others. The whole of reality for Whitehead is in process and always changing. The universe is less a universe of discrete things, substances, or beings than of things continuously becoming through relational processes. The universe, and all of reality, is a relational event comprised of interrelated and intrarelated events. Nothing exists independently of other things. This does not mean that each thing is related to *all* other things, but that nothing that exists, exists apart from *many* other things, and those relations through which things exist are internally *constitutive* rather than merely externally *correlated*. In other words, things do not first exist independently and then relate to one another; rather, things become what they are in and through relationships to others. Things at all levels and scales become what they are through their relations to the relational becoming of other things. Whitehead, who was originally a mathematician, evocatively described this relational understanding of reality as the process whereby the "many become one and are increased by one."[3]

This picture of reality is pervasively relational and dynamic. It runs against the tendency, especially among those who have been enculturated in the modern West, to perceive, experience, and think about the world and their own identities as individual, isolable, and independent. These patterns have become sedimented into the psychic lives and cognitive habits of many of us in countless subtle ways—from the subject-predicate structure of language to patterns of classification, from the idea that religious traditions are monolithic, self-subsisting entities to atomistic views of the self. This leads to thinking about things in isolation from one another, such that a thing or person is identified by way of its independence, difference, and even opposition to other things and persons. But for Whitehead and the broader tradition of process philosophy, all reality, including people, symbols, and cultural and religious traditions, are who and what they are through their relation to other things and people. We become who and what we are through innumerable relational events, just as is true of everything else that exists.

Paul Knitter illustrates the interreligious resonance of this way of thinking. Alluding to Whitehead, he writes, "The many are called to be one. But it is a one that does not devour the many. The many become one precisely by remaining the many, and the one is brought about by each of the many making its distinct contribution to the others and thus to the whole."[4] Knitter's concern here is to show that although a process orientation to the world is deeply relational, the differences between and among things, including people and traditions, are not subsumed into one another. A relational vision of interreligious life does not dilute religious identities or reduce religious differences, although it can, as we are suggesting, lead to a way of imagining and engaging differences as (potentially) mutually enriching contrasts rather than mutually exclusive oppositions. Along this vein, Knitter continues, "Whereas individualization is weakened, personalization is intensified; the individual finds its true self as part of other selves. So there is a movement not toward absolute or monistic oneness, but toward what might be called 'unitive pluralism': plurality constituting unity."[5]

Sometimes when we work with students to think through the social implications of process philosophy, we make a culinary distinction. An old and, we think, problematic culinary metaphor for US American diversity is the image of a "melting pot." We call this the "stew" metaphor. Diverse ingredients are dropped into a pot and, if cooked long enough, their distinct flavors and textures reduce into a single flavor and texture—for instance, the carrots feel like potatoes, and both the potatoes and carrots taste something like the beef. This stew metaphor is problematic as a social ideal because the homogenous something that the diverse ingredients reduce into is dominated by a single ingredient—in our version of the metaphor, the beef (or "Americanness," or even more specifically, "White Christian Americanness").

The melting pot is a bad metaphor for society and interreligious engagement and leadership for two reasons. First, it reinforces the idea that for a diverse society to function, the cultural, religious, and other differences that shape our identities need to be dissolved into a mushy, least common denominator. And second, the mushy, least common denominator that diversity is supposed to dissolve into is not neutral but is instead normed by the identity of a dominant cultural and racial group (or stew ingredient).

In place of the "melting pot" or "stew" metaphor, we believe process philosophy supports a "stir fry" metaphor. As in a stew, a stir fry includes diverse ingredients—for instance, carrots, pea pods, peppers, onion, chicken, cashews, broccoli. But in a good stir fry, those diverse ingredients are cooked and combined in such a way that they enhance one another's differences rather than reduce to a mush. Somehow the carrots taste and feel more like carrots, as do the peppers, chicken, cashews, and other ingredients, not despite the other ingredients, but because of their contrasting textures and flavors.

In addition to process thought, many aspects of postmodern thought are useful in thinking about interreligious leadership. The importance of context, the multifaceted notion of truth, and the complexity of essentialism, along with the depth and nuance of language—which embeds and reflects power and culture, even as it constructs both—are important and will be discussed in various parts of this book. In a similar vein, much of literary criticism and postmodern thinking raises issues and questions that are central to interreligious encounters. Michel de Certeau, for example, in *The Writing of History*, notes that historians begin from present determinations and current events and they assemble signifiers, not facts. All historical interpretation depends upon a system of reference; history is less the "real" than the "intelligible"; and history occupies a social place, such that historians civilize, colonize, and change nature. Like so much else, truth has consequently become seen as more relational and perspectival than absolute.[6] As such, the emphasis and skill building around relationship dynamics seem particularly relevant in interreligious leadership. At the same time, the emphasis in postmodern thinking on the role of interpretation, which itself provides meaning to a text or situation, necessitates the cultivation of hermeneutic skills and sensitivities.[7]

One additional aspect of postmodernism that is important relates to the ideas of otherness and alterity and the relation of self and other. These ideas have been significant in a good deal of philosophical writing and literary theory since the middle of the twentieth century and have intersected with advances in interreligious dialog as well as a host of academic disciplines and developing academic fields. Postmodern sensibilities, and associated historical ideas, often revolve around concepts of selectivity and self. For historians, for instance, everything begins with setting aside and collecting (for historians, this is the case with documents and archives). The choices we make about which documents and archives to examine, what to include and exclude, are powerful. They constrain and are constrained by our worldviews, experiences, and social location. But selection also assumes separation, another important postmodern concept. The discipline of historical research begins with the differentiation of present and past, and yet we never succeed in dissociating the past and present completely. History is played out along the margins that join a society with its past and with the very act of separating itself from that past. The study of religion, especially as developed and defined (in Western ways) in the nineteenth century, has also often contended with questions about boundaries and separation. What are the rituals, beliefs, myths, and practices that define and differentiate religious traditions? What are the categories and concerns that bind and forge identities, how do those compare across traditions, and how do encounters with and inquiries about other traditions shape our religious self-understanding of our own religious lives?

Questions such as these illustrate how interreligious engagement and leadership entail an encounter with alterity and careful thinking about the relation of self and other. Emmanuel Levinas's ethics of responsibility is helpful in this regard. For Levinas, "Only a being who is responsible for another being can enter into dialogue with it. Responsibility, in the etymological sense of the term, not the mere exchange of words, is what is meant by dialogue, and it is only in the former case that there is meeting."[8] We cannot really understand cultural and religious others through our own lenses or religious or cultural categories. Thus, Levinas argues that we must be responsible for the other before we can meet the other in genuine dialog.

Summarizing Levinas's ideas about this, philosopher of religion and interreligious scholar Ryan Urbano writes that receptive learning from and about the other stems from an initial "vulnerability to the ethical appeal of the Other . . . with the aim . . . to respect the radical alterity of the Other."[9] Dialog is a meeting of two or more participants who share an active intention to communicate with one another and share experiences.[10] Interreligious dialog is thus much more than a mutual exchange of information and very different from the academic study of religion.[11] Serious interreligious dialog requires mutual respect, deep listening, sincerity, openness, and the willingness to be in a relationship with others.[12] According to Francis Cardinal Arinze, such dialog is "a meeting of heart and mind between followers of various religions. It is communication between two believers at the religious level. It is a walking together towards truth and a working together in projects of common concern. It is a religious partnership without hidden agendas or motives."[13] Interreligious dialog, therefore, requires trust between partners, and it is a dynamic and not a static activity.

Similarly, Raimon Panikkar has argued that our relationship with the other is not external, but rather part of our innermost constitution:

> When we limit our field to human relationships, we see that the other is not just a producer of ideas with which we agree more or less, or just a bearer of affinities that make possible a number of transactions; it is neither a mere (other) subject nor a mere (other) object. It is a person who is not my ego, and yet it belongs to my Self. This is what makes communication and communion possible. This awareness is the dawn of the *"dialogical dialogue."* The thou emerges as different from the non-I.[14]

The other plays a truly vital role—in short, it is another source of self-understanding.[15] To really get to this point, Panikkar suggests that we need to be vulnerable and examine our own presuppositions: "But this we cannot do alone. We need the other. We are more or less conscious of our assumptions, that is, of the axioms or convictions that we put at the starting point and use as foundation of our views."[16] While we do not need to forego our beliefs and convictions, we must dispense with apologetics and polemics.[17] Panikkar writes that "A religious dialogue must first of all be an authentic dialogue, without superiority, preconceptions, hidden motives, or convictions on either side."[18] Dialog for Panikkar, therefore, must involve two languages encountering each other and passing through the intellect to encounter the whole person.[19] He concludes: "I foresee a new and fundamental function of dialogue in the encounter of religions. The first aim was to better know each other, to dispel fears and misinterpretations. A second role was that of mutual influence and fecundation. I envisage now a third function: that of positively contributing to the new self-understanding of both sides."[20]

This possibility of new intrareligious self-understanding through interreligious resilience is a significant concern for us in this book. This "third function" of interreligious engagement invites interreligious leaders to participate in the creation of something new for themselves and for the religious people and communities they serve—a new mode, insight, or dimension of religious life. This is the reason we use the acronym VITA, the Latin word for "life," to name the practices of interreligious resilience. We believe interreligious leaders can cultivate new possibilities of intrareligious life by bringing the practices of interreligious resilience into everyday interreligious encounters. We ourselves have experienced this with each other and through working with religious leaders and students from many traditions through the years. These institutional and personal experiences in combination with our scholarly inclinations provide us with perspective on the many challenges and blessings of interreligious leadership which we look forward to sharing with you in the chapters ahead.

Chapter Summaries

The chapters of the book contextualize and advance the case for interreligious resilience in several steps. Part I is comprised of Chapters 1–4. Chapter 1 articulates the motivating theses of interreligious resilience, offers a brief history of interreligious engagement, and surveys exemplary theories of interreligious leadership. Our critical thesis is about the structure and societal effects of religious supremacy. We define religious supremacy as a structure of reinforcing patterns of belief and belonging—monopolistic truth, oppositional identity, exclusionary belonging. Following the important work of intercultural and interreligious scholar Perry Schmidt-Leukel, we argue that these patterns have a fractal structure, such that they show up across traditions and are not directly correlated to specific religious doctrines or religious traditions.[21] As Schmidt-Leukel describes it, "The nucleus of the [fractal interpretation of religious diversity] is that the diversity that we observe *among* the religions globally is mirrored in the diversity that we find *within* each of the major religious traditions."[22] Our constructive thesis argues that religions themselves possess the antibodies to the poison of religious supremacy and that interreligious resilience, as a pathway for constructive interreligious leadership, can catalyze an antidote.

Chapter 2 addresses the question of what is different, and uniquely difficult, about interreligious leadership in today's world. Religions and religious people have interacted all through human history, so the facts of religious diversity and interreligious encounters are not new. But certain historically specific social, cultural, and political aspects of contemporary life make the work of interreligious leadership both especially difficult and important. This chapter illuminates the historical specificity of the contemporary context by tracing linkages between globalization, postsecularism, social acceleration, polarization, and religious supremacy. We show how polarization and the religious supremacy fractal mutually amplify one another and function as vectors of other types of hierarchy, suspicion, and supremacy. Even if these phenomena are not often consciously understood or explicitly articulated in all interreligious encounters, they are not merely background contexts of interest to sociologists and historians. Rather, they should be understood as foreground realities in the lives of actual people, including the people with whom interreligious leaders work. A basic understanding of these phenomena and their relation to one another provides critical context for interreligious leadership in today's world.

Chapter 3 critically examines several of the most prominent and frequently discussed theories of leadership generally. We note both the valuable insights provided by these studies as well as some of the core assumptions and limitations that are inherent in their approaches and models. We then review some of the most recent work on interreligious leadership, pointing out the similarities to, and differences from, the general leadership literature. Much of the work in this chapter is based on surveys we conducted with diverse religious leaders; discussions we had with students (clergy, seminarians, and chaplains) in a course we co-taught on vulnerability, resilience, and religious leadership that enrolled nearly thirty students from North America, South America, Europe, Asia, and Africa, from a variety of Christian, Jewish, Muslim, Hindu, and Buddhist traditions; feedback from a dozen workshops on the themes of vulnerability, resilience, and interreligious leadership with a variety of groups of clergy, educators, and communal service professionals; and a broad literature review. In the concluding section of this chapter, we present some overarching concepts from studies of resilience and vulnerability and suggest a new model of leadership that we believe is particularly well-suited and attuned to interreligious leadership in the volatile and ever-shifting conditions of today and the future.

In Chapter 4, we discuss several classic and contemporary theories of religion and present a new way of thinking about religion and interreligious engagement through the prism of vulnerability and resilience theory. Our purpose is not to present a new general theory of religion that seeks to replace others, but to articulate a set of bridge concepts that can empower interreligious leaders to think in novel ways about the substance and purposes of interreligious engagement in a globalizing, postsecular, accelerating, and polarized world. Our point, in other words, is not that resilience and vulnerability theory can finally explain what religion is, but that reimagining religion and religious life through the lenses of resilience and vulnerability can be useful to interreligious leaders working in the peculiar contexts of the contemporary world. A core idea is that interreligious resilience is not simply a characteristic of individual leaders, but that it is an intercommunal and social aim, one that can help us to transform a diversely religious world into a more creatively pluralistic one.

In Part II we turn to a practical application of the ideas and theories developed in Part I. In Chapter 5 we draw from the resilience and vulnerability approach to religion developed in Part I to craft and shape the VITA pathway into a suite of strategic and interpretive practices. The aim of VITA is to cultivate interreligious resilience and move us toward a more pluralistic world.

Chapter 6 concludes the book with fourteen case studies in which readers can experiment with VITA and the interreligious resilience pathway. These are not cases drawn from the headlines but rather composites (with made-up names and organizations) based on interreligious scenarios shared with us in our survey of diverse religious leaders and our own professional experiences. They are not extraordinary cases, or cases that one might find in a dramatic docuseries. Instead, and quite pointedly, they are cases that are as fraught and complex as everyday life is in our globalizing, postsecular, acceleratory, and polarized world. The cases attend to various issues and contexts of interreligious leadership, including, among others, chaplaincy in interreligious settings, interreligious space sharing, interreligious leadership in contexts of intercommunal violence, addressing interreligious stereotyping and prejudice, questions of interreligious conflict mediation and education, interreligious responses to natural disasters and care for displaced people, and working across religious divides to address broader social and communal concerns and needs. Questions for reflection, based on VITA, are included at the end of each case study. These cases offer a valuable means of applying theory to practice and helping interreligious leaders to approach the complex range of questions and challenges they face in new and productive ways. As we have learned in our own work, the VITA framework is also valuable in other areas of leadership and can be applied in diverse settings.

We believe the pathway of interreligious resilience that we present in this book is especially useful for several reasons. First, it integrates theory and practice by situating the practical tasks of interreligious leadership in the contexts of broad social trends and conditions. Second, it provides a systemic framework for interreligious leadership that can be applied to diverse issues and challenges of interreligious engagement. And third, rather than being focused primarily on interpersonal interreligious encounters or interreligious dialog, it presents a multidimensional framework that is relevant at different scales. For these reasons, this book is specifically for interreligious leaders and other community leaders working with diversely religious people in the contemporary world.

We hope that this book will show why interreligious leadership is more important now even though it is in some ways more difficult than ever before, especially given the challenges and uncertainties that have plagued and will continue to plague us individually, organizationally, communally, and socially in the future, even in ways we cannot predict or comprehend. A second aim of this volume is to introduce a resilience and vulnerability theory of religion and religious life, drawing from a rich and exciting literature and applying it to contemporary challenges and questions. That is, we seek to demonstrate the relevance and efficacy of resilience and vulnerability to interreligious leadership and introduce interreligious resilience as a new integrative, systemic, and multidimensional approach to interreligious leadership. We hope that this book will provide readers with real-world cases so they can practice working with the interreligious resilience pathway. In that way, this book is a modest, but we hope a useful, development of some new practices and approaches to interreligious leadership and, by extension, leadership in other contexts as well.

Part 1

Building a Model of Interreligious Resilience

1

Interreligious History and Models

Addressing Religious Supremacy and Religious Pluralism

Religious Supremacy and Religious Pluralism

We have written this book because we are deeply worried about the kind of world we are living in and that our students and children are inhabiting—a world of increasing cultural and political polarization, religious intolerance, rising social and economic inequality, racial hostility and grievance, unprecedented global ecological, social, and health crises, and surging ethnonationalism and right-wing authoritarianism. These are global challenges, although locally they manifest and are experienced in different ways. But a world that is as divided and polarized as ours, a world of mutual suspicion and radical inequality, is incapable of effectively responding to social, moral, and political challenges such as these.

As Pope Francis wrote in a recent encyclical, *Fratelli Tutti*, global problems like the Covid-19 pandemic expose the false securities and profound fragmentation of the world.[1] Too many of us think of ourselves, and the planet, as invulnerable, and despite global digital interconnectivity and economic and ecological interdependence, the many ways we divide ourselves from one another persist. The divisions within our communities of identity and belonging, national, religious, and otherwise, can be as debilitating as the divisions between them. While our global challenges must be addressed by global initiatives, global initiatives cannot get off the ground if we are fragmented and polarized at local levels.

Although there are many legitimate approaches to the overwhelming challenges of life in the twenty-first century, our interest in this book is on the constructive role of interreligious leadership. Our view is that a resilience and vulnerability approach to interreligious engagement can help us not only to cross over, learn from, and collaborate with religious others, but that learning how to do these things can help us to work across other types of differences, including racial and political differences. Thus, although our focus is on interreligious issues, this focus is imbricated with, and to no small extent motivated by, a concern with the challenges of relating across other kinds of difference as well, all within a context in which globally entangled social, political, and ecological challenges require cross-difference collaboration and trust-building.

Since we are not politicians, journalists, or policy makers, but religious educators and scholars, we exorcise our anxieties and exercise our responsibilities by teaching and writing books. Through numerous conversations, as well as co-teaching and research, we have shaped our anxieties and our sense of responsibility into two orienting theses, one critical and the other constructive.

Our critical thesis is that much of the fear and loathing pervading our world, present and past, is culturally formatted by patterns of religious supremacy. More precisely, we believe that the logic of religious supremacy is fractal.[2] By this we mean that it is not exclusive to any religious tradition, historical moment, or religious doctrine, but is a pattern of belief and belonging that shows up across and within traditions, and that it functions as a vector and amplifier of other contemporary social challenges, from political polarization to racial supremacy and the global surge of ethnonationalism. Our constructive thesis is that interreligious resilience is a counter-fractal to religious supremacy and that the cultivation of interreligious resilience is conducive to the broader ideal of social pluralism. In other words, we believe that interreligious engagement can be a direct path to undoing patterns of religious supremacy, and that theories of resilience and vulnerability offer a new set of tools for interreligious leaders as they navigate various types and levels of interreligious engagement.

The connections between religious and other social pathologies have long been recognized. As interreligious scholar Diana Eck has observed, "[T]he past 100 years have provided ample evidence that religions are still powerful producers of symbolic weaponry for the strife of humankind."[3] There is no religion and no place in the world that is immune from religiously stoked and sanctioned violence: "[R]eligious rhetoric and the communal power of religious identity have been employed in Northern Ireland, the Middle East, and Sri Lanka, in the Sikh separatist movement in the Punjab, and in the competition between Muslims and Christians in sub-Saharan Africa."[4] The same is true in Europe and the United States, where recent years have seen an increase in white Christian ethnonationalism and anti-Semitism, and in India, with the ascendance of Hindu chauvinism and the Bharatiya Janata Party.

Nor are religiously fueled violence and hatred recent phenomena. Religious supremacy, organized around particular practices of religious belief and belonging, has legitimated and intensified human conflict and division throughout history. According to the Christian philosopher of religion John Hick, "almost all human conflicts have been validated and intensified by a religious sanction." And the reason for this, according to Hick, is that "each of the great world faiths has either assumed or asserted its own unique superiority as the one and only true faith and path to the highest good. . . . These exclusive claims to absolute truth have exacerbated the division of the human community into rival groups, and have repeatedly been invoked in support of oppression, slavery, conquest, and exploitation."[5]

Absolutist and exclusive modes of religious belief are constitutive of what we mean by religious supremacy, and there is no doubt that they have contributed to the history of religious violence. But along with Eck we would add that these modes of belief create divisions within the religions at least as much as between them. As Eck writes, "At present, the greatest religious tensions are not between any one religion and another; they are the tensions between the fundamentalist and the pluralist in each and every religious tradition."[6] If this is so, then religious supremacy, and the strife, conflict, and violence sanctioned by it, is not an essential feature of all religions or specific religions. Rather, religious supremacy emerges through patterns of belief and belonging that show up across and within them. Comparative theologian John Thatamanil illustrates these patterns well: "I can understand God without help from you. In the quest for religious truth, I don't need you if you aren't part of my tradition."[7]

While it is undoubtedly true that people throughout history have caused great harm in the name of religion, it is also true that the religions are and have been existentially and socially liberating, morally orienting, aesthetically inspiring, and intellectually deepening. The religions and forms of religiosity certainly have divided people, but religions also contain wisdom that attunes minds and hearts to sacred ideals and values that transcend individual and group interests and inspire works of compassion, love, and justice. As Hick puts it,

> religion has been responsible for the saintly lives of men and women who have risen above self-centeredness to serve God or to live out the Dharma; it has been a major influence in such developments as the abolition of slavery, the beginning of the liberation of women, the struggle against racial discrimination, the rise of political concern for the unjustly disadvantaged and the search for international disarmament and world peace.[8]

And yet "religion has [also] sanctioned human sacrifices and the torture and burning of 'witches' and 'heretics'; it has blessed almost every war that has ever been fought; and it has been used as an instrument for gaining power over and exploiting large groups of people, bestowing its validation upon massively inequitable social systems."[9] In short, all religions are guilty of inciting conflict and violence, and all religions have worked for compassion, justice, and peace—no religion has a monopoly on violence or good. If it is true that religions have been an agent and accomplice of transformative good as well as great harm, then perhaps the religions themselves contain the antidote to their own poisons.

The tools of resilience and vulnerability theory can help us to engage religious others, even those within our own traditions who practice belief and belonging differently, in constructive new ways. They can help us to sustain these engagements and build relational rapport across our differences by helping us discover that our religious values are not the only important religious values, our religious ideals are not the only ideals worthy of reverence, and our rituals are not the only meaningful rituals. This can lead to modes of belief and belonging that are faithful to our traditions and can also foster pluralism, mutual learning, and collaboration.

We believe the concept of interreligious resilience that we develop in this book is an antidote to religious supremacy. It is a personal and communal condition for the broader social ideal of pluralism, which we will now examine a bit more closely. By pluralism we are not merely referring to the differences and diversities that are "out there" in the world, but to a mindset or attitude toward difference, one that individual religious people can cultivate, and religious communities can nurture and transmit. Pluralism does not presume the abandonment of deep religious commitment to a specific religious tradition. As Eck describes it, rather than "giving up the distinctiveness of [one's] own tradition," pluralism is about "engaging the other in the mutual education, and potentially, the mutual transformation of dialogue."[10] Eck articulates four aspects of pluralism: (1) pluralism is not merely respect for diversity, but energetic engagement of diversity; (2) pluralism is not merely the tolerance of difference, but the active effort to build understanding across difference; (3) pluralism is not the abandonment of commitments or religious ambivalence, but the encounter of commitments; and (4) pluralism is based on dialog.[11]

Pluralism is thus a way of embodying and expressing religious identity and interpreting and navigating religious difference, such that those differences are not experienced as a threat to be avoided or defeated. A pluralist mindset explores religious differences as opportunities for mutual learning that can lead to the creative deepening of diverse religious paths—the learning does not lead one away from one's own religious commitments, but more fully into them. Pluralism is a mindset and a social aim that can be developed within all religious traditions. It is not a departure from the truths of distinctive religious traditions, but an interpretation of religious difference that can be understood as internally compatible with, even entailed by, a commitment to those distinctive truths.[12] To speak of religious diversity, on the other hand, is simply to speak of the objective reality of religious difference in the world—there are different religious truths and different religious aims; diverse accounts of the divine, sacred, and holy; diverse conceptions of God and religious ideals; diverse ways of worshipping and practicing; different institutional and organizational forms of religious life; and much of this diversity exists within as well as between the religious traditions.

Pluralism is also different from tolerance. Tolerance presumes a negative understanding of religious difference, whereas pluralism presumes a positive appreciation of religious difference.[13] Tolerance is a relatively low bar. At its best, tolerance is an attitude of indifference to religious difference, a "live and let live" attitude; but it is often embodied as a patronizing response to religious difference. As Goethe once put this, "To tolerate is to insult."[14] With this in mind, Jewish philosopher Paul Mendes-Flohr argues that the ideal of tolerance is problematic for numerous conceptual and practical reasons. Practically, for instance, does tolerance entail that the intolerable should be tolerated? If not, where should lines be drawn, and on which or whose terms? As Mendes-Flohr notes, law in liberal democratic societies is "crafted to ensure the maximal freedom and thus diversity of opinion and practice," but often "has difficulty in drawing the lines between toleration and legal censure. The civic duty to tolerate and the moral injunction to oppose what is objectionable are often in conflict, if not seemingly irreconcilable."[15]

Besides the legal and moral dilemmas of tolerance, there is something condescending in the very idea of tolerance. An implicit assumption of those who claim tolerance is that that they are following the true and right way, and others are not, but so long as the others are not causing harm (especially to them), or somehow infringing upon or challenging what is really true and right, there is no need to worry. Or, tolerance could be rooted in a humanistic or ethical universalism, which holds that there is something essentially the same beneath all the cultural and historical accretions of religious difference. Because the distinct particulars of different religious traditions do not substantively matter according to this view, they can be ignored, or dismissed. The problem with this type of tolerance, of course, is that it is not really a way of engaging difference at all. Rather, it is a form of intercultural minimization, presented in the guise of philosophical sophistication or cultural liberalism; but it treats differences as superficial, and in so doing illiberally dismisses the self-understanding of the practitioners of different traditions.

As a social ideal, pluralism aims for the possibility that religious differences, as well as other kinds of difference, can be positively appreciated and mutually enriching. The pluralist assumes not only that different religions possess or aim for different truths but also that encounters with those different truths can help to enlarge, deepen, or further illuminate one's own religious path. Thus, an important difference between pluralism and tolerance is that the pluralist seeks to appreciate and learn from religious differences, rather than merely to put up with them, avoid them, or deny that there is anything possible to learn from them.

What we are suggesting, then, is that appreciating and learning from religious difference entails a certain interreligious vulnerability, the risk of opening oneself to learning with and from the religious other. The practice of engaging this interreligious vulnerability is essential to the cultivation of interreligious resilience since vulnerability is at the core of resilience (and the first key component of the VITA pathway to interreligious resilience). And interreligious resilience is spiritually deepening and contributes to the social aim of religious pluralism by enabling us to continue risking the vulnerability of ongoing religious learning.

So, interreligious resilience is an antidote to religious supremacy as well as a step toward pluralism, and interreligious vulnerability is a pathway to interreligious resilience. This may seem counterintuitive, especially if one thinks of resilience and vulnerability as opposed and distinct from one another. But, as we will discuss more fully in Chapter 4, the reality is that resilience is developed through vulnerability: resilience is a learned personal, communal, or systemic capacity that can only be cultivated through the experience of vulnerability. The task of interreligious leaders, as expressed in our constructive thesis, is to facilitate interreligious encounters such that the practice of interreligious vulnerability can lead to interreligious resilience. The benefits of interreligious resilience are multiple: from personal spiritual growth to deepened interpersonal interreligious friendships, from more effective interreligious collaborations to increased religious literacy, the reduction of religiously fueled prejudice and bigotry, and broader civic and social goods.[16] A resilience and vulnerability approach to interreligious engagement equips interreligious leaders with tools that can help them lead their communities toward the aim of interreligious resilience. We now turn to an overview of broader historical trends in US interreligious engagement.

History of Interreligious Engagement in the United States

To understand the nature, challenges, and opportunities of interreligious engagement today, it is instructive to provide a brief historical overview of interreligious engagement and the notions of religion that underpin it. But even a brief review of the history of interreligious engagement in the United States raises vexing methodological, theoretical, and historical questions. At what point in history should one begin such a review? What counts as "interreligious engagement"? Wherever different religions and religious people have come into contact, there has been an engagement of some kind, sometimes through conflict and violence. Another question is whether one should begin prior to the founding of the United States as a modern nation. After all, there were advanced civilizations and complex religious communities and traditions that preceded the founding of the US government. Long before the arrival of European colonizers, there were a multitude of indigenous nations and ways of being religious. During the settler-colonial period, enslaved Africans brought their Muslim, animist, and shamanistic traditions with them to this country. Since the seventeenth century, there have been Puritans from England, Catholics from Spain, Italy, and Ireland, and Sephardic Jews from Spain and Portugal. Ashkenazi Jews arrived somewhat later, from Western Europe in the early eighteenth century and from Eastern Europe in the late nineteenth. Chinese Buddhists, Taoists, and Confucians have had a presence since at least the middle of the nineteenth century. In these respects, then, this country has been interreligious as far back as the historical record goes. But organized interreligious engagement in the United States, aiming for mutual interreligious learning and collaboration, emerged in the late nineteenth century. In what follows, we will briefly describe three eras of interreligious engagement since that time.[17]

The first era, which began near the end of the nineteenth century, emerged in response to new waves of immigration, rapid industrialization, and urbanization, which brought ethnically and culturally diverse people together in major cities. These initiatives focused on learning about religious diversity and were organized in large part by white liberal Protestant Christians. In response to rising nativist and xenophobic sentiments, liberal Christian leaders in Chicago organized the first World Parliament of Religions, which took place in 1893 during the

World's Fair in Chicago. The events, speeches, and presentations during the Parliament were shaped and interpreted through a Protestant Christian lens and the Parliament unfolded in the context of a fair that exoticized the world's cultures for a US American audience. As Diana Eck has written, "For many of those at the Parliament . . . the universal gathering in of the religions was nothing more than an extension of the vision of a united Christendom."[18] This ethnocentrism is evident, for example, in the address given by Parliament chairman John Henry Barrows, a Presbyterian minister, who opened the events with the rhetorical questions, "Why should not Christians be glad to learn what God has wrought through Buddha and Zoroaster—through the sages of China, and the Prophets of India and the prophet of Islam?"[19]

Implicit in these questions is the assumption that the God behind and within the various religious traditions represented at the Parliament was the God of Christianity. As Eck observes, Barrows's "conception of the universal was but a larger and more expansive Christianity."[20] This tends to be the case with universals, which are invariably the projection of ideas, principles, values, or categories that have roots in some specific tradition of thought and practice. Nevertheless, the "prevailing spirit of the Parliament was a kind of welcoming universalism or inclusivism on the part of the Western and largely Christian hosts."[21] Through this inclusive spirit, thousands of US Americans were introduced to global religious diversities and to the alluring possibilities of interreligious harmony. This vision and the interreligious curiosities it provoked were soon diminished, however, by the upheavals of the Great Depression and the horrors of two world wars.

Interreligious efforts regained energy after the Second World War. During this time, up until the end of the Cold War in the late 1980s, interreligious efforts shifted from local US religious education efforts to internationally organized peace-focused initiatives. The world was traumatized by the violence of war, the unspeakable inhumanities of the Jewish Holocaust, and the horrific devastation of the atomic bombs dropped by the United States on Hiroshima and Nagasaki. In response, interreligious efforts took on a new urgency and international focus, exemplified by the emergence of the World Conference of Religions for Peace in the late 1960s and early 1970s.[22] The WCRP's work was less focused on educating about religious difference than on coordinating multireligious efforts around global challenges such as nuclear nonproliferation, gender equality, freedom of religion, and the environment. This time period was also the context for Vatican II and *Nostra Aetate*, the Catholic Church's Declaration on the Relation of the Church to Non-Christian Religions, which was especially focused on

Christian-Jewish relations and the long history of Christian anti-Semitism. Around this same time, interreligious scholars Leonard Swidler and Rabbi Arthur Gilbert started the *Journal of Ecumenical Studies*, and a few years after that, Temple University, where Swidler taught, launched the Institute for Interreligious and Intercultural Dialogue. These academic initiatives represented a pedagogical and a social turn for interreligious engagement. It was increasingly recognized that interreligious initiatives and learning had broader social and civic significance and thus that they should not be confined to the efforts of religious elites.

From the end of the Cold War to the present, interreligious efforts have taken shape as localized and regionally networked grassroots initiatives led by local clergy and lay religious activists. The new interreligious leaders are less concerned with hosting high-level dialogs among religious elites than with organizing to build civically and socially oriented interreligious coalitions. While international interreligious initiatives continue to focus their efforts on global issues and seek to articulate and disseminate interreligious statements of conscience, the newer grassroots movement focuses on local expressions of global challenges such as rising Islamophobia and environmental and social justice issues. Exemplary in this regard are initiatives such as Reverend Dr. William Barber's and Reverend Dr. Liz Theoharris's leadership of the Poor People's Campaign, as well as organizations such as the Interfaith Youth Core, which trains youth and young adult interfaith leaders; Faith in Place, which works with diverse religious communities in Illinois to discover and apply the ecological wisdom in their own traditions; and Interfaith Worker Justice, which engages faith communities in efforts to organize workers and advance initiatives for a living wage, health benefits, safety, and dignity for all workers.

The changing forms and foci of interreligious efforts over the past century have paralleled and to some extent shaped different models of teaching and learning about religion in the United States. The earliest model emerged in the wake of the 1893 Parliament of Religions. In this model, different religions are viewed in universalist terms, as though there was a general essence of "religion" that was expressed in diverse ways through particular historical and cultural forms. The focus of interpretation and comparison was on beliefs, doctrines, and myths. This way of teaching and learning about religion reflects the Parliament's framing of religion in a couple of ways. It simplifies the complexity and internal differences within the traditions to make them accessible as objects of curiosity for a primarily Christian audience—one could pejoratively refer to this as the museumification of religion. Rather than the fullness of the traditions, the focus of study in this model is on religious worldviews, or the beliefs, doctrines, and myths that are taken to provide the universal infrastructure of religion. This theologically oriented model of teaching and learning about religion is not without value but it formats the study of religions through universalized or projected Western and largely Protestant Christian categories. This is understandable, given the historical connections between this model and the Parliament. As Eck writes, "Just as the spirit of universalism dominated the Parliament and the religious outlook of the late 19th century, so did it dominate the emerging study of religion" in the United States.[23]

During the middle period of US interreligious history, from the end of the Second World War through the Cold War, a different approach to the study of religions in the United States began to emerge. The study of religion in the United States became increasingly formalized and academically institutionalized, paralleling the formalization and internationalization of interreligious engagement described earlier. The field of religious studies emerged as an independent and secular academic discipline, in contrast to the earlier theologically oriented and faith-based model. Rather than exploring the religions as unitary systems of belief, scholars developed increasingly sophisticated theoretical approaches to religion. Phenomenological, functionalist, comparative, historical, and social scientific methods engaged the diverse social, historical, behavioral, cultural, and political complexities of religion and religious life. While these developments led to ways of teaching and learning about the religions that did greater justice to their fullness of religion, the focus often remained on the study of religions as discrete traditions in isolation from one another.

At present, shifts in the academic study of religion are paralleling the grassroots shift in interreligious engagement. Increasingly, scholarship, teaching, and learning about religion focus on interactions between different religions and the intersections of religion and everyday life. As Eboo Patel puts it, this emerging approach to religious studies is interested in "how people who orient around religion differently interact with one another."[24] Rather than studying the religions in isolation from one another, scholars and students explore the contacts between different religions and religious people, how and why they conflict and collaborate, how diverse religious beliefs and values and cultural patterns lead people to navigate their social worlds in different ways. And rather than investigating the philosophical, ethical, ritual, narrative, and historical dimensions of religions by abstracting them from their lived social contexts, there is increasing interest in exploring how religion manifests in the intricacies of everyday life among diverse religious people. This turn away from a view of religions as monolithic carriers of a universal essence of religion reflects a growing recognition that, as Eck puts this, religions are "far more like rivers than stones," "flowing and changing" as a result of the ripples and eddies created by religious people swimming in and against their currents.[25]

The changing approaches to the study of religion just summarized reflect the reality that today we live in a world in which the experience of religious difference is internally constitutive of our own religious communities, religious beliefs, and religious identities. This reality has led to new initiatives and theorizing about interreligious dialog and engagement. In what follows, we will briefly discuss three exemplary interreligious scholars' contributions to thinking about models, conditions, and purposes of interreligious engagement in our interreligious world.

Models of Interreligious Engagement

Given this historical and conceptual review of interreligious engagement, what kind of models and approaches have evolved and been developed? Jeannine Hill Fletcher distinguishes between Parliament, Activist, and Storytelling models of interreligious dialog and gives particular attention to the contributions of women to the emergence of the latter two models.[26] The Parliament model, as the name suggests, refers to the model associated with the 1893 Parliament of World Religions. As Hill Fletcher describes it, this model "puts forth 'religions' as objects available for comment, explication, and comparison."[27] The focus is on beliefs and worldviews, the participants in the dialog are expert representatives, and the aim is not only to explain and defend one's tradition but often to do so in such a way as to demonstrate its truth relative to other traditions.

The Parliament model has historically privileged male leaders and voices, reflecting the fact that for much of history in many traditions, religious leadership and training have excluded or been biased against women.[28] The gender bias of this approach, as Hill Fletcher writes, is due to the realities that, for example, the traditions of "'the Catholic Church' . . . [have been] formulated exclusively by men in its authoritative doctrines and magisterial teachings. The practices of Hinduism, if centered on the temple, are also the domain of male priests. Gendered divisions in Islam, Judaism, and Buddhism similarly take male space as the normative religious space."[29] Insofar as the expert representative in the Parliament model is typically male, and the representative in this model is in the position of speaking for the whole of the tradition, male religious perspectives and experiences are presented as the defining perspectives and experiences for the whole tradition. However, "women's engagement with a tradition is often different from the androcentric male perspective. . . . What women contribute [to interreligious dialogue] as formerly obscured subjects may bring into greater relief the dynamics of religion in its sheer multiplicity and the recognition that 'religions' are ultimately unrepresentable in any totalizing of comprehensive sense."[30] The problem is not that the male perspective is invalid, but that it is incomplete and typically uninterrogated by its male representatives. Representing men's religious experience and perspectives as normative for the whole of a tradition neglects the gendered partiality of their representations.

This discussion illuminates three critical realities: the gendered pluralism of religious traditions, the perspectival nature of representation, and the inevitable partiality of dialog. Recognizing these realities need not foreclose the significance of a Parliamentary model of interreligious dialog, but it can shift the purposes of dialogue from formal explanation and apologetic defense to interpretation and mutual learning across multiple perspectives, gendered and otherwise.

Some of these shifts give rise to what Hill Fletcher identifies as an Activist model of interreligious dialog. As she describes it, the Activist model emerges out of the Parliament model even as it represents an alternative to it. The timing of the Parliament of Religions in 1893 coincided with the early stirrings of the global feminist movement. Although a vast majority of speeches at the 1893 Parliament were given by men, several were given by women, including the US American suffragettes Julia Ward Howe and Elizabeth Cady Stanton. Howe and Stanton, along with other women who gave speeches at the Parliament, brought a critical, subjugated perspective to the task of representing the nature and history of their religious traditions. In contrast to the androcentrism and apologetic purposes of the Parliament model, the Activist model "seeks the transformation of the world and the transformation of religions."[31]

In addition to illuminating the gendered pluralism of the religions and aiming for transformation rather than explanation, the work of the Activist model takes place amidst the porous boundaries of the "religious" and "secular." While the Parliament model, as described previously, tends to represent the religions in ahistorical and idealist terms, the Activist model, through its commitment to the mutual transformation of society and the religions, elucidates the entanglement of religious and social power. The global feminist roots of the Activist model engendered an approach to interreligious understanding that cultivated relational solidarities across traditions through a commitment to shared social and political projects. From its origins in the early feminism of the late nineteenth century up to the present, the Activist model has brought the work of addressing "the suffering rooted in the oppression of sexism, and the social conditions that acutely impact poor women and women of color," as well as other social justice and ecological concerns, into the center of interreligious dialog.[32] In sum, the Activist model focuses on the social conditions and contexts of lived religious experience, in addition to the beliefs, symbols, practices, and truth claims of religious traditions; it presents the religions as internally plural, morally ambiguous, and intertwined with historical and social conditions; and it aims to increase mutual religious understanding by cultivating relationships and social change.

Like the Activist model, the Storytelling model has feminist roots. Whereas the Parliament model presents the religions as discrete monolithic entities, and the Activist model illuminates the religions' internal multiplicity and religious-secular porosity, the Storytelling model prioritizes the lived, everyday experience of women's religious lives. Like the Activist model, the Storytelling model emerges out of the marginalized experience of religious women and responds specifically to the exclusion of women "from formal networks of communication within hierarchically organized institutions."[33] As Hill Fletcher describes it, this model is arguably the most explicitly feminist model of interreligious dialog—not only by occupying marginalized space as a space of creative interreligious agency, but also methodologically, by claiming the interreligious significance of informal, everyday interreligious relationships. This model "brings home ever more clearly the superfluity of religion itself as every participant necessarily represents her or his tradition through the filter of his or her biography. . . . The expressions of any given tradition are thus irreducibly diverse, making the reality of dialogue an overflowing abundance of possibility."[34] The Storytelling model's embrace of the biographical and lived experiential contexts of religious life subverted the conceit involved in offering a representative, definitive account of any religious tradition. As Hill Fletcher summarizes the strengths of this model, "it reminds us that 'religion' cannot be reduced to doctrines and scriptures, to 'what I believe' or 'what I do.' 'Religion' is always 'found' embedded in and intertwined with other aspects of our lived condition: economics, gender, social relations, material conditions, life stages, family relationships, and more."[35] Rather than dis-embedded or disembodied representations of religious traditions, the Storytelling model "enables the presentation of 'religion' in a way more akin to the way it is lived."[36]

While Hill Fletcher's models analyze the spaces and aims of interreligious dialog, Catherine Cornille articulates the conditions, virtues, and practices required for mutual interreligious learning. Effective interreligious dialog, for

Cornille, should not aim for an apologetic defense of the superiority of one tradition over another, but for mutual learning and growth. Cornille's case for her virtues-based approach to dialog stems from her view that encounters between religious individuals are often "governed by mutual fear and aversion rather than by friendship and attraction, and by feelings of superiority and condescension rather than by mutual respect."[37] These tendencies and attitudes obviously do not support dialogical learning and growth. Cornille responds to this challenge by identifying virtues she takes to be necessary to genuine dialog. As she articulates them, these include virtues that orient one within one's own religious tradition, as well as virtues that inform how one relates to other traditions. With respect to one's own religious tradition, Cornille advocates for the importance of humility, commitment, and interconnection. With respect to other traditions, she articulates the importance of empathy and hospitality. The embrace and practice of these virtues, Cornille writes,

> requires a certain hermeneutical effort and creativity, a reinterpretation of traditional teachings or a mobilization of latent resources hidden within one's own religious texts and teachings. . . . Religious symbols and concepts that at one time and context were used to insist on the superiority and uniqueness of one's own religion may in a different context become the basis for openness and receptivity toward the truth of the other religions.[38]

Cornille's point is that "the possibility (or impossibility) of interreligious dialogue is less a matter of the hard and fast teachings of a particular religion than of the hermeneutical principles that may be brought to bear on its self-understanding."[39] This is consistent with our view, stated earlier, that the problem of religious supremacy is not intrinsic to specific religious traditions, but is an effect of fractal patterns of believing and belonging that occur within all traditions.

The importance of humility, for Cornille, is rooted in the premise that the motivation to genuine dialog is learning not only about others but also about oneself. This motivation presupposes that one is aware of the limitations, incompleteness, and partiality of one's own tradition and experience, as well as the incompleteness and possibly distorted understanding one may have of other traditions. Cornille writes, "Insofar as religions lay claim to possessing the absolute truth or the ultimate means to salvation, dialogue cannot but be regarded as a form of redundancy or a threat."[40] Given this, humility is a necessary condition of dialog. The humility entailed for genuine dialogue is partly epistemic or doctrinal, and partly spiritual. Spiritual humility is, in part, an openness to other ways of being religious, cultivated through spiritual practice and self-examination. This can lead to epistemic or doctrinal humility, which is a relation to the truth claims of one's own tradition that opens one to the possibility of learning from other traditions. Spiritual humility can lead to epistemic humility, and epistemic humility can engender a will to learn about the truths and practices of other religious traditions. As one genuinely explores the truth of other religious traditions, this can further reinforce epistemic and spiritual humility. Thus, humility, as a condition and effect of genuine dialog, is a core virtue of interreligious learning.

In addition to humility, Cornille argues that commitment is a necessary ingredient of interreligious dialog. The combination of humility and commitment reflects a complicated balance between openness to learning from other traditions and investment in one's own tradition. Although interreligious dialog will be viewed as redundant or threatening if one is committed to the absolute and exhaustive truth of one's own religious tradition, mutual interreligious learning is not possible if the dialogical partners are not willing or able to articulate the beliefs, values, and practices of their own traditions. While no one person has exhaustive knowledge of their own traditions, it is also the case that people belong to specific religious traditions for reasons, some of which are philosophical and moral. Cornille writes, "Religious commitment is generally understood as a deliberate identification with the teachings and practices of a particular tradition. It thus entails assent to the truth-claims of a particular tradition and recognition of the authority of the tradition in matters of doctrine and discipline."[41] However, as Cornille understands it, commitment is not only about reasons. "On closer inspection," she writes, "the process of committing oneself to a particular religion generally includes both voluntary and involuntary dimensions. Many come to adopt a religious conviction through a process of socialization and education in which particular views of the world and of the meaning of life are absorbed with little or no reflection."[42] Nevertheless, "Mature religious commitment presupposes a certain degree of critical reflection on its teachings and practices and a conscious embrace of its truth."[43] The commitment required for interreligious dialog is always embodied and contextual, as Hill Fletcher would remind us. But in addition to being embedded in social and cultural identities, such as gender and sexuality, Cornille makes the important point that commitment is also always particularly rooted in sub-traditions. Interreligious dialog is not between Muslims and Christians and Buddhists in general, whatever that might mean, but between, for example, Sunni Muslim college students from Indonesia, Catholic women activists from the United States, or Mahayana Buddhist educators from South Korea.

Humility and commitment are necessary but insufficient to mutual interreligious learning. In addition to these, a sense of interconnection is also necessary. Of this, Cornille writes: "One of the basic conditions of interreligious dialogue is a sense of commonality or solidarity among religions, and of the relevance of the other religion for one's own religious tradition. Any notion of the radical singularity or the fundamental incomparability of religions would render dialogue superfluous, if not impossible."[44] A condition of dialog, then, is the sense or agreement that the religious perspectives in dialog have something in common. What is held in common will vary with the nature and purposes of the dialog. The common ground could be an exploration, for instance, of what different religious perspectives have to say about something philosophical, such as truth or beauty; or perhaps it is a moral exploration of what different traditions have to say about particular social or environmental issues, such as climate change, women's rights, or racism; or it may be something practical, such as a discussion of the nature and purposes of spiritual practice in different traditions. Cornille's point in stressing the importance of interconnection is not that there is a universal essence at the core of different religious traditions, but that the practical possibility of mutual learning across religious differences requires that the dialog take place within a field of shared concerns, questions, and themes.

This field of shared concerns, questions, and themes, however, needs to be cultivated, which leads Cornille to argue for the importance of interreligious empathy. She writes,

> The ethos of a dialogue presupposes a certain reciprocity in which, just as I would like the other to understand me in the depth of my religious experience, the other also appeals to my willingness to enter into his or her self-understanding. Empathy thus represents the means to gain understanding of the affective dimension of the other religion, of the religious desires and needs that lie at the origins of particular beliefs and practices and of the experiences generated by them.[45]

The importance of empathy in interreligious dialog, and of emotion and desire, corresponds to the recognition that the religions and religious experience can never be fully or finally expressed conceptually. This of course does not mean that dialog need not include concern with concepts, ideas, and language, but that if one seeks genuinely to have a dialog, and genuinely to share about one's own tradition as well as to learn from religious others, then the empathic work of "crossing over" into the affective textures of another's religious lifeworld is necessary.[46]

The importance of empathy, for Cornille, affirms that interreligious learning is about something more than learning the doctrines, rituals, and myths of religious others. Despite the importance she grants to empathy, Cornille also rightly understands the danger of naïve empathy, which flows from the uncritical assumption that one can bracket or suspend one's own perspective and experience to understand fully the religious other from within their own perspective. Cornille looks to the phenomenologist Edmond Husserl's concept of "analogical apperception" to articulate the importance and limits of interreligious empathy. As a form of "analogical apperception," interreligious empathy aims to understand something of the cognitive and affective experience of the religious other, but also recognizes that the form and motivation for such understanding cannot help but be one's own experience. The concepts of "analogy" and "apperception" underscore simultaneously "the impossibility of ever fully duplicating the primordial experience of the other" while also suggesting "the presence of at least structural or formal similarities or points of rapport that allow for some level of mutual comprehension."[47] Thus, interreligious empathy does not presume the possibility of knowing the religious other from the inside of the other's perspective. It grants that, as Cornille puts it, "The meaning of any religious phenomenon is always complex and fluid and can never be fully grasped, either from within or from outside a tradition."[48] But this impossibility, paradoxically, is a contributing condition to the possibility of mutual interreligious learning: "The impossibility of fully entering into the experience of the other is here thus regarded as a potential source of creative growth for both partners engaged in dialogue."[49]

This paradox of impossibility leads Cornille to argue that "hospitality" is the "sole sufficient condition" for interreligious dialog. An analogy may help to explain what Cornille means by this. A common understanding of hospitality is conveyed by the image of a gracious host, one who welcomes a guest into their home, or to a dinner, and serves the guest with the comforts and nourishments of a specially prepared meal and congenial conversation. The practice of genuine hospitality, in contrast to an obligatory etiquette of hospitality, could be said to consist of a combination of generosity, care, and curiosity. The hospitable host generously shares something, such as food, comfort, or shelter, with the guest. This generosity is motivated, in part, by care for the guest as a person, whether they are a stranger or a friend, and in part by curiosity about the life of the guest.

The generous sharing and care create conditions for curiosities to be explored, for instance through conversation about ideas and experiences. As such, the practice of hospitality, while we may commonly think of it as generosity extended by a host toward a guest, opens an event of mutual exchange between guest and host.

Cornille's understanding of interreligious hospitality structurally resonates with this account of hospitality between host and guest but defines it as an orientation to religious truth. Such an orientation toward religious truth "involves the recognition of actual truth in another religion" and "hospitality toward integrating that truth in one's own tradition."[50] The practice of hospitality toward other religious truth entails the practices of dialog identified earlier: "the recognition of truth in another religion presupposes some humility about the truth of one's tradition, commitment to a tradition which exercises hospitality, a general sense of the interconnectedness between religions, and genuine understanding of the other."[51] Hospitality toward religious truth need not require the recognition of truth in all religions, or in every aspect of a religion, but "the discovery of any single inspiring thought or practice may or should lead to a constructive engagement."[52] Hospitality is thus a practice of humility toward the truth of one's own religious tradition that welcomes at least the partial truth in some other religions. But, as with the analogy to the hospitable host, whose generous care and curiosity about the guest is rooted in the host's own lifeworld or home, the "starting point or basic norm" for hospitality toward other religious truth is "one's own religious tradition."[53] While one may practice epistemic and spiritual humility in relation to one's own religious tradition, the interreligious dialog still presumes commitment to that tradition. In relation to the truth in other traditions, there is no getting outside of the perspective of the truth(s) of one's own religious tradition. If this is so, how then is it possible to integrate other religious truth? Cornille describes alternative perspectives on the truth of one's own religious tradition as it relates to the truth in other traditions. One can adopt minimal or maximal or negative or positive norms for relating to other religious truth: "When the teachings of one's tradition operate as maximal or positive norm, only those teachings or practices in the other tradition which are identical to one's own will be regarded as valid or true."[54] In contrast, "In functioning as a minimal or negative norm, one's tradition serves as a basis to exclude only those teachings and practices which are irreconcilable with one's own," or to "affirm teachings and practices which are compatible with one's own."[55]

While Hill Fletcher investigates the role of gender in different models of interreligious engagement, and Cornille makes a case for the conditions, practices, and virtues of interreligious learning, Eboo Patel articulates the knowledge, skills, and qualities conducive to what he describes as civically engaged interfaith leadership.[56] Patel's case for the knowledge, skills, and qualities of interfaith work is calibrated to his interfaith leadership vision, which is to help to build a more pluralistic society.

To elaborate this vision, Patel draws upon Diana Eck's distinction between diversity and pluralism, according to which diversity describes the social fact of people with different identities, and pluralism identifies a social aim. He describes pluralism as "the energetic engagement of diversity toward a positive end," and adumbrates the "positive end" or aim of pluralism as "respect for identity, relationships between different communities, and a commitment to the common good."[57] As Patel defines it, respect for identity entails accommodating other persons' rights to form and express their religious and other identities. Thus defined, respect for identity does not require the full endorsement or affirmation of others' identities, but a commitment to shaping a world that supports learning about and making room for diverse religious identities.

As necessary as respect for other identities is for pluralism, it neither ensures the elimination of conflict between diverse religious people, nor is it sufficient to the fuller positive aim of pluralism. In fact, respect alone, in the limited sense that Patel advocates, is perfectly compatible with a fragmented social world of diverse identity enclaves. Such a world can be described as diverse, but it is not pluralist. Thus, Patel argues for the importance of building relationships across religious differences. He writes:

> By "relationship," I mean positive, constructive, warm, caring cooperative engagement. This takes the form of conversation, activity, civic association, and friendly contact. It almost always involves some dimension of concern for the other's well-being. These are not connections based on the fiction of total agreement across all dimensions of identity, but rather engagement in full awareness that there are areas of both commonality and divergence and a commitment to care for one another in recognition of both.[58]

Building relationships with people and groups with diverse religious and other identities presumes at least minimal respect for those identities, and through the relationship, the respect can grow into the complexity of genuine friendships and solidarities. But respect and relationships across religious differences do not spontaneously arise—they presume a society that upholds principles and institutions that enable them. These principles and institutions are what Patel refers to as the common good, which includes abstract principles such as, in the

US American context, freedom of speech and association and equality before the law, as well as concrete material goods such as public schools and civic institutions. Shared commitment to common goods such as these provides a social context and set of social conditions that make respect and relationship building possible. And yet, while the common good can be specified in a limited, formal way, it is also the case that people with diverse identities, traditions, and values who orient around religion will interpret the foundations and purposes of the common good within the context of religiously diverse accounts of what is ultimately good and true. As Patel writes, "It is impossible to overstate how real, and how challenging" it is to gather "people who disagree on ultimate concerns."[59] For this reason, neither respect, relationships, nor a shared commitment to the common good is sufficient to a pluralist society, but these three together support a vision for interfaith work that aims for pluralism.

With this vision, Patel next turns to the knowledge, skills, and qualities necessary to the interfaith labor of pluralism. We should note that Patel utilizes the term "interfaith" as opposed to interreligious, which we have adopted in this book, but by that means much the same as we do. (See the Introduction.) Patel advocates for a knowledge base that includes appreciative knowledge of other religious traditions, familiarity with theologies of interfaith cooperation, acquaintance with the history of interfaith cooperation, and an understanding of shared values across religious difference. By "appreciative knowledge," Patel has in mind effective religious literacy and knowledge of other traditions, awareness of positive contributions diverse religious people and communities have made, and sympathetic understanding of diverse religious views. A theology of interfaith cooperation, as Patel explains it, entails knowledge of texts and stories about interfaith relationships within one's own tradition—in other words, familiarity with exemplary figures and lessons about cross-religious interaction within the scriptures and history of one's tradition. Acquaintance with the history of interfaith cooperation is less focused on tradition-internal interfaith stories than the social history of interfaith dialog and interfaith movements, such as the history we outlined earlier in this chapter. Knowledge of shared values entails understanding that while there are common concerns across traditions with things such as justice, love, compassion, and humility, these values are interpreted in different ways. As Patel puts it, following Paul Knitter, the aim is to "identify *commonality without the pretense of sameness*."[60]

The interfaith skills Patel identifies include a radar screen for religious diversity, building a public narrative of interfaith cooperation, creating activities that bring diverse religious people tougher, and facilitating interfaith conversations. In discussing the need for a "radar screen for religious diversity," Patel observes that although many people are increasingly aware of and sensitive to racial, sexual, and gender identities, fewer people are accustomed to navigating the world with an awareness of diverse religious identities. By developing a "radar screen for religious diversity" interfaith leaders learn to scan the world, from current events in the news to their local civic spaces and historical trends, for the presence and role of religious identities and traditions. Patel also recommends the importance of crafting a public narrative. Building from the work of Jewish community organizer and leadership theorist Marshall Ganz, an interfaith public narrative includes three interrelated stories: a "story of self" that narrates in personal terms one's commitment to interfaith work, a "story of us" that conveys the values and purposes of one's communities of belonging, and a "story of now" that shows the importance of interfaith work in the contemporary world. Interfaith relationship building, for Patel, is enabled through cooperative activity and conversation.

The importance of interfaith projects and activities is a signature element of Patel's Interfaith Youth Core pedagogy and leadership. In contrast to the discursive or dialogical foci of Hill Fletcher's and Cornille's work described previously, Patel advocates for the importance of shared activity as good itself and as a means to interfaith conversation. But not all activities are equal. As he writes, "Good interfaith activities bring together a wide range of people who orient around religion differently in compelling projects that highlight shared values and create the space for powerful sharing, storytelling, and relationship building."[61] Appropriate activities are ones that reflect widely shared as well as deeply held values. The combination is important, for if the values are not widely shared and are overly specific to a particular religious group, there will be little to bring different religious people together. And if the values are not deeply held, there will be little investment in the project.

The character qualities Patel identifies include grit, relatability, leading with pluralism, and craft. Grit, Patel suggests, "is the foundational quality of effective interfaith leadership. You have to play the long game and know that you are going to encounter prejudice, tension, disagreement, and conflict along the way."[62] Though he doesn't specify what he means by grit, he implies that grit is a quality that makes it possible to work with other religious people even when one experiences their different beliefs, values, and language as offensive. This does not mean, of course, that interfaith leaders must subject themselves to hate speech or threats of violence, but interfaith work exposes one to differences one may not like. That this is so underscores the importance of relatability. It can be tempting to respond confrontationally to people whose beliefs are not only different but offensive. But if one is playing the interfaith long game, as Patel advocates, then righteous indignation is not a useful tactic. "To be an effective social change agent," he explains, "people have to want to listen to you. And for that to happen, you have to make yourself relatable."[63] This quality of relatability is consistent with the priority Patel places on relationship building generally. Mutual learning across religious differences is unlikely if there is no rapport between interfaith partners, which requires that interfaith leaders practice relatability. One effective way to go about this, according to Patel, is by "leading with pluralism." To lead with pluralism, as Patel describes it, entails "choosing to highlight the inspiring things you have in common with another person or community," which presumes that one has knowledge of "the resonances between different traditions."[64] Here we see how the knowledge, skills, and qualities of interfaith leadership overlap and reinforce one another. The work of integrating these elements of interfaith leadership through reflective practice is what Patel means by the quality of "craft." While craft presumes work, it is far from drudgery. Craft is work that one invests oneself in because one finds meaning in the work itself and one loves the end or purpose of the work—which, in Patel's case, is the vision of pluralism.

Conclusion: Resilience in Interreligious Contexts

As the summary in the previous paragraph indicates, there is a rich history and there has been an efflorescence of scholarly work on interreligious engagement in recent years. A sign of this is the number of readers, anthologies, edited volumes, companions, handbooks, and encyclopedias that deal with interfaith and interreligious topics. This scholarly productivity is an indication of several generally important trends, including a growing number of courses on interreligious topics being taught in colleges, universities, divinity schools, and seminaries and even new faculty positions for educator-scholars working in interreligious areas. There are new book series and academic journals and at the annual American Academy of Religion meetings there is even a new Interreligious and Interfaith Studies Unit.

This new interreligious scholarship is related to but different from longstanding work in the areas of comparative religion, history of religions, and theology of religions. Scholarship in these areas has tended to be more historically, textually, and theologically oriented and geared toward an audience of other scholars. As the review of Fletcher, Cornille, and Patel indicates, the newer interreligious scholarship is different. It is primarily concerned with the conditions, possibilities, and challenges of lived interreligious experience, and the work of theology, history, and textual studies, while still important, is in service of interreligious understanding.

We have learned a great deal from the interreligious scholars we reviewed earlier, as well as others. Our approach builds upon aspects of their work but is distinct in several ways. Like Patel, our approach is specifically interested in the question of leadership. But whereas Patel focuses on the knowledge, skills, and qualities of individual interfaith leaders, our work explores issues of leadership from a systems perspective. Like Cornille, we explore conditions and practices of interreligious engagement, but the occasions of interreligious engagement that concern us are not exclusively dialogical or pedagogical. As our case studies reflect, we are interested in the practical challenges and everyday circumstances of interreligious engagement in an interreligious world. And in keeping with Hill Fletcher's analysis, we also think of our approach as a model.

Our model (the VITA pathway, Chapter 5) builds on the important history and insights we have noted throughout this chapter. But it is also informed by, and applies, the vast and increasing work on resilience and vulnerability more generally. We will explore resilience and vulnerability in greater detail in Chapter 4, after examining the changing contexts for interreligious engagement (Chapter 2) and the key areas of focus in leadership in an interreligious setting (Chapter 3). What distinguishes our model from others, therefore, is the use of theories of resilience and vulnerability rather than the identities of the interreligious participants or leaders, which has more typically animated work in and thinking about the field. Hill Fletcher is right to be concerned with questions of identity, difference, and social power in interreligious engagement, and we believe a resilience and vulnerability model provides a relevant set of tools for attending to those issues in deep and nuanced ways.

Although the concepts of interreligious resilience and vulnerability have meaning at multiple levels, including personal, communal, organizational, and even societal, the personal level is fundamental. Interreligious vulnerability in this context means empathic openness to religious difference. This includes not only willingness to interact with persons from different religious traditions but also openness to thinking, and even attempting to experience, different religious ideas and truths, valuing different religious ideals, encountering other religious identities, and imaginatively engaging other religious symbols and rituals.

In addition to other religious people, we understand encounters with religious difference to include interaction with diverse religious symbols, texts, stories, and practices. With respect to the many types of religious others, and the various contexts in which we can engage them, the cultivation of interreligious resilience entails the cultivation of an empathic imagination, which itself entails making oneself vulnerable to learning with, from, and through encounters with religious difference. This means opening space in one's own mind, heart, and spirit for the vital complexity and genuine difference of other religious symbols, texts, and persons. Doing this takes intellectual, emotional, moral, and spiritual energy, as well as humility, curiosity, and a bit of courage. So, interreligious vulnerability at the interpersonal level is the work of empathically and imaginatively opening oneself to the reality and value of other religious possibilities. And through practice, this process can lead to interreligious resilience, which enables one to learn and grow through, rather than to be threatened by, encounters with religious difference.

The concept of resilience at the heart of this book, then, is not merely about adapting or coping or "bouncing back," all of which are common tropes in the popular resilience literature. We think of adaptation, coping, and bouncing back as "simple resilience." There is a need and a place for simple resilience in our lives—we need buildings and bridges, for example, that can cope with severe weather and gusting winds and earthquakes. But we believe simple resilience is insufficient to the social complexity of human life, let alone to interreligious learning.

For this reason, we distinguish "complex resilience" from the popular understandings of simple resilience. If simple resilience is about adapting to change to stay the same, then complex resilience is about engaging change to learn from and through it. If simple resilience is about coping with risk, threat, and disturbance, or if it is merely about the maintenance of sameness and identity in the face of difference, then complex resilience enables purposive learning through change and growth of one's religious identity through encounters with different ways of being religious. If simple resilience enables one to tolerate the fact of religious diversity in ways that maintain or insulate one's own preexisting religious identity and truth, complex resilience enables one to openly engage religious diversity with competency and curiosity.

In short, complex resilience is a capacity for learning in contexts of diversity and change, and as such it supports forms of religious identity and modes of religious belief and belonging that are conducive to the social ideal of pluralism. In this sense, complex resilience is best understood as something that can be developed through reflective experience and intentional practice, rather than a set of essential characteristics that is inherent in some but not all persons.

We will further elaborate this idea of complex resilience in Chapter 4 and will also introduce, through the VITA pathway, a suite of practices that activate it for interreligious leadership. However, to set the stage for that work, in the next chapter we will explore further some of the contemporary contexts and conditions of interreligious life—what is it about the contemporary world that makes interreligious and other forms of cross-difference engagement so difficult and so important?

2

Interreligious Contexts

Globalization, Postsecularism, Acceleration, and Polarization

Introduction

In the last chapter we examined the historical development and models of interreligious engagement and we extracted important foci and lessons that resonate with an approach that we have termed "Interreligious Resilience" (building on discussions of resilience and vulnerability). In this chapter we expand this discussion by considering the most pressing societal issues that are impacting and playing out in many fields of human life and community and especially in interreligious work. These include globalization and postsecularism, social and technological acceleration, and polarization and religious supremacy. In what follows, we dig a bit deeper into each of these in order to understand them and their implications for interreligious engagement and leadership.

Providing a context for this discussion, at a recent interreligious event at the Spertus Institute for Jewish Learning and Leadership in Chicago, Interfaith Youth Core founder Eboo Patel, who we discussed in the previous chapter, shared stories that led the audience to think about some of the contemporary challenges of working across religious and cultural differences. A gifted speaker, Patel expertly gathered the attention of the audience of about 200 people—Jews from various traditions, students from a midwestern Christian college, and seminarians from a Unitarian Universalist theological school. The stories he told evoked for the audience the fraught nature of contemporary interreligious life. They helped us not only to see but also to feel how interacting across differences in the contemporary world is both increasingly important and difficult. The stories were about the challenges faced by several prominent writers and leaders, which helped to make the point that the struggle many of us have with relating across differences are not ours alone, nor are they due entirely to lack of interreligious experience or literacy. Many others, even people we esteem as interreligious experts, also seem to experience the contemporary context of interreligious engagement, and cross-cultural encounters generally, as especially vexing.

Why is this? What makes our encounters with difference especially complicated these days? Why is it that our political, religious, racial, and cultural differences seem so electric and supercharged? Chasms of mutual suspicion divide us from one another to the point that even everyday interactions at the supermarket, on playgrounds, or at school functions, can be paralyzing. We interpret others' mannerisms, speech, and dress for clues as to who they are and what they represent, or which "side" they are on. Sometimes it seems like we live in completely different worlds, as if we are aliens to one another, rather than fellow citizens inhabiting a shared world. "Yes," many of us were thinking and feeling as Patel told his stories, "This is right, this is what it's like." We live in a world of multiple worlds, of suspicion and aversion, a world in which we sort and divide ourselves into factions, friends, and enemies. Of course, the world has always been this way. But the factions today seem to be more fractious, the differences more divisive, and the way to common ground, dialog, and relationship, more treacherous.

Patel did not present in his talk an analysis of what makes cross-difference encounters so fraught in today's world. Nor did he offer many practices or principles in his presentation to help us to navigate the contemporary dynamics of difference. Instead, he turned that task back to the audience. He asked us to turn to one another at our various tables—which had been intentionally diversified—to share examples of difficult cross-difference encounters and how we dealt with them. We think it is fair to surmise that Patel was implicitly making two points by asking the small groups to move into conversation with one another. The first was to reinforce the point that, although it may seem otherwise, the difficulties of navigating culturally charged differences are not ours alone—whether we are Jews, Christians, Buddhists, atheists, or otherwise, Democrats, Republicans, Independents, libertarians, or anarchists, liberal, progressive, radical, or conservative—we all have our own complicated stories about dealing with challenging differences in our families, workplaces, and other settings. The second point was that the work of finding ways to connect with others who are different from us requires meeting and talking with people who are different from us! It requires vulnerability and takes intentional effort and practice!

This book is very much about these ideas. But the purpose of this chapter is to explore some of the background conditions that make interreligious and other cross-difference engagements so important in our time and so distinctly challenging. Human history is in part a long story about the many ways we have used cultural, religious, ethnic, racial, and other differences to simultaneously bind ourselves together and divide ourselves from others. In fact, a common strategy human groups have used to bind themselves together has been to stereotype and disparage other groups of people. These tendencies are not new, but a new set of historical conditions reinforces them.

Soon after the event with Patel, we met with some of our students to discuss the question of what it is about the present world that makes interreligious and cross-cultural engagement so distinctly challenging. Themes that emerged included the sense that, perhaps especially in the United States, we are increasingly polarized politically and culturally. Insofar as religious identities are entangled with political and racial identities, as well as ways of thinking about race and politics, interreligious encounters will tend to be politically and racially charged. We also talked about the anxiety that many of us have about how rapidly the world is changing. We discussed, for instance, the incessant churning of news cycles, the velocity of information in a digital world, and the tempo of social change, all of which can lead to emotional fatigue and cognitive overload. Everyday life seems to be speeding up, and it seems to take all our time and energy just to keep pace, let alone to cultivate relationships across challenging cultural and religious differences. What is more, our cultural and political differences are hardened by informational segmentation—our cognitive biases have been hacked and monetized by social media, cable news, and political campaigns. Profit-driven social media and search engine algorithms prey upon our ideological and cultural differences, intensifying our divisions and amplifying our mistrust of one another. We also talked about the struggles of life in an interconnected, globalizing world of economic uncertainty, precarious employment, surging ethnonationalism in the United States and around the world, and other global moral crises such as the climate emergency. In short, we are living in a volatile world wracked with social and moral challenges whose urgency is as clear as their complexity is confounding. And just when we most need to work across our differences to collectively address these challenges, just when we most need to build interreligious and cross-cultural collaborations, we are less able to do so because we are also increasingly divided from and suspicious of one another.

The processes just described are systemically reinforcing, which is to say that they compound and amplify one another. Polarization fuels and is fueled by social and news media echo-chambers. The increasing pace of social life fuels and is fueled by the economic and cultural dynamics of globalization. Social and economic inequalities are culturally and politically mobilized in ways that fuel the racial resentments and nationalist retrenchments that drive rising ethnonationalism. The cumulative effect of these feedback loops is a sense of existential insecurity and social anxiety. This puts pressure on the cultural identities and traditions through which we navigate our lives and contributes to the fraught complexities of contemporary interreligious engagement and leadership.

In this chapter we will look more closely at these issues and how they impact our human quests for meaning and belonging. Specifically, we will explore linkages between globalization and postsecularism, and between social acceleration and polarization. Although globalization, postsecularism, social acceleration, and polarization are complex system changes that create uncertainty and anxiety, and can fuel religious supremacy, they can also seed the potential for novelty, including new approaches to pluralism through interreligious resilience. But finding and nurturing the seeds of interreligious resilience require interpreting the causes and conditions of our changing world more closely.

Globalization and the Postsecular

The world, and the religions of the world, have long been interreligious. There have always been diverse religious traditions, forms of piety, and types of faith. Religious leaders, practitioners, and communities shaped by diverse religious traditions have always interacted and learned from one another and argued and fought and sometimes killed one another. But many people imagine and learn about the religions, if they learn about them at all, in the singular, as if they are monolithic, and as if they emerged and developed independently of one another. Of course, in addition to their differences from one another, the religions also contain a great deal of internal religious diversity. There are many ways of being Buddhist, Hindu, Christian, Muslim, Jewish, Taoist, Confucian, Humanist, and so on. The truth is that the religions are internally plural, and they have evolved in relation to and through contact with one another. So, in this basic sense, the world has been interreligious for as long as it has been religious: there have always been different ways of being religious; religious difference has always existed within as well as between religious traditions; and diverse religions have interacted with and mutually influenced one another all through their histories. Although this is true, it is also true that contemporary cultural conditions and social processes shape the interreligious present in distinct ways. Accelerating globalization, along with access to other cultures and religions (and representations of them), and broad and growing hybridity of religious identities and faith traditions are central for understanding the challenges and opportunities of relating to others of different geographies and backgrounds.

For example, some years ago, Mike began listening to the music of an artist with a style that was unlike anything he had heard before. It was not exactly hip hop, and it was not exactly reggae, and it was not exactly rock, but it was a bit of all these things—syncopated beats, Caribbean rhythms, screeching guitars, rapping, and a melodic voice thrown in here and there. The sound was a mix of struggle, longing, adoration, and praise. The lyrics were not always telling a straightforward story, but they were spiritually allusive and storied, layered with narrative references and symbols.

The artist we are talking about is a guy with a Hebrew stage name, Matisyahu. Matisyahu grew up as Matthew Paul Miller in the suburbs of Philadelphia and New York in a family affiliated with Reconstructionist Judaism. Reconstructionism is a modernist, ethical branch of Judaism founded by Mordecai Kaplan, who was committed to the idea of Judaism as a civilizational project. Reconstructionism is committed to the work of building, sustaining, and repairing the moral world. Reconstructionist Jews, through Kaplan's teachings, aspire to live as moral exemplars and resist what they take to be Judaism's more traditionally exceptionalist self-understanding. Kaplan's concept of God was as modernized as his concept of Judaism: God is not a supreme, personal, conscious being who intervenes in history, but a symbolic synthesis of the historical processes and moral principles that contribute to the human good—God is thus an ethical force more than a supernatural being.

Matthew Miller's life and art appear to be deeply imprinted by Reconstructionism, and especially by its syncretistic interpretive ethos, or what we might playfully refer to as its hermeneutic of sampling and remixing. After dropping out of high school and spending some time following the jam band Phish, Miller took a trip to Israel and eventually discovered and embraced Hasidic Judaism. Hasidic Judaism emerged as an Orthodox spiritual revival movement in eighteenth-century Poland in reaction to the academic tendencies of the dominant modes of Rabbinic Judaism. In contrast to the rabbinical intellectual focus on Talmudic study and interpreting Jewish law, or Halakah, Hasidic Judaism emphasized a mystical personal union with the divine. It rapidly grew as a Jewish spiritual movement through the nineteenth century in Europe but was tragically decimated by the Holocaust. Today, Hasidism is considered an Ultra-Orthodox sect, and is concentrated mainly in Israel and New York City.

Perhaps in reaction to what he perceived to be the modernist, assimilationist, and secularist characteristics of Reconstructionism, Miller embraced the separatist, spiritual, ritualist, Ultra-Orthodox culture of Hasidism. He dressed in full Hasidic garb in observance of traditional codes of dress—the long black suit, black brimmed hat, bearded with sidelocks, or payot. His lyrics allusively expressed mystical reverie at times and were saturated with references to the Torah and to the stories and symbols of Hasidic Judaism. The lyrical content was a long way from Phish, but there were extended trance-like instrumental sequences reminiscent of the improvisational styling of a jam band. Although spiritually, theologically, and culturally Ultra-Orthodox, Matisyahu's musical aesthetic was highly heterodox and contemporary. A blend of reggae, hip hop, and rock, his music was a sonic fusion of unlike things that somehow worked, as mixed and provocative as his spiritually allusive lyrics and his cultural hybrid personae!

Musical genres or styles are commonly imagined as having essential characteristics that distinguish them from one another—for instance, that reggae, hip hop, and rock are sonically, historically, and culturally distinct. But as with religion, the reality of music is much more complex and interesting. Reggae, for instance, is not a pure type, but an emergent musical mélange of African and Caribbean traditions and African American Rhythm and Blues. It grew from roots in the staccato off-beat rhythms of Jamaican Ska and Rocksteady, which were themselves seeded by Caribbean mento, calypso, and American jazz. But from these seeds and roots, and through the fertile soil of Rastafarianism, reggae evolved into a slowed, off-beat, syncopated rhythmic vehicle for postcolonial Afro-Caribbean consciousness, protest, pride, and social change. Reggae, then, is already mixed. To combine reggae with hip hop and rock, both of which are themselves also mixed, is to deepen the musical and cultural hybridity. And then, to realize that a suburban-secular-Jewish-white-kid-turned-Haredi seems to be pulling it off is a little mind-blowing.

Matisyahu is a global postsecular artist. He embodies and musically expresses a creative form of cultural remixing that is characteristic of our globalizing and postsecular religious present. His life history—being raised in a highly modernist form of Judaism, and then choosing and creatively adapting an Ultra-Orthodox form of Judaism—parallels the passage of religion through modernity, in which religion, including religious orthodoxies, increasingly becomes a matter of choice. His mixing of musical genres, too, illustrates aspects of cultural globalization and postsecularity. As reggae's syncopated beats are a creative, off-beat disruption of standard rhythmic lines, cultural globalization interrupts the standard lines and assumptions of classical secularization theory. As reggae creatively advances elements of Ska, Rocksteady, Jazz, and the Blues, postsecular religious trends creatively advance and remix globally diverse cultural and religious traditions. Postsecular religious identities in a context of cultural globalization tend to be chosen and reflexive, aware of their own historical and cultural contingency in a context of alternative religious options, including the option of mixing different religious traditions or not being religious at all.

Interpreting the cultural dimensions and aspects of globalization is a complex undertaking that, as cultural theorist Jan Nederveen Pieterse has evocatively put this, "resembles eating soup with a fork."[1] This is partly due to the reality that cultural globalization "is a long-term, uneven, and paradoxical process" that generates both "widening social cooperation and deepening inequality," as well as seemingly contradictory processes of cultural homogenization and differentiation.[2] Sifting through these paradoxes and contradictions, Pieterse offers an insightful overview of cultural globalization that is a useful background for interpreting the postsecular context of interreligious engagement. He helpfully summarizes three interpretive models regarding the impacts of cultural globalization on questions of cultural identity and difference.

One such model is the clash-and-conflict model, which is associated especially with the work of Samuel Huntington.[3] This model emphasizes the essential and enduring differences of cultural and religious traditions, not despite increasing economic, technological interconnectivity, but even because of it—economic interconnection and integration, fueled by technological innovation and economic policy, generate cultural friction. According to this thesis, cultural and religious traditions are treated as relatively monolithic, non-dynamic, and immutable, and contact between them is likened to collision. The borders and boundaries that matter for interpreting and navigating the world are civilizational and cultural rather than geopolitical and national. One positive effect of this model is that it brings the frequently neglected influence of culture and religion into international relations and policy making. Negatively, however, this model of cultural globalization is organized around an oppositional logic, one that reflects a "West" against the "Rest" mentality. As such, this thesis reinscribes the Cold-War binary of capitalism and communism in cultural and civilizational terms. As Pieterse writes, "While Huntington reproduces standard enemy images of 'the Rest,' he also rehearses a standard self-image of the West. 'The West' is a notion conditioned by and emerging from two historical polarities: the North-South polarity of the colonizing and colonized world, and the East-West polarity of capitalism-communism and the Cold War."[4] As Pieterse points out, these polarities elide the differences and diversities within the global North and South, as well as within capitalist and socialist nations. These internal diversities are neglected by way of a culturally essentialist theory of civilizations. The result, as Pieterse sharply puts it, is that Huntington's version of the clash-and-conflict model of cultural globalization reflects both "Orientalism and Occidentalism."[5] It is shaped by the colonialist stereotyping of Asian and Middle Eastern nations, on the one hand, and the valorization of the strength and innocence of the West, on the other.

Quite different from the clash-and-conflict model is the homogenization model, according to which global interconnectedness generates patterns of global cultural convergence. According to this model, cultural differences yield to, are subsumed within, and are flattened by global interconnectedness. In other words, cultural globalization leads to growth of cultural sameness. Whereas cultural differences within the clash-and-conflict model tend to be interpreted as essential and enduring, cultural differences within the homogenization model are interpreted as "erasable and being erased."[6] Sociologist George Ritzer evocatively describes the cultural homogenization model as a process through which the world becomes McDonaldized. McDonalidization is "the process whereby the principles of the fast-food restaurant are coming to dominate more and more sectors of American society as well as the rest of the world."[7] The McDonalidization metaphor draws attention to the globalization of such modern industrial and manufacturing emphases as standardization and efficiency. Embedded within the metaphor and the broader model of homogenization is a diffusionist theory of cultural change according to which a powerful cultural influence moves from center to periphery. The classical sociological sources for this theory of change include Karl Marx and Max Weber, according to whom, respectively, European modernity would increasingly remake the world in its own capitalist and rationalist self-image. This model of cultural globalization assumes change is unidirectional, from center to periphery, and from Europe and the United States to the rest of the world. It neglects the degree to which, in keeping with the metaphor, McDonalds franchises in Delhi and Moscow localize their menus and their décor to reflect their own culinary and cultural contexts. By neglecting the reciprocal dynamics of cultural influence and assuming a center-periphery diffusion of cultural change, the homogenization model of cultural globalization inscribes a form of cultural imperialism.

To summarize this point, whereas the clash-and-conflict model emphasizes unchanging, essential differences between cultures and imagines the world as "a mosaic of immutably different cultures and civilizations," the homogenization model asserts the mutability of cultural differences and imagines the world moving toward global cultural sameness. A third model, which Pieterse describes as a hybridization model, highlights the ways in which cultural globalization leads to the mixing and remixing of cultures, along the lines that we have illustrated with Matisyahu. According to this model, the globalizing world is, and has long been, a world of open cultural mixing, syncretism, and crossing. Hybridization does not mean a loss of difference. Against the conflict model, the hybridization model does not assume that contact is inevitably conflictive. And against the homogenization model, the hybridization model assumes neither the unidirectional cultural influence nor the flattening of cultural differences into a singular common culture.

Although the recent history of globalization has accelerated the processes of intercultural mixing, hybridization has a long history. As Cees Hamelink observes, "The richest cultural traditions emerged at the actual meeting point of markedly different cultures, such as Sudan, Athens, the Indus Valley, and Mexico."[8] There is something Eurocentric in the claim that globalization is a recent, relatively modern phenomenon. As Pieterse puts it, if it is "primarily a *modern* phenomenon, then it belongs to the historical chain of the European journeys of reconnaissance followed by expansion, imperialism, colonialism, and decolonization. Then the world was an archipelago of fragments that existed in bits and pieces until [European] modernity and the [European] moderns united it."[9] The integrative aspects of recent globalization should be interpreted against a "backdrop of much older and ongoing intercultural traffic," including the deeper history of long-distance cross-cultural trade, technological and artistic diffusions, and the spread of religions.[10] This is why it makes sense to think of contemporary cultural globalization as an "acceleration" of these and other historically integrative processes.

However, while it is true that cultural "mixing has been perennial as a process," it is "new as an imaginary."[11] It runs against the grain of the "boundary fetishism" that results from having been "trained and indoctrinated to think of culture in territorial packages."[12] Through the practice of remixing, we do not cease to inhabit or express particular religious traditions and cultural identities, but we learn to inhabit them differently. Keep in mind the earlier reflection on Matisyahu. Though he mixed diverse cultural styles and musical genres, those styles and genres remained present and detectable—but by mixing them, or bringing them into aesthetic resonance, novel modes of sonic, lyrical, and even religious expression and experience emerged.

Against the homogenization model, hybridization claims that interreligious engagement does not compel diverse religious perspectives to collapse into the sameness of a singular generic religious landscape. And against the conflict model, hybridization affirms, simultaneously, that interreligious engagement need not be conflictive, and that traditions, perspectives, and identities can be remixed in mutually edifying ways. But the possibility of mutual religious learning in a context of cultural globalization requires the cultivation of a particular approach to religious identity and difference, one that resists the "boundary fetishism" of religious and cultural essentialism on the one hand, and a culturally imperialist diffusionism on the other.[13] We agree with Pieterse that in important respects our cultural and interreligious futures depend on which model of cultural globalization we seek to enact, for the different models are organized around "different politics of multiculturalism." The conflict model of essential cultural differences "translates into a policy of closure and apartheid," the homogenization model translates into a "politics of assimilation," while the hybridization model offers the possibility of a "politics of integration" and "new cross-cultural patterns of difference."[14] The accelerated mingling and mixing of different cultural and religious differences are effects of the compression of the world, the technologically mediated sense that culturally and even geographically the world is shrinking. This sense of global compression generates a growing awareness of, and sensitivity to, cultural difference, which in turn is correlated with, as Pieterse puts this, "a general cultural turn" toward self-reflexivity.[15]

The religious effects of this cultural turn toward self-reflexivity shape the postsecular. What then do we mean by the postsecular? We do not think the postsecular is best understood as a time frame or period after the secular. If the "secular" is meant to signify a time without religion, then there never really was a secular. This is not to say that there was not a time when theories of secularization were ascendant. Theories of secularization positing that modernity inevitably leads to the decline of religion, and ideological secularism actively seeking the marginalization or abolition of religion, do have a history—they are common ways many intellectuals, scholars, and social scientists have imagined religion over the past several decades. By the postsecular, then, we are not referring to the return of religion after a time without religion. Rather, we think of the postsecular as a set of cultural conditions that leads to new ways of imagining, inhabiting, and enacting religion.

Kristina Stoeckl and Dmitry Uzlaner describe this cultural sense of the postsecular when they describe the postsecular as "a novel constellation of pluralism. Such pluralism applies also to the religions themselves, which are no longer studied as monoliths, but as multivocal bodies, as part of highly pluralized societies, with which they interact in multiple ways."[16] And, as Charles Taylor has compellingly argued, a pervasive effect of this "novel constellation of pluralism" is the "fragilization" of religious belief.[17] Increasing cultural interconnectedness and global consumerist ideology have relativized religious meanings, purposes, desires, and institutions. The instabilities and uncertainties of these dynamics lead some to turn to orthodoxy and denominationalism, and others to experiment with new religious and spiritual options. The rise of new forms of fundamentalism, religious, cultural, and political, as well as the swelling ranks of the "spiritual-but-not-religious," of religious "nones" and nomads, are all aspects of the postsecular.

In contrast to ideological secularism, then, postsecularism is a way of naming how modernity changes religious traditions, religious communities, and the beliefs and practices of religious people. This raises the question of modernity. When modernity begins and/or ends is a subject of endless debate, as is the question of whether it is a globally homogenizing process of Westernization and capitalist hegemony, or if it is something that, though it may have emerged out of the West, has taken shape in different places through different cultural programs in diverse ways.[18] Rather than enter these debates, we identify modernity as a culturally and geographically variable set of social, material, historical, and intellectual processes that accelerate the pace of social change, interconnect the world, and change the way people imagine and communally organize themselves in relation to truth, meaning, and value. Aspects and effects of these modernizing processes include, among other things, urbanization, industrialization, bureaucratization, new differentiations and fusions of public and private life, expanding education and literacy, innovative communication and transportation technologies, and the ascendance of individualistic and consumerist expressions of human agency.

Through these processes, along with the proliferation of new social media networks and the digital dematerializing of culture, modernity stretches our social relations and internalizes our awareness of cultural difference. This generates, as Pieterse observed, more culturally reflexive self-understandings and identities, or the increasing awareness that our affiliations, beliefs, and values are culturally and historically contingent—that the patterns of belief and belonging with which we identify could very well be otherwise, and that there are a multitude of options for what and how to believe and belong. This reflexivity and sense of contingency releases modern subjects from the experience of their identities as solid and fixed—in short, as sociologist Zygmunt Bauman argues, modernizing processes liquify identity and put it into motion.[19] This melting of solids—of fixed traditions, identities, and social boundaries—creates postsecular conditions for embodying cultural and religious identities and negotiating cultural and religious differences and impacts our human quests for meaning, truth, and belonging in diverse ways.

For some, these social conditions illuminate the cultural and historical contingencies of beliefs, values, and social practices, unfinalizing meaning and deabsolutizing truth, including religious meaning and truth, which are core to postmodern sensibilities and require us to think about and engage with others (and ourselves) differently than in the past. The awareness of historical contingency and cultural context makes it possible for some people, such as Matisyahu, to explore, sample, and remix religious options in new ways. The phenomena of dual-belonging, inter-spirituality, and some liberal and progressive expressions of belief and belonging across traditions, reflect this type of postsecular religiosity. For others, these very same social and cultural conditions generate the opposite response. Sensing that their religious traditions are at risk or jeopardized, they seek to insulate and protect their beliefs, practices, and institutions from what they take to be corrupting influences. Often the sense of religious threat is entangled with a sense of racial and political grievance. Some respond to cultural globalization and postsecularism by turning toward religious pluralism while others turn toward religious fundamentalism. As Diana Eck puts this:

> Both fundamentalism and pluralism are responses to modernity, with its religious diversity and competing values. Fundamentalists reaffirm the exclusive certainties of their own traditions, with a heightened sense of the boundaries of belonging that separate "us" from "them." Pluralists, without giving up the distinctiveness of their own tradition, engage the other in the mutual education and, potentially, the mutual transformation of dialogue. To the fundamentalist, the borders of religious certainty are tightly guarded; to the pluralists, the borders are the good fences where one meets the neighbor.[20]

As varied as these and other religious responses to modernity are, they are all examples of postsecular religion, at least as we use the term. For us, the postsecular refers to a theoretical desire and an empirical reality. Theoretically, it signals the desire to move on from the classical theory of secularization, according to which modernity would lead to the decline of religion, to new ways of interpreting the interplay of modernity and religion. And this theoretical desire emerges from an empirical reality—the contemporary world remains deeply and pervasively religious, and yet the place, function, and forms of religion and religiosity have changed through their passage through modernity. Postsecular theories of religion seek to interpret and explain the interaction of modernity and religion. New pressures for meaning lead people to look for meaning in new ways in their traditions; modernity creates new challenges for individual and communal identities, which leads to performing and expressing religious identities in new ways; modernity changes the way we imagine and inhabit the world, which leads to imagining and inhabiting religion in new ways.

Benjamin Schewel has insightfully leveraged the concept of narrative to interpret the way different theories of religion seek to represent these changes. Theories of religion seek to offer a coherent account of what is going on with religion in the present, as well as where it has been and where it is going. In other words, theories, like stories, are shaped around a causal arc that narratively sequences events, circumstances, observations, and data into a plot. Theories seek to explain in a meaningful way the connections between the history, present, and future of religion and religious life. As stories show how characters respond to and are affected by challenges in their world, theories of religion seek to explain how and why religion and religious people respond in particular ways to a changing world. In postsecular theories of religion, the focal event of social change is modernity. As characters in stories have distinct personalities and traits, which are affected by the events and circumstances they face in their story, so also do theories of religion assume some things about the nature and character of religion, about its structure and function in human life.

In Schewel's first narrative, the "subtractionist" narrative of classical secularization theory, religion is characterized as something that provides humans with a way of coping with what they do not know and cannot do. It is a way of dealing with human ignorance in a complex and mysterious world and with relative human powerlessness in a world of abundantly powerful processes and patterns that we cannot control. According to the "subtractionist" narrative, as human knowledge and power increase, the human need for religion will decrease. Since modernity has brought about an exponential increase in human knowledge and power, in effect shrinking the field of what we cannot do and do not know, "subtractionist" theories argue that the processes set into motion by modernity will inevitably lead to the decline of religion. As Schewel summarizes this narrative, "The basic idea is that there is an inverse relationship between religion and the progressive patterns of social transformation that characterize the modern world. The more modern we are, the less religious we should be, and vice versa."[21] The trouble with the subtractionist narrative, or classical secularization theory, is at least twofold. First, and most pointedly, the modernizing processes of social transformation have not led to the decline of religion. Second, modernization is not a uniform process. As mentioned earlier, theories of multiple modernities show how modernizing processes such as industrialization, urbanization, democratization, and the expansion of capitalism unfold at different paces in different places and impact regional cultures and local communities in diverse ways. While it may be fair to argue, as we have suggested, that modernity has certain common characteristics, it is neither historically nor empirically accurate to say that the processes of modernization are uniform, nor that they inevitably lead to the decline of religion.

According to Peter Berger, a sociologist of religion who was once a proponent of the secularization thesis, "the assumption that we live in a secularized world is false. The world today . . . is as furiously religious as it ever was."[22] It is interesting that Berger used the word "furiously" to describe the status of religion in contemporary life. The context of the comment was a reflection on the rising forms and expressions of religious fundamentalism, which, ironically, are products of modernity. To the extent that fundamentalisms are characterized by a type of belief and commitment that is aggrieved, angry, and oppositional, then "furiously religious" may be a relevant way to describe this phenomenon.[23] But the postsecular is not only about the rise of fundamentalism. It is true that modernity has generated a rise of fundamentalist forms or styles of religiosity, but it is also true that it has transformed religion in other ways as well. Matisyahu, for instance, is hardly a fundamentalist—he embraces Orthodox Judaism and is devoutly and intensely pious, but there is little in his life or his music that expresses fury, anger, or a sense of being aggrieved.

Another way of understanding "furiously" is as a synonym for "frenzied," "intensely," or "passionately." This description of the contemporary religious world may be more accurate. After all, the world today is intensely and passionately religious. But what of the clause "as it ever was"? Perhaps this is accurate if it indicates a lack of an historical break or rupture, such that the religious world is still intensely religious, or remains intensely religious. But if this clause indicates a comparison and is meant to suggest homology or symmetry, such that the world is as intensely religious today as in the past, and in the same way, then the clause is perhaps less accurate. For it is not just that people are as intensely or passionately religious as in the past, but that they are intensely and passionately religious in new and different ways.

So, how does someone like a Matisyahu come about? According to what Schewel describes as the "transsecular" narrative of religion, modernity and religion do not exist in an inverse relationship: modernity is not the antagonist of religion and the processes of modernization do not marginalize religion. Transsecular theories agree with subtractionist theories on a basic point: modernity and modernizing processes affect religion. They disagree, however, about the nature of the impact. Instead of religious decline, transsecular theories posit religious metamorphoses. Modernizing processes such as consumerization, individualization, and the idealization of autonomy, among other things, create relativizing conditions that influence religious behavior, thought, and community in ways that lead some people, for example, to relate to religious traditions, beliefs, and modes of belonging as matters of choice or lifestyle options.

For instance, Berger interprets the postsecular persistence of religion through the paradoxical concept of heresy. The paradox is that although we tend to associate heresy with religious eccentrics, special cases of religious rebellion, or rejections of inherited orthodoxies, Berger sees heresy as a pervasive contemporary religious sensibility, even among those who identify as orthodox or fundamentalist. Berger's point is that, nowadays, it is increasingly impossible to be unaware of, or untouched by, diverse ways of being religious, and therefore we are compelled to make choices about our religiosity. As mentioned previously, this can have a relativizing effect on our religious commitments. As a result of our increasing awareness of, and contact with, different ways of being religious, more people come to experience the inherited religious traditions and identities into which they are born as options they must decide upon—they can choose to affirm them, or not. On this view, one feature of postsecular religion is that more religious people choose their religious commitments and identities, rather than simply living into their religious inheritance. Since "to choose" is a root meaning of "heresy," this feature of postsecular religion can be descried as heretical. The cultural, technological, social, and economic dynamics of modernity means that many people conceptualize and experience religion as an option or choice.

This postsecular transformation of the concept and experience of religion has altered the way people inhabit and abandon religious traditions and inherit and disinherit religious communities and identities. This is what Berger means by the "heretical imperative"—choosing among religious options, including the option of rejecting religion, is itself non-optional. According to this way of thinking about it, the postsecular is characterized by the necessity of religious choice. This does not mean that everyone invents their own idiosyncratic religious paths. Indeed, conversions to orthodoxies, conservatisms, and fundamentalisms, to the extent that they are self-consciously chosen options among alternatives, express the heretical imperative as much as the choice to reject religion or to mix religious traditions. Berger's interpretation of the postsecular illuminates the way modernity "reduces the scope of what is experienced as destiny" by expanding the range of choice and multiplying options, not just with respect to consumeristic goods and services, but also with respect to religious belief and belonging. The emphasis on choice in the realm of religion can have an empowerment aspect to it as well. As Melanie L. Harris describes this, in an adjacent scholarly context, "it has also been observed that millennials, as well as many in older generations, see the world of religion as a cornucopia of choices and religion itself as a place of agency and self-naming."[24] The heretical, in this case, is a mode of self-expression and empowerment.

The postsecular normalizes heresy by necessitating religious choice: "the modern individual is faced not just with the opportunity but with the necessity to make choices" about their religious traditions, practices, and beliefs.[25] This expansion of the realm of choice into the innermost, existential aspects of religious conviction and identity is an effect and a vector of other aspects of modernity such as the expansion of consumerist behaviors generated by global capitalism. Consumer choice is one of the animating logics of free-market capitalism—businesses, manufacturers, and firms compete with one another to sell goods and services to consumers. Consumers must choose among competitors but the metrics of value that consumers use to make their choices, such as a cost-benefit metric, are themselves partly produced by the marketplace through advertising and other means of persuasion. Because of the reach and the depth of capitalism in our everyday lives, even what we think of as a cost or benefit is shaped by the marketplace. And not only our metrics of choice and value, but even our desire for certain goods and services is to some extent manufactured by the market—as consumers we are not only shaped to want more than we may need but also to want certain brands of things more than others. So modern capitalism is not only a free-market system of production and consumption in which businesses, manufacturers, and firms compete with one another to produce the best services or goods. It has also become a cultural context that shapes people's desires and values, and our behavioral and thought patterns in spheres of life that are not explicitly economic.

In addition to consumer capitalism, postsecular religion is also shaped by the multiplying forms of social interaction and social networking across geographic distances and cultural differences. The field of social relationships is massively enlarged, and cross-cultural encounters are more frequent and intensified. This enlarged sociality, in combination with the expansion of choice, relativizes and mobilizes religious structures of belief and belonging, which in prior historical contexts seemed to be absolute and static. Modernity, in this sense, makes more visible the dynamic nature of religion and religious identity. The transition from static to dynamic, from the given and inherited to the chosen and elected, from solid to liquid, can fuel the sense that even the grandest myths, the deepest worldviews and cosmologies that fund the basic categories and concepts through which we interpret and engage the world, are relatively limited perspectives on the world, incomplete and culturally variable perspectives on reality.

Postsecular religious life emerges through the combined material and social dynamics of cultural globalization and modernity. While modernity has not led to the decline of religion, modernity has not left religion unchanged either. Religious commitments and identities are rendered vulnerable by proximity to, and encounters with, multiple religious alternatives. For some, this can lead to an insistence on the absolute truth and rightness of their religious and moral positions, to an aggressively reactive response to the perceived threat of other ways of being religious. It can also lead to an emancipating embrace of religious pluralism and the possibilities of mutual learning. But to understand these options and their implications for interreligious leadership more fully, it is helpful to consider how they are related to the pace of social change.

Social and Technological Acceleration

In our surveys and workshops, many participants have expressed that they are frustrated by the sense that life seems to be speeding up and that there just is not enough time to do everything that is important to do. The challenge for the religious leaders and students with whom we have worked is not a lack of meaning and purpose, but a perceived lack of time—there is so much going on in their families and communities, their personal and professional lives, so many demands on their attention and time, so many emails and meetings, that it is easy to become overwhelmed, exhausted, and even disoriented. Life becomes a blur, and time seems scarce. Pope Francis, in his recent encyclical *Laudato Si'*, spoke to our changing sense of time: "The continued acceleration of changes affecting humanity and the planet is coupled today with a more intensified pace of life and work which might be called 'rapidification.'"[26] Pope Francis acknowledges that change is part of the way complex systems work, and yet that the pace of change today is putting unsustainable pressures on us as individuals and on our social systems and the natural world.

We feel these pressures ourselves and our guess is that most of you who are reading this book do so as well. The contemporary experience of the increasing pace and pressures of time is pervasive for a reason. They are experiential effects of what social theorist Hartmut Rosa calls social acceleration, which he argues is the constitutive dynamic of late modernity.[27] As he explains, "you really cannot understand modern society and also the throbbing heart of capitalism if you don't understand that it permanently speeds up social life. . . . That is to say, the world around us does not stay the same, it changes in ever shorter intervals. And this in turn leads people to try to increase their pace of life."[28] These claims about the linkages between contemporary society, capitalism, and the pace of life provoke several questions. Does the theory of social acceleration claim that time itself is speeding up, and if not, what is it claiming? What are the causes of social acceleration? What, if anything, is wrong or problematic about an acceleratory world? And last, what does social acceleration have to do with the distinct challenges of contemporary interreligious leadership?

First, social acceleration is not about the acceleration of time itself. It is not a cosmological claim. The length of a day on planet Earth is still comprised of the same number of hours, minutes, and seconds and the Earth still rotates on its axis and orbits around the Sun at the same velocities. But if time is not speeding up cosmologically, what accounts for the pervasive sense that life is speeding up and the prevalent anxieties of time scarcity? What is acceleration about if not the velocity of time? Acceleration theory is not about time itself, but about the causes and conditions of our changing perceptual and sensory experience of time. And it turns out that, since we are temporal beings, our changing experience of time influences many aspects of our lives, including our relation to physical space and place, our generational sensibilities, our connectedness to history, our relations to other cultures, and even patterns of religious belief and belonging.

According to Rosa, our changing experience of time is caused by three primary phenomena: the speeding up of technological innovation, the velocity of social change, and the pace of everyday life. The speeding up of these phenomena is fueled by the capitalist imperative of growth and, correlatively, by a cultural drive to prosperity and security in an increasingly unsettled world.[29] In combination, these realities help to explain not only our personal experiences of temporal anxiety but also provide context for understanding broader societal and cultural issues, including deepening cultural and political polarization. But before we explore the social and cultural impacts of acceleration, it is important to examine how the increasing tempos of technological innovation, social change, and everyday life reinforce one another.

For many, the most obvious and easily understood aspect of social acceleration is the increasing rate of technological change—every few days or weeks, we are given notice of the need to run new software updates on our computers and apps; every few months, we are subject to an onslaught of advertising for new and (allegedly) improved smartphones; and every year, car manufacturers desperately appeal to us to buy the latest models of their cars. These examples provide a snapshot of the current pace of innovation in consumer technology. But if we widen our lens to gain a view of the broader historical scene, we can see that over the past several generations our lives, communities, and social patterns have been dramatically transformed by the production and management of new transportation, manufacturing, and communication technologies.[30]

For example, over the past century, transport technologies have radically changed our perception and experience of the relation between time and space. It wasn't so long ago that we were amazed by the first high-speed trains travelling at 60 miles per hour, but now, electromagnetic trains can speed along at 375 miles per hour; where it was once the case that we used diesel and gas engines to drive our cars, now there are driverless electric cars with computers that drive us; similarly, in aviation, we have transitioned from an age of propellers to supersonic jets and pilotless drones. The changing speeds and forms of transportation, through which it takes less time to travel or transport goods, compress our sense of space. The distances remain the same but experientially, as well as in our imaginations, we are more proximately connected to distant people and places. Similar transformations have taken place in communications. Within the span of a single lifetime, we have shifted from using typewriters and organizing our information with physical file folders and floor-to-ceiling cabinets, to desktop computers and floppy disks, laptops and micro-drives, and now, notebooks, tablets, phones, and cloud-based storage. We send emails and social media messages to one another instantaneously, effectively collapsing the communicative and relational tissue between people, time, and space. In these ways among others, the increasing velocity of communication and travel technologies leads to the experiential compression of geographic and cultural space.

As the physical world virtually shrinks through the accelerating speeds of new technologies and the increasing rate of innovation, our social worlds dilate and our sense of proximity to diverse social and cultural others intensifies. As a result, our sense of ourselves in the world, of where we and others are located, physically and culturally, and of how communal and personal identities are shaped by particular places have been fundamentally transformed. One important impact of these transformations is the abstraction of social and cultural relations from localized geographic, social, and cultural contexts. Material technological changes affect immaterial social and cultural conditions insofar as "patterns of association and relationship are no longer or to a lesser extent bound to one common geographic space."[31] Thus, the technological changes that make it possible for us to span physical distances in new ways and at increasing speeds also create new opportunities and challenges for spanning social and cultural differences. Cultural difference is made proximate through technologically mediated temporal synchronization and spatial deterritorialization. This is of course not to say that cross-cultural and interreligious interaction is historically novel—for as long as there have been migration and trade, diverse cultures and religious traditions have interacted with one another. The point is that encounters with cultural and religious difference, often mediated through new technologies, saturate the everyday life experiences and consciousness of many more people than ever before.

Another cultural and religious effect of these processes is the correlation between portability and commodity. As the deep historical connections between cultures, people, and particular places are loosened, cultural and religious traditions can be perceived as products to be tested, brands to be loyal to or identified with, and styles to be enacted. As traditions are made portable and commodious, the authenticity of cultural and religious identities can seem increasingly dependent upon individual expressive facility rather than historically sedimented and intergenerationally formed inheritances. As a result of this, cultural and religious identities can be experienced as tenuous and contestable, adding to the sense described earlier of the "fragilization" of religious belief. By intensifying our awareness of cultural difference and increasing the frequency of cross-cultural encounters, technological acceleration impacts the way we inhabit religious traditions and enact religious identity by bringing images and experiences of diverse religions and cultures into the temporal and spatial textures of everyday life.

A second element of social acceleration that is important for interreligious leaders to be aware of is the increasing speed of social change. Social change includes such things as "attitudes and values, as well as fashions and lifestyles, social relations and obligations as well as groups, classes, or milieus . . . [and] forms of practice and habits," all of which are changing at increasing rates.[32] The speed of social change has led some social theorists to introduce new metaphors for interpreting the contemporary social world. Modern sociology traditionally focused on relatively stable and fixity entities, such as institutions, firms, organizations, and industries, and used spatial metaphors like spheres, sectors, and forms to describe how and where social actors interact. In contrast, postmodern social theorists are increasingly using more organic, de-spatialized metaphors to describe the social experience of contemporary life. As we mentioned earlier, the sociologist Zygmunt Bauman uses the metaphor of "liquidity" to represent the increasing dynamism of postmodern life, including everything from social and geographic mobility to institutional and identity destabilization.[33] The evocative power of the metaphor, in the context of social acceleration, comes from the contrast to solids and the way this contrast reflects the changing experience of time—whereas solids hold their shape over time and are identified with the spaces they occupy, liquids change shape as they flow across spaces and move through time. In this way, the metaphor of liquidity helps to represent the shape-shifting effects on identities, traditions, and communities as the rate of social change increases.

Think of the changing rates in work and family cycles, which, over time, have shifted from intergenerational to intragenerational.[34] In the premodern and early modern world, it was typical in many cases for children to take up the type or sphere of work that their parents did. Later, this intergenerational pattern shifted to a generational one, in which it was more common for children to do work that was different from their parents. And yet, although the type of work might be different, it was typical for a person to hold the same job or at least to work in the same field for the whole of their working lives. But now, it is much more common for people to change jobs, and even fields of work, multiple times during their working life. Similar changes are evident in family cycles. It used to be typical for a family structure to remain stable across a few generations, whereas now, with increasing rates of divorce and remarriage, of stepparents and stepchildren, it is much more common for family structures to change within a single generation.

Accelerating social change, as illustrated in the changing rates in work and family cycles, contribute to our changing sense of time by contracting the temporal range of experience we draw from to orient ourselves in the world. The past that is experientially relevant to us as we navigate our social worlds recedes away from us in direct proportion to the increasing speed of social change; so also does our sense of what we can reliably anticipate or expect about the future. The intensifying experiences of personal uncertainty and social unpredictability impact not only individual persons but also contribute to sharper divisions between generations and age groups, which can further destabilize social institutions and cultural norms.

Thinking about the accelerating pace of everyday life brings us back to the visceral experience of time scarcity with which this whole discussion began. The accelerating pace of life and the sense of time scarcity generally have to do with new personal and social patterns in which we attempt to do more things during a given span of time—for example, fitting in a phone call to our parents or other family members during a commute, or catching up on the news while cooking dinner, or checking and responding to emails during a meal with family. What is ironic, however, is that we are feeling more hurried, and that we sense that we have less time than before, even though new technologies were designed to increase efficiency and, allegedly, give us "more time." After all, since transportation and communication innovations are often aiming to reduce the time it takes to do certain things, we should feel as if we have more rather than less time for everyday-life activities.

Consider email.[35] Email accelerates the flow of communication; it takes much less time to write, send, and receive emails electronically than it does to write, send, and read letters sent through the postal service. Thus, if we were communicating with the same number of people with the same frequency as we were before email existed, email should free up significant time. But this is not true for anyone we know! This is because although email has accelerated the speed of communication, it has also substantially increased the daily frequency and volume of written communication and the number of people with whom we are communicating. In this way, an innovative communication technology that accelerates the speed of communication and could in theory provide us with more time to do other things, has reduced the time we have for other things. But because we still need or want to do the other things (whatever they are, some combination of other work responsibilities and family or personal activities), and since the length of a day does not change, we end up having to fit more into less time. And trying to do more in less time leads both to the sense of time scarcity, the compression of experience, and to task anxiety. We tend to be hurried throughout the day and must regularly face challenging decisions about prioritizing our tasks, which compels reflection on what matters to us, what we value, and why. We feel pressure to decide between pace and quality, tasks and relationships, urgency and importance, and this pressure forces reflection on the moral, cultural, and religious traditions that shape our values and beliefs at the very moment when these traditions have been relativized by the globalizing and postsecular processes described earlier.

In sum, as Rosa puts this, "social acceleration produces new experiences of time and space, new patterns of social interaction and new forms of subjectivity, and by consequence, it transforms the ways human beings are set or placed in the world."[36] The acceleration of technological innovation compresses space, by diminishing the spatial obstacles to communicative interaction with others, and effectively contracts the space of cultural difference. Accelerating social change reduces the relevance of the past to the future, effectively compressing the present. And the accelerating pace of everyday life compresses experience—we feel compelled to do more, to fit more in, within a given unit of time, thereby producing the conditions of time scarcity. And all of this together contributes to a sense of the precarity of meaning: the proximity of cultural and religious difference can relativize cultural and religious commitment, cultural and religious identities are made portable and commodious and seem to depend on our facility to perform them adequately, and the cultural and religious meanings and moral values through which we navigate the world are increasingly pressured by the frequency with which they and we are burdened by the important everyday life decisions an acceleratory world force upon us. The increasing pace of social change, which becomes intragenerational, and the frenetic rate of technological innovation, which compresses our sense of space and brings us into more proximate relation with diverse others, contribute to a growing postsecular awareness of the contingency of our cultural and religious traditions.

Thus, the increasing tempos of technological innovation, social change, and everyday life reciprocally reinforce and mutually accelerate one another, and effects of this include a sense of the precarity of cultural and religious identities in relation to our performance of them and the vulnerability of cultural and religious traditions in relation to the vagaries of speed. The sense that everything that matters to us could be otherwise, and the ever-present awareness that for many others it is, produces, for some, a liberating release into intercultural curiosity and interreligious experimentation, and for others, a reactionary retreat into the comfort of fixed identities and traditions, which brings us to the topic of polarization.

Polarization and Religious Supremacy

Let us now turn to a final context for thinking about the challenges of interreligious engagement and leadership—the context of polarization, which is related in interesting ways to our discussion of postsecular globalization and social acceleration in the previous sections of this chapter. There has been much analysis and anxiety recently about increasing political polarization in the United States. Some of the most illuminating new studies about this have important implications for interreligious engagement, and specifically for understanding religious supremacy. These studies show that political polarization today is less correlated to political ideas or policy preferences than to a moralized sense of partisan identity. This is indicated by research showing that people will shift their policy preferences and values to match their party affiliation, rather than shift their affiliation to match their values.[37] Drawing from a foundational religious metaphor, some scholars are referring to this emerging form of polarization as "political sectarianism."[38] The term's religious resonance is intended to reflect the moral absolutism and identity-based construction of contemporary partisan politics. Members of political sects, researchers argue, are bonded by an identity-based and emotional commitment both to their sect's moral superiority and to a strong sense of the moral inferiority of other sects.

Political sectarianism has many sources and causes. One contributing factor to this sectarianism is the changing media landscape in recent decades. This includes the political fragmenting of old media, or legacy media, such as radio and cable news, which was fueled in the United States by the Federal Communications Commission's repeal of the "Fairness Doctrine" in 1987. This allowed radio and cable news stations to politically consolidate their programming and target an ideologically like-minded audience with news and commentary that reinforced their preexisting political leanings: "People who are already sectarian selectively seek out congenial news, but consuming such content also amplifies their sectarianism."[39] Thus, while it was once the case that social conservatives and liberals sorted across partisan political lines, such that liberal Republicans and conservative Democrats were broadly distributed, this is now much less common. Liberals are aligned much more closely with the Democratic Party and conservatives with the Republican Party. For anyone following politics over the past couple of decades, this should not be surprising; nor should it be surprising that by capitalizing on the phenomenon of confirmation bias and doing so in ways that caricature and even demonize other partisans, radio and cable news media have helped to fuel political polarization.

Social media has only compounded and accelerated the polarizing trends of legacy media. One of the ways it does this is by employing "popularity-based algorithms that tailor content to maximize user engagement," which has the effect of "increasing sectarianism within homogenous networks, in part because of the contagious power of content that elicits sectarian fear or indignation."[40] While older media is editorially centralized, and its audience is relatively passive, newer social media is editorially decentralized, and its consumers and audience actively create, curate, and amplify content. Increased engagement on social media is the means to increased advertising revenue, and emotionally charged, incendiary, and polarizing content increase engagement. In short, polarization is a primary profit stream for corporate social media and political fundraising. The political fragmenting of legacy media and the amplifying effects of newer social media have combined to create increasingly polarized information ecosystems. As a result, news media consumers are sorted into ideologically homogenous echo-chambers that reinforce their political identities and partisan biases, intensifying the phenomenon of political sectarianism.

Political elites are also driving political sectarianism. This is reflected by the prevalence of negative political messaging that aims to galvanize and mobilize partisans rather than positively to persuade citizens on the merits of policy. Elite polarization is also influenced by a campaign finance system that drives politicians into relations of dependence on ideologically extreme donors. Adding to these factors is the use of new mapping technologies in the partisan gerrymandering of congressional districts, which effectively allows politicians to choose their voters rather than voters to choose their representatives.[41] While political sectarianism broadly affects the whole of the political spectrum, the polarization of Democratic and Republican Party elites is not symmetrical. Since the late 1970s, "Republican politicians [have moved] further to the right than Democratic politicians have moved to the left."[42] The causality of asymmetrical elite polarization, which is a driver of political sectarianism broadly, is complex but is historically correlated with the civil-rights era alignment of white Southerners with the Republican Party and the deep historical ties between white Evangelical Christianity and systemic anti-Black racism.[43] In other words, race and religion are historically and structurally comingled with, and help to fuel, asymmetrical polarization and political sectarianism.

This brings us to the fusion of political and demographic identities, which is the most relevant aspect of political sectarianism to our work in this chapter.

The Republican Party is much more racially and religiously homogenous, less formally educated, and more rural than the Democratic Party. Specifically, the Republican Party is whiter and more Christian than the Democratic Party, which is comparatively more multiracial and more religiously diverse. As of 2019, 81 percent of registered Republicans were white, compared to 59 percent of registered Democrats; 79 percent of registered Republicans identified as Christian, compared to 52 percent of registered Democrats; 29 percent of registered Republicans have a college or graduate degree, compared to 41 percent of registered Democrats.[44] Evidence such as this supports the post-ideological, identity-based construction of political sectarianism, and shows that partisan political identities are increasingly fused with race, religion, and culture.

The effect of this demographic sorting of partisan sects is the transformation of "political orientation into a mega-identity that renders opposing partisans different from, even incomprehensible to one another."[45] That partisans view one another as different and even incomprehensible to one another, however, is putting things mildly. In a highly moralized politically sectarian landscape, the fusion of demographic mega-identities with political orientation makes opposing partisans view one another as if from morally inverted worlds, worlds whose boundaries are marked by social, religious, and racial identities.

Interestingly, evidence shows not only that the rise of political sectarianism is driven more by identity than ideas or policies but also that the identities of political sectarians are formed more by out-group aversion than by in-group affiliation. Political sectarianism is constituted by three elements: "othering—the tendency to view opposing partisans as essentially different or alien to oneself; aversion—the tendency to dislike and distrust opposing partisans; and moralization—the tendency to view opposing partisans as iniquitous."[46]

Political sectarianism, then, is the effect of mixing racially and religiously inflected mega-identities with a moralistic politics of essentialist othering and aversion. This helps us to understand the toxic societal cocktail of mutual suspicion we described at the opening of this chapter, which Patel and our students have said, and we agree, contributes to the urgency and the difficulty of cross-difference engagements generally and interreligious leadership specifically. The lens of political sectarianism, which represents a trifocal fusion of politics, religion, and race, also helps us to see the linkages between polarization and our critical thesis about the religious supremacy fractal.

Our aim in these concluding reflections is not to make a causal argument about the role played by specific religious traditions or beliefs in the rise of political sectarianism. Rather, we will look at how different religious dispositions are correlated to the ingredients of political sectarianism noted earlier: othering, aversion, and moralization. In suggesting that the logic of religious supremacy is a vector and amplifier of other contemporary social challenges, we are not assuming that religious supremacy can be easily isolated from, for example, ideas about racial and national supremacy. We understand religions as historically dynamic, existentially potent, sociocultural systems of meaning, value, and practice oriented around transcendent ideals and correlated to a sense of ultimate reality.[47] As such, religions are deeply entangled with other human systems of meaning, value, and practice, including cultural, racial, and political systems.

In the United States, as well as around the world, anti-Semitic, Islamophobic, and white nationalist hate crimes and mass shootings are on the rise.[48] As noted by Robert Jones of the Public Religion Research Institute, "There is clear evidence that we are witnessing measurable upticks in hate crimes and hate groups."[49] Jones cites reports from the FBI that indicate a 30 percent increase in hate crimes in 2017. In addition, the Southern Poverty Law Center also shows a 30 percent increase in the number of hate groups in the United States from 2016 to 2017, reaching the highest number of such groups since their record keeping began in 1999. And according to the Anti-Defamation League, there was a 57 percent spike of anti-Semitic incidents in the United States in 2017, representing the largest single-year increase in the past fifty years. Federal law enforcement agencies in the United States are clear about the threat of domestic right-wing white nationalist terrorism. In recent congressional testimony, FBI director Christopher Wray reported that between 2017 and 2021 the number of domestic terrorism investigations had doubled, and the number of arrests of white supremacists had tripled.[50] In the United States, the increasing frequency of hate crimes corresponds to the increasing prevalence of xenophobic public and political discourse. As Jones observes, "Remarkably, the wink-and-nod behavior of [former President Trump] has been so prevalent, and the resulting increase in violence so pronounced, that a 2018 PRII survey found that a majority (54 percent) of Americans said they believe that President Trump's statements and behavior have encouraged white supremacist groups."[51]

Thus, in the context of the United States, the politically sectarian fear-driven trifecta of othering, aversion, and moralism, described previously, is especially resonant with particular fusions of religious and racial identity: those who are feared and loathed tend to be people who are not Christian, or presumed not to be Christian, or not white, or neither white nor Christian; and those who are afraid tend to be conservative white evangelical Christians. None of this means that being politically or socially conservative, or white, or white evangelical naturally causes one to be xenophobic, or to subscribe to an inverted persecution complex, or to be hateful and violent. But it does mean that in the United States, a xenophobic politics of racial grievance is disproportionately produced, activated, and circulating within the cultural contexts of white American Evangelical Christianity, compared to other religious and racial communities.[52] What is going on here? Are these patterns unique to white evangelical Christians in the United States, or are there similar dynamics among other groups in other settings?

As we said earlier, no tradition has a monopoly on fear and hate. Hate, fear, xenophobia, and intolerance circulate and have always circulated within a variety of religious and cultural communities, and for diverse historical, sociopolitical, cultural, and economic reasons. In India, for example, the marginalization of minority Muslims by majority Hindus, and the periodic outbreaks of violence between them, cannot be understood apart from the historical legacy of the "divide-and-rule" strategies of British colonialism. Similarly, the oppression of Tamil Hindus by Sinhalese Buddhists in Sri Lanka, and the long-standing historical conflict between them, has a colonial history. In addition to colonial histories, the cultural and racial identities of perpetrators and victims, and internal domestic politics, also matter. In India, conflicts between Muslims and Hindus are aggravated by the rise of the Hindutva over the last century, an ethnonationalist movement of Hindu chauvinism mobilized by the BJP. While cases in other parts of the world could also be cited, our point is simply that the roots and motivations of fear and loathing around the world, now and in the past, are irreducible to singular causes, religious or otherwise, are not confined to specific traditions or national contexts, and cannot be resolved by simplistic solutions.

But the critical concern that motivates our work on interreligious resilience in this book is focused on the amplifying role of religion in all of this. What is it about some forms of white Christianity in the United States, and other religious and ethno-racial fusions in different cultural contexts, that accounts for the resonance of fear and loathing? Granting that sociopolitical, historical, and economic variables matter, as well as other factors such as racial socialization and media consumption, our constructive argument on behalf of interreligious resilience requires a basic understanding of the psychological structure and social expression of religious supremacy. If religious supremacy is not exclusive to any individual religious tradition and is not correlated to specific religious doctrines, then what is it and how does it arise? We need to address these questions, at least briefly, to offer a context for additional work in the next chapters.

As we briefly introduced it previously, we think of religious supremacy as a fractal phenomenon. By this we mean that it is constituted by mutually reinforcing patterns of religious belief and belonging—specifically, monopolistic understandings of religious truths and ideals, oppositional and racially coded religious identities, and exclusionary logics of religious community. To describe religious supremacy as fractal is to say that it is structured by a system of patterned relationships that repeat themselves in diverse contexts and at various scales, within and across traditions and historical time periods. As defined by Perry Schmidt-Leukel, the originator of the fractal interpretation of religious diversity, a fractal "refers to certain patterns, structures, or forms that display either a rough or strict self-similarity across various scales. A component of the pattern or structure constitutes an identical or similar copy of the whole. Recursiveness and scale invariance are the two key elements of fractals."[53] Thus, even though religious supremacy manifests in different religious traditions in contextually particular ways, it tends to show up, as we define it, as a pattern of relationships of self-reinforcing approaches to religious truth, identity, and community. To describe this fractal pattern as "supremacist" is to identify it as one that leads to the sense that one's own community or tradition is immune to error, it is innocent or pure and, for these reasons, superior to other communities and traditions—patterns of belief and belonging that parallel the trifecta of othering, aversion, and moralism constitutive of the politically sectarian form of contemporary polarization.

Thus understood, the supremacist fractal helps to explain why some religious individuals and communities are more susceptible than others to the dynamics of fear and loathing. If one's view is that one's own religious community has a monopoly on religious truth, then one will tend to view the truth claims of other religious people and their communities and traditions as wholly in error, or at best incomplete—as infidels, kafir, heretics, unenlightened. This leads one to approach religious others as people who need either to be corrected, defeated, or at best educated into the higher truth of one's own religious way. To approach other religious people in any of these ways is to have an oppositional religious identity. For someone with an oppositional religious identity, religious others will be perceived as threats that need to be vanquished, problems that need to be solved, souls that need to be saved or converted, or people who do not matter or count and are even dehumanized. People with oppositional identities and monopolistic understandings of truth tend to have been formed within exclusionary religious communities, whose exclusionary ways they in turn reinforce through their participation. These reinforcing approaches to religious truth, identity, and community create the fractal of belief and belonging that we define as religious supremacy, which in turn channels and amplifies other forms of prejudice and supremacy, and functions as a reinforcing vector of politically sectarian polarization.

Conclusion

Returning to the questions posed at the beginning of this chapter, we now have more context for understanding why our encounters with difference seem especially complicated these days and why our political, religious, racial, and cultural differences seem so electric and supercharged. We are living through a unique time in human history, a time of spatial and cultural compression, accelerating social change, and new fusions of religious, political, and racial identities. In such a time, "The encounter of worlds and worldviews is [our] shared experience," as Diana Eck has observed; and this shared experience of difference provokes some common questions: "What do we make of the encounter with a different world, a different worldview? How will we think about the heterogeneity of our immediate world and our wider world?"[54] In this globalizing, postsecular, acceleratory world of political sectarianism and religious supremacy, these are the questions that make interreligious leadership so important and so challenging. In the next chapter, then, we turn to a discussion of theories and models of leadership generally and for interreligious leadership in particular for a world and time such as this.

3

Interreligious Leadership

Challenges and Opportunities

Introduction

As we argued in Chapter 2, the globalizing, postsecular, acceleratory, and polarizing dynamics of the contemporary world create pressures that can be mobilized in ways that reinforce tendencies toward the supremacy or resilience fractal. We are at an inflection point. The same pressures, changes, and disruptions (i.e., the various effects of these trends and developments) that can strengthen the appeal of supremacy (racial, nationalist, religious, etc.) can also create the opportunity and the need to practice religious and interreligious life in more constructive ways.

Although these developments of modernity and postmodernity are not uniformly experienced—they vary in a wide range of contexts and can result in very diverse conditions and situations—the challenge for religious leaders committed to cultivating interreligious resilience and the social ideal of pluralism is the same. It is to recognize (literally, rethink) the dynamics named in Chapter 2, and intervene in them within their spheres of influence, in ways that resist the seductions of monopolistic truth, oppositional identity, and exclusionary belonging and instead reinforce the resilience counter-fractal of pluralistic truth, relational and coalitional identity, and inclusionary and solidaristic belonging.

Globalization

The development and proliferation of technology have helped to create a tangible sense that culturally and even geographically the world is shrinking. Such shrinkage affords opportunities for encounters with others who have different cultures, mores, and worldviews (including religious ones) from us. At times, this is quite positive, and we can learn and acculturate in creative and beneficial ways. And yet, such encounters—along with the associated increasing economic and technological interconnectivity—can lead to clashes and conflicts. When we neglect the reciprocal dynamics of cultural influence and exaggerate or flatten difference, we may enact a form of cultural imperialism or create polarizing conditions that feed and are invigorated by religious supremacies. Indeed, we live increasingly in a world of complex and multiple worlds, where suspicion of others and factionalism inform a good deal of interactions and decisions. Finding ways to connect with others who are different from us requires meeting and talking with people who are different from us! It takes intentional effort and practice! While good leadership often stresses the need to understand diverse opinions and perspectives and the value of "bringing the outside in," something more than that is needed given both the vast diversity and the entrenchment that we find all around, and often within, us.

The acceleration of change and the feeling (and at times the reality) of instability—in the form of global economic uncertainty, precarious employment, surging ethnonationalism, and the climate emergency, for example—have led to a sense of the precarity of meaning. Given the proximity of the cultural and religious (and other) differences of others, we can easily question the worldviews and values of others, even as we question, or often more likely reinforce, our own. But, as we will see, leading with an eye toward vulnerability is one of the keys to adaptation, innovation, and development, especially in complex systems. Though vulnerability has generally been eschewed in discussions of the best practice of effective leadership, new approaches emphasize the importance of some aspects of vulnerability, such as humility. In Chapters 4 and 5 we will offer a much fuller notion of vulnerability that we believe is core to resilient leadership in all contexts, and especially in the context of interreligious engagement and leadership.

Social and Technological Acceleration

Modernity has ushered in social acceleration, with the rapid global changes and churning of fast-paced information noted previously, as well as the potential for fatigue and overload. People regularly complain of a lack of time—though that is sometimes a code for a lack of meaning and purpose. Some scholars have used the metaphor of "liquidity" to represent this increasing dynamism of postmodern life. Not only are things around us more fluid, but our response to them needs to be less fixed and more fluid as well. How does the sense of time scarcity created by social acceleration impact religious leaders? How does the intergenerational compression of social acceleration impact issues related to formation and transmission of religious identities and traditions? What implications and opportunities does this have for interreligious work?

The Postsecular

Many scholars have identified secularism and postsecularism with decreasing and changing religious engagement. Even individuals who do engage with religion are increasingly choosing what aspects of religion to engage and adopt and their own religious commitments are often impacted by proximity to, and encounters with, multiple religions and religious alternatives. In one direction, we find the increasing retreat or withdrawal into sectarian ways and the hardening of religious, political, and social positions. In another direction, there are relativizing commitments that often become diluted and meaningless.

Religion nonetheless remains a vital force across the globe. It can help to organize people and communities. It can offer valuable ways for meaning making and connection, even when it can be divisive. And, while some forms of religious supremacism may challenge notions of collective good and responsibility, religion can also provide valuable ethical and moral frameworks. How can the various, often oppositional trends of a postsecular world impact interreligious leadership?

Polarization

We have witnessed in recent decades growing sectarianism. One contributing factor to this sectarianism is the changing media landscape, in which the proliferation of new social media networks and the digital dematerializing of culture stretches our social relations and increases our awareness of cultural difference. Our cultural and political differences are hardened by information segmentation. At the same time, we tend to develop confirmation bias, often leading to the demonization of others and the magnification of political polarization. The other postmodern realities noted earlier also contribute to this challenging tendency. How does the increase of out-group aversion (via polarization) play out in religious traditions and communities, and even in the lives of religious leaders themselves who are not immune to those pressures? While effective leadership training often focuses on the importance of communication, are there additional considerations and new approaches to communication that must be taken account of in the accelerating world around us?

Religious Leadership

Despite, or perhaps precisely because of these and other developments, it is more important than ever to deepen and, in some cases, rethink our approach to religious and interreligious leadership for today and the future. Contemporary religious leadership, regardless of the context, can be quite demanding, especially in the globalized, rapidly changing, and complex world we just referenced. In addition to more general leadership challenges, religious leaders often face very unique denominational, communal, and institutional issues and concerns. What is more, the leadership responsibilities and expectations imposed on religious leaders can differ quite a bit depending upon the larger structures within which they work as well as their particular roles—religious leadership today includes more than traditional clergy roles (religious knowledge and ministering functions), but also lay and professional work (as in an institution's board members or organization's executive director).

Given the nature of contemporary society and the myriad challenges and opportunities created by postmodern conditions, religious leaders are almost never sequestered in their own faith traditions. They, like the people for whom they serve in a leadership role, face larger societal and global issues, and interact with people from other faith traditions (including those who espouse no faith traditions) on a daily basis. In a real sense, then, religious leaders today are by default—consciously or unconsciously, willingly or not—in some way participants in interreligious engagement. In such an interreligious environment some of the issues faced by religious leaders reflect "internal" faith tradition concerns and broader religious interests, while also surfacing some unique (often individual or communal) challenges and opportunities.

Having outlined the importance of resilience in interreligious work, what we have termed interreligious resilience, in this chapter we explore how leading in interreligious contexts can be enhanced by ideas and actions inspired by resilience. Just as recent studies of leadership have emphasized that leadership is situational, and not simply top-down and hierarchical, in this chapter we consider the challenges facing religious leaders and communities and those people engaged in interreligious work, regardless of their formal "leadership" title or position. Interreligious resilience, as we have outlined it, is a type of resilience that is manifest in an interreligious context and is beneficial to it.

Interreligious leadership is leadership attuned to interreligious contexts and needs, and our notion of interreligious resilience offers a path toward a deeper and more nuanced idea and practice of leadership generally, and especially within the context of interreligious work.

Interreligious leadership can benefit from the vast literature on leadership more generally and religious leadership more specifically, as well as the rich tradition of interreligious engagement itself. At the same time, new ways of thinking about interreligious leadership (in theory and practice) are required to navigate the challenges and developments in areas of human life and organization. The emphasis on systems thinking and vulnerability, for example, are important components of resilience and along with other skills and qualities they expand the scope and potential efficacy of leadership.

We begin, therefore, with a brief overview of some of the most frequently discussed general principles of leadership. We then turn to a discussion of the leadership skills and approaches associated specifically with interreligious engagement. This discussion is based on some key, recent studies and insights from the field—in feedback we received from three dozen colleagues through a survey of religious leaders involved in interreligious work and through students (clergy, clergy in training, and chaplains) in a course we co-taught for thirty students from North America, South America, Europe, Asia, and Africa, from a variety of Christian, Jewish, Muslim, Hindu, and Buddhist traditions. With the insights from the "literature" and the "field," we chart the key inflection points that these two have in common and where they diverge. In the next chapter, we apply these themes and present some overarching concepts from studies of resilience and vulnerability and suggest a new model of leadership that we believe is particularly well-suited and attuned to interreligious work—work that we believe is essential for overcoming the religious (and other) supremacies we identified in the Introduction and that is necessary for more nuanced and effective leadership in the volatile and ever-shifting conditions of today and the future.

Traditional Approaches to Leadership

There is a vast literature on leadership, much of it drawn from the field of business and organizational psychology. In what follows, we highlight some key findings from a few core studies to identify some of the best practices in leadership generally so that we can assess what elements are important for religious leaders engaged in interreligious work and also identify areas that have received less attention and that can profitably be developed further through an interreligious resilience approach.

Bill Joiner and Stephen Josephs in *Leadership Agility: Five Levels of Mastery for Anticipating and Initiating Change* point out that "The prevailing approach to leadership development moves from the outside in: You identify a leader's external challenges and then determine the competencies required to meet these challenges effectively. An inside-out approach has also emerged in recent years, focusing on the mental and emotional capacities needed for effective leadership."[1]

Joiner and Josephs argue that leadership agility requires both approaches in the kinds of complex and rapidly changing contexts that we have been discussing. Unlike more passive and reactive competencies such as flexibility and adaptability, they assert that "agility implies an intentional, proactive stance."[2] What they term "creative agility" is, they claim, particularly well-suited for "problem solving that uses both critical and breakthrough thinking to generate uniquely appropriate responses." The essence of their concept of leadership agility revolves around a reflective action cycle: assessing situations and results; diagnosing issues—understanding the causes of problems and preventing them; setting intentions; taking action; and (again) assessing situations and results.[3]

They distinguish between types of leadership that fall into heroic levels (pre-expert, expert, and achiever) and post-heroic levels (only 10 percent of leaders in total: catalyst, co-creator, and synergist).[4] In the first category, experts rely on a tactical and problem-solving set of skills and believe that they will be respected for their authority and knowledge. They tend to have a style in which they strongly assert their opinions and do not seek to accommodate others. They generally avoid giving or soliciting feedback. They often work one-on-one and assemble individuals rather than a team, leading to incremental improvements. Achievers are strategic but similarly believe that leaders motivate others. Primarily assertive or accommodative, they accept and at times initiate feedback. Achievers often call meetings to gain buy-in to their own views, though they also seek some form of stakeholder input.

Leaders in a post-heroic level have a different orientation. Catalysts have a visionary orientation and believe they must "articulate an innovative, inspiring vision and bring together the right people to transform the vision into reality." As such, they empower others. They are interested in learning from a diverse range of viewpoints and seek to create highly engaged and participative teams, resulting in an empowering culture. Co-creators orient toward shared purpose and collaboration—seeing leadership as service to others and the development of a shared vision. They are, therefore, integrative and take seriously negative feedback, with a preference for consensus decision-making and deep levels of stakeholder relationships and genuine dedication to the common good. The highest level in this rubric is the synergist (only 1 percent of leaders), who has a holistic orientation. The synergist "experiences leadership as participation in a palpable life purpose that benefits others while serving as a vehicle for personal transformation." The synergist cultivates a "present-centered awareness" along with external feedback, moving fluidly and adjusting between leadership styles and "develops and maintains a deep, empathetic awareness of conflicting stakeholder interests, including the leader's own."

Heroic skills associated with knowledge and motivation skills are important, and they tend to be hierarchical and directive. They literally reflect the "great man" approach to leadership. Post-heroic approaches, by contrast, are more concerned with catalyzing, empowering others, open and vulnerable to critical feedback, fluid and adaptive, aware of broader systems of stakeholders and contexts, and to some extent decentralized (or depersonalized, or perhaps better, less person-centered than the heroic models). These qualities reflect some of the more recent leadership skills that have been identified in consulting, research, and a wide range of leadership literature as most successful in the complex and radically changing environments that animate human life, communities, and organizations with which we began this chapter and which (as we will see further), contemporary religious and interreligious leaders have identified as the most pressing concerns they are facing.

Contemporary Leadership Approaches

Traditional approaches to leadership, which often focused on leadership as mastery and invulnerability, and along the way reinforced perceived masculine leadership traits, regularly resonate with, and can lead to, a supremacist fractal. Much of contemporary leadership literature, by contrast, has come to embrace the complexity, vulnerability, and humility that we all share, including those in leadership positions. The most frequently cited leadership work offers nuanced and reflective advice for those in leadership positions, those who aspire to occupy those positions, or those who leverage the lessons to improve their work and to lead from whatever positions they happen to hold.

Among the many themes addressed in leadership literature are self-awareness; knowledge and learning; contextualizing and meaning making; inspiring and motivating (oneself and others); and adapting and growing from change. These are all helpful in addressing the diversity inherent in a postsecular world, the expansion of globalization, the acceleration of society, and the increasing polarization that we find in the world today. These are necessary, but insufficient for the resilience stance that is prescribed and activated by interreligious resilience. After a quick review of these ideas as reflected in some of the major leadership writers of the past generation—which have themselves helped to differentiate the heroic and post-heroic notions of leadership outlined previously—we turn to some newer emphases and directions in leadership thinking that align with a resilience approach and that we believe advance interreligious leadership for the future.

Self-Awareness

Psychologist Daniel Goleman, in his famous work on "Emotional Intelligence," stressed the importance of several qualities that he found to be effective in leadership development and practice. These included self-awareness, or knowing one's emotions, strengths, weaknesses, drives, values, goals—and their impact on others. Beginning with the self is a significant leadership statement, as it recognizes the central role we play in our interactions with others—in all dimensions of our affect and behavior. Self-regulation, controlling or redirecting disruptive emotions and impulses, similarly builds from internal conditions. For Goleman, and perhaps a bit different from some other early theorists, the emotional side of the person is essential in leadership, as is the relational aspect of leadership, which asks us to consider ourselves as well as our impact on others.[5]

Knowledge and Learning

The guru of leadership, often quoted in rather diverse settings, Peter Drucker, argued—among many other things—that effective executives have a few leadership qualities in common. Leaders know how to acquire knowledge in diverse settings and for various reasons. But while knowledge is in and of itself important, leaders must also have the ability to convert that knowledge into action, through the development and execution of action plans.[6]

Peter Senge in *The Fifth Discipline* famously noted that leadership is about systems thinking—a core component of much of our discussion about vulnerability and resilience and reflective of the broader and more complex system in which interreligious dialog and leadership is situated. Leadership also involves knowledge and learning—in aspects of personal mastery in a number of areas (proficiency, lifelong learning, personal visioning, etc.). For the purposes of interreligious leadership, Senge also points to the value of the construction of mental models. Thoughtful leaders must understand deeply engrained assumptions, generalizations, and the images that influence the world and how we take action. They practice the art of turning the mirror inward—learning to unearth internal pictures, bringing them to the world, and scrutinizing them. They also regularly balance inquiry and advocacy, and they expose their own thinking and make it open to the influence of others.[7]

Central to Senge's model is a "fifth discipline" that relates to learning (and especially team learning—the intelligence of teams, he notes, exceeds the intelligence of individuals; and there is great value in dialog and thinking together). For Senge, real learning is about shifting the mind rather than just taking in information. "Through learning we become able to do something we never were able to do. Through learning we re-perceive the world and our relationship to it. Through learning we extend our capacity to create, to be part of the generative process of life."[8]

Contextualizing and Meaning Making

Ronald Heifetz[9] and Donald Laurie assert that the work of leadership involves providing broad vision through getting up on the metaphorical balcony to see the bigger picture(s). This work bridges knowledge and learning (above) with inspiring and motivating (below). Leadership entails the process of identifying adaptive challenges (so that we may overcome them), regulating distress (through debate, clarification, definition, control), maintaining disciplined attention on an issue, instilling collective self-confidence and a sense of responsibility, and uncovering and protecting the leadership voices from below. These are quite active attributes, and they revolve around providing context and perspective, identifying and maintaining focus, and bringing people along—leading them through change—that have proven to be essential in religious and interreligious leadership efforts.[10]

In a well-known study, Warren Bennis and Robert Thomas inventoried what they found to be essential leadership skills. Among the most important skills, they noted engaging others in shared meaning (and we might add meaning making) and developing a distinctive and compelling voice. Like others, they also maintained that leadership involves the qualities of integrity and the capacity to be adaptive, the latter closely related to the concepts of resilience noted in this book. Indeed, as we will discuss, interreligious work is often focused on narratives—especially around personal experiences; exploring (though not always finding) common ground, seeking to elicit and construct meaning; and practicing agility and adaptation.[11]

Inspiring and Motivating

Goleman also identified some more traditional or classical aspects of effective leadership. These include motivation (being driven to achieve for the sake of achievement), empathy (considering others' feelings, especially when decision-making), and core social skills (managing relationships to move people in desired directions)—all of which are related to our ability to engage with others. As we will see, these are essential characteristics and skills for leaders working in what can be complicated interreligious environments, ones which require knowledge and comfort with oneself and one's beliefs on one hand and an ability to empathize and engage with others and their feelings and beliefs on the other.[12]

For Drucker, successful executives take responsibility for their decisions, communicate effectively, and, as a result, consequently foster buy-in and accountability from supervisees and others with whom they work. For Drucker, good leaders are less concerned with problems than they are with opportunities. The emphasis on knowledge and constructive use of knowledge is central to interreligious leadership, but so is the orientation toward responsibility and entrepreneurialism (in the positive sense) and the skills of communication and inspiration.

In a more constructivist sense, for Senge leadership is also about building a shared vision—finding ways to bind people together around a common identity and sense of destiny and unearthing shared pictures of future that foster genuine commitment and participation rather than mere compliance.

John Kotter, another leading leadership expert, famously contrasted leadership and management—an issue that resonates deeply with many of our communal service students, who often get bogged down in what are ostensibly "management" issues, issues which often divert them from the long-term, strategic, and transformative work they need to do. For Kotter, leadership is about setting directions, aligning people, and motivating and inspiring people. Management, on the other hand, is generally related to what appear to be more tangible (sometimes measurable) skills such as planning and budgeting, organizing, staffing, and controlling and solving. Management skills are important (even, perhaps particularly in the on-the-ground work of interreligious dialog), and at times they do overlap with leadership skills (leaders often need to be managers as well!); but it remains important to remember the differences too, especially as we grapple with some of the challenges related to motivation and alignment.[13]

Adapting and Growing from Change

For Bennis and Thomas, leaders find meaning in crisis. But in doing so, they must understand context, recognize and seize opportunities, and identify reasons for hope and chart appropriate or useful courses of action. Successful leaders are imbued with creativity, optimism, and, importantly, a sense of curiosity. Effective leaders have a deep adaptive capacity, through which they possess an ability to look at a problem or crisis and see in it an array of unconventional solutions; remain comfortable with uncertainties, mysteries, and doubts; thrive in chaos, tolerating ambiguity and change; are willing to understand the benefit of entertaining opposing views and multiple options; and see that conventions and habits can at times be comforting, but can also at times be limiting. While some interreligious work is borne of crisis—acts of violence, bias, and prejudice, for example—and so afford leaders opportunities to engage such skills and approaches, some of the interreligious work is also animated by a sense of common concern and a spirit of love, understanding, and curiosity. Here, the search for meaning and shared understanding and concerns—at times through social activism—are also related to the insights provided in the leadership literature.

Bennis is well known for his work on the "crucibles of leadership." He writes that "Whenever significant new problems are encountered and dealt with adaptively, new levels of competence are achieved, better preparing the individual for the next challenge."[14] The challenges of leadership—the crucibles—can have positive, strengthening roles, help develop and enhance wisdom, and provide a locus for essential questions and reflection—a tipping point where new identities are weighed, values are examined and strengthened or replaced, and judgment and abilities are honed.[15]

* * *

We are aware that this quick survey of some of the most common leadership studies features only male scholars and practitioners. While these approaches are quite diverse, and certainly do address many of the key components of what we will define as resilient leadership, new approaches to leadership that take account of the massive changes that we have outlined throughout this book and in this chapter, and that engage with a more diverse range of perspectives and experiences—including gender and other academic disciplines—will be very helpful and instructive. Such an approach draws on notions of creative vulnerability and on systems and resilience thinking and science (discussed at greater length in Chapter 4).

Similarly, a good deal of recent work on leadership, which emphasizes decentralization, self-organization, and the nature of systems, also emphasizes the importance of networks.[16] In a recent study, "Designing for Networked Leadership: Shifting from 'What?' to 'How?,'" a guide for designing and delivering cohort-based leadership and professional development programs for the Jewish social sector prepared for the Jim Joseph Foundation, Valerie A. Futch Ehrlich and Brendan P. Newlon identify a number of values of networks. These include the idea that field-wide collaboration and resource sharing are necessary to address changing complexity, increase program impact, grow and adapt, and build cultural and social capital.[17] Networked leadership, they maintain, requires collaborative action, systems thinking, developing and engaging networks, and effective communication.[18] In designing programs that support and leverage networks, they recommend selecting with intentionality, establishing trust, preparing learners, delivering powerful content, redefining prestige, launching to a larger network, and changing how we gauge impact.[19] In assessing the value of cohort programs, Futch Ehrlich and Newlon assert that they "are uniquely positioned to create a space for vulnerability and communal support in which participants can be encouraged to reflect on their own leadership and/or life struggles and leverage them to extract new learning and personal growth."[20]

Some of these orientations and skills have been associated in several recent studies, in which women were rated significantly more positively than men in leadership effectiveness during crises, most recently and most notably during the initial phases of the Covid-19 pandemic.[21] In fact, women were rated more positively in all but one of nineteen (and in thirteen of nineteen with statistical significance) competencies measured in one study. Areas measured included initiative, learning agility, leading others (inspiring and motivating others, developing others, building relationships—women appear to have been more aware of the fears and concerns of their followers and excelled in a range of interpersonal skills), high integrity and honesty, powerful and prolific communication, collaboration and teamwork, championing change, making decisions, innovating, problem-solving and analyzing issues, driving for results, valuing of diversity, establishing stretch goals, developing strategic perspectives, and taking risks. The only area in which men rated more positively (55 to 53 average percentile) was technical or professional expertise.

A quick review of some select (albeit well-known and recent) leadership studies given earlier suggests a few broad conclusions about how we think about leadership today. Much of history has been littered with descriptions and discussions of the great men (and we literally mean men) and associations of leadership with power, authority, and office or position. Leadership studies today proffer a different notion of leadership and leaders. Leadership is behavioral and situational. Leaders occupy many different positions, and they may assume many different roles. The qualities of leadership are much more significant (and diverse) than mere position or authority, even as we still recognize that sometimes positions and authority can make a difference in what can be accomplished.

Leadership implies the possession, acquisition, and constructive use of knowledge. But knowledge can be static and focused on ends and acquisition and not on evolution and process. As such, learning is often a preferred substitute for knowledge in education (and we think in leadership as well), stressing as learning does the process of knowledge building and application and the transference of skills beyond specific content areas or particular contexts. The ability to shift mindsets and the importance of curiosity often associated with learning have become key qualities of contemporary leadership. Similarly, the ability to provide broad (internal and external) perspectives and to understand contexts and changes, often discussed in studies on learning more broadly, are valued leadership skills. Consider, for example, the pioneering work of Carol Dweck, which contrasts fixed mindsets and growth mindsets. For Dweck, a fixed mindset operates from a sense that our "qualities are carved in stone" creating an urgency constantly to prove ourselves. By contrast, a growth mindset "is based on the belief that your basic qualities are things you can cultivate through your efforts, your strategies, and help from others. Although people may differ in every which way—in their initial talents and aptitudes, interests, or temperaments—everyone can change and grow through application and experience."[22]

Leadership today is focused on responsibility, which is especially important given the moral and ethical lapses we have witnessed in some recent leadership. Leaders must demonstrate responsibility in all they do, but perhaps nowhere more than when and how they interact with others. Leaders must regularly balance inquiry and advocacy; they must possess true (and not self-negating) humility; they must be comfortable with themselves and their beliefs, even as they practice and demonstrate the ability to empathize and engage with others and their feelings and beliefs.

Key to leadership in a contemporary setting is the ability to communicate effectively. Communication in this context is about constructing and sharing meaningful narratives that animate and inspire. Such communication brings to life the experiences we have, allowing us to connect with and draw in others. They also serve to inspire conversation and the development of consensus, along with shared beliefs, ideas, and motivations.[23] They usher us through change, even as they root us in traditions. Communication is essential in constructing a framework for people of different backgrounds to participate in genuine conversation rather than simply comply with traditional boundaries and particular expectations.

Leadership today is closely linked with systems thinking and particularly understanding how the various components of systems operate together or in opposition and at various levels. Systems thinking requires leadership that examines changes over time and space and that involves many levels of complexity and interaction, with cause and effect being minor and often undecipherable categories of understanding.

Much of the leadership work is related to setting strategic direction, based on internal and external forces and considerations. It requires agility and adaptation, on one hand, and identifying and maintaining focus, on the other. Given the complexities of postmodern life, leadership is often most palpable and on display in times of, and in response to, crises. At times, leadership is expressed in the actions we take in such conditions, frequently through some social activism. The experience of Covid-19 and recent episodes of racial injustice in the United States and elsewhere have made that quite evident.

Of course, the classic differentiation between leadership and management skills does not negate the reality that leaders need to possess and utilize a range of skills, some that appear to be more managerial than visionary. In the same way, effective leadership requires that leaders balance strategic thinking and acting with flexibility that allows them to take advantage of changed conditions and opportunities as they arise.

Religious and Interreligious Leadership

Religious leadership is not (necessarily) the same as interreligious leadership—the latter can (though does not always) require leaders to work more regularly outside of their religious tradition. In what follows, we will identify the key issues associated with religious leadership—many echoing those in the general leadership literature—and then consider in what ways they intersect with interreligious concerns and leadership.

In approaching religious leadership, it is important to note that religious institutions are in fact complex systems—living organisms, which require a good deal of contextualization and which are full of organizing principles, universal and particular dynamics, and a range of relationships.[24] As one religious leadership scholar notes, "congregations are complex, multilayered, intergenerational, and multigenerational institutional relationship systems."[25] Israel Galindo identifies four core challenges for leaders of religious institutions (here specifically referring to congregations):[26] identifying the congregational life stage, understanding the hidden life dynamics affecting the congregation, identifying and providing the leadership necessary for the state of the congregation, and ministering successfully for the current life stage as well anticipating the leadership functions needed for the future. Drawing from many traditional leadership studies, he further isolates six leadership functions: providing vision, leading in crisis, staying connected, serving as the resident theologian, managing, and influencing.[27] Another writer on religious leadership similarly points to some key leadership skills required in religious institutional work today, namely visioning, coaching, affiliating, being democratic, pacesetting, and commanding.[28]

Indeed, many of the traditional observations about good leadership are repeated in the literature on religious (and also interreligious) leadership. According to Jeffrey Jones, to take one example, leadership is simultaneously always and never about the leader.[29] Leadership, he notes, is about servanthood (echoing the literature on servant leadership), change (change that we can only lead when we are ourselves willing to change),[30] and style.[31] Building on the work of Robert Greenleaf, others have developed an inventory of qualities that reflect servant leadership, including listening, empathy, healing, awareness, persuasion, conceptualization, foresight, stewardship, commitment to the growth of others, and building community.[32]

Here, as in many other studies, the work of Ronald Heifetz on the difference between technical and adaptive change is cited.[33] Particularly important is the concept of modeling values[34] or leading by example. What is more, Jones notes that in our leadership work we must be careful and transformative in our language. There is great potential value, for example, in shifting from a language of complaint to commitment; from a language of blame to personal responsibility; from a language of rules and policies to public agreement; and, from a language of constructive criticism to deconstructive criticism encouraging "a new understanding of power and authority."[35] Jones also discusses the importance of teamwork.[36] At the same time, he writes that leaders must enhance, not reduce, conflict. For many of us, taking deliberate actions that will lead to conflict runs counter to both personal desire and our image of our role in the congregation. The very thought of it may make our stomachs tighten, our hearts pound, and our palms sweat. And yet, at times inciting conflict is what effective and faithful leadership demands.[37]

Along similar lines, another writer notes that "Conflict is ultimately a gift to a leadership community when it helps to clarify values, mission, or a strategic direction."[38]

As discussed in previous chapters, what we mean by interreligious can be multifaceted, and have different emphases and concerns depending upon specific contexts. Before jumping into a brief review of some recent thinking about interreligious leadership, it is worth highlighting, therefore, some of the key leadership skills that emerge from one articulation of interreligious dialog. According to one of the leading interreligious thinkers, Paul Knitter, what is required to practice interreligious dialog is to "a) speak one's own conviction clearly and respectfully; b) listen to the convictions of others openly and generously; c) be open to learning something new and changing one's mind; and, if that happens, d) be prepared to change one's way of acting accordingly."[39] That is, interreligious dialog requires the skills of self-awareness, self-knowledge, and self-assurance; active listening and genuine openness and curiosity; and willingness to consider and actually to implement change. As we will see, these and other skills and characteristics are important for effective interreligious leadership. And, while these resonate with the broader literature on leadership, they can also take on different nuance in the context of interreligious leadership. For now, let's turn to some of the recent discussions about the needs and characteristics associated with interreligious leadership.

As we pointed out in Chapter 1, Catherine Cornille argues that necessary prerequisites for interreligious dialog are simultaneously humility (for example, epistemic, doctrinal, spiritual) and commitment to particular religious traditions—without which one would have mere new age syncretism.[40] At the same time, genuine dialog requires a sense of interconnection, possibility of understanding, and empathy.[41] But the same is true for effective leadership in general and interreligious leadership more specifically. Humility is often discussed in leadership studies. In the context of interreligious leadership, it plays a particularly central role. In the most recent leadership literature, humility reflects a leadership stance that is simultaneously self-reflective, open, and vulnerable—aware of limitations and the fact that nobody is an expert in everything—and committed to understanding multiple perspectives and learning as a means to growth. As Cornille writes:

> The impulse to dialogue arises from the desire to learn, to increase one's understanding of the other, of oneself, or of the truth. It thus presupposes humble awareness of the limitation of one's own understanding and experience and of the possibility of change and growth. . . . Humility may also be understood, however, in a more radical sense to denote a genuine acknowledgement of the limitation and imperfection of one's insights and accomplishments, as indeed of all human realization and self-expression.[42]

Many of the traditional approaches to leadership resonate with and are reflected in the discussions about, and the actual practice of, interreligious leadership. Many of the key observations of Eboo Patel highlight important aspects of interreligious leadership, noting different contexts and types of leadership approaches and concerns, such as transformational, transactional, spiritual, and pastoral.[43] While we discussed many aspects of Patel's work in Chapter 1, we rehearse several key themes here as well, as they draw from, and contribute to, the most recent thinking about interreligious leadership. For Patel there are bases of knowledge and skill sets that are essential for people involved in interreligious work. These revolve around some of the core themes we identified previously in the general leadership literature. Reflecting the value of self-awareness, knowledge, and communication in leadership, Patel writes that "An interfaith leader is someone who can create the spaces, organize the social processes, and craft the conversations such that people who orient around religion differently can have a common life together."[44] Interreligious leaders should attempt to be intelligible and convincing to others;[45] an interreligious leader does not need to "check her identity at the door, but does need to be aware of how her various views and positions might affect her engagement in any particular situation."[46] Indeed, interreligious leaders (and people more generally) have a right (and really the obligation) to form and express their own identities,[47] making their own case for the religious traditions, which have real social value.[48] This is particularly the case with the rich text and textual interpretations within religious denominations.[49]

And yet, interreligious (Patel uses the term "interfaith") work must be about more than advancing one's own view.[50] As a result, for Patel, there is an important difference between diversity and pluralism—which we unraveled in Chapter 1. The former is simply the fact that people have different identities; the latter is about trying to achieve understanding and cooperation[51]—core issues of leadership more generally. According to Patel, pluralism includes respect for identity, but also relationships between different communities and a commitment to what he terms a common or civic good.[52] The five civic goods of interfaith cooperation he articulates in this regard are increasing understanding and reducing prejudice;

strengthening social cohesion and reducing chances for identity-based conflict; bridging social capital and addressing social problems; fostering the continuity of identity communities and reducing isolation; and creating binding narratives for diverse societies.[53] Cultivating such goods leads to fostering and building relationships through learning, inspiration, communication, and networks—all crucial in the most contemporary approaches to leadership more generally.

Much of the work that Patel does, and much of what he recommends, revolves around constructing narratives and sharing stories, especially ones of connecting interfaith experiences.[54] Citing the work of Howard Gardner, another key figure in the leadership literature, Patel argues that effective leadership requires "the ability to relate an influential story to the world and embody that story in your life."[55] Communities, he asserts, are constructed through stories,[56] and as a result, "Stories of now move into answering that choice with a plan of action, a plan that will move the world closer to operating by the values that the community cherishes."[57]

Effective interreligious leadership also requires "appreciative knowledge of other traditions, a theology of interfaith cooperation, and a history of interfaith cooperation."[58] In conducting this work, as many have stressed (e.g., Frank Sesno[59]), leaders must facilitate dialog through asking poignant and relevant questions and eliciting meaningful stories (and not simply personal opinions).[60] Interreligious leaders, for Patel, must work to create an environment in which different people can be seen engaging with their own traditions[61] and similarities between groups can be highlighted and cooperation can be facilitated;[62] and yet, he cautions that commonality cannot be mistaken for sameness.[63]

Part of what makes interreligious conversation possible—in fact necessary— is the observation that there can be significant doctrinal diversity within every tradition and every community. Combined with the reality that today we all have hybrid identities, which bring together various perspectives, worldviews, and identities that in the past would never have been possible together and that often go far beyond only religious ones,[64] complicates, but makes even more urgent, the work of interreligious engagement. As a result, interreligious leaders must be attuned to trends in their own faith traditions and in religion more generally, along with current developments and changes in their own communities and in broader (local, regional, national, and global) society.[65] Interreligious leaders need to gain knowledge of other traditions—not merely some mechanical or superficial familiarity[66]—and they must be prepared to recognize the contributions that other religions and members of other religious traditions have made to humanity.[67] Further, they must also interact with real-world situations and people,[68] not simply distilled (no matter how nuanced) or unidimensional representations of others.[69]

Key to Patel's presentation are self-awareness and self-knowledge, which are required to engage with others effectively. At the same time, real interreligious leadership requires respect for others and a willingness to engage in constructive questioning, communication, and conversation. And while interreligious leadership assumes working on common problems and constructing bonding narratives, it also recognizes the importance of discerning, understanding, and, when appropriate, even celebrating difference.[70]

From the Field: A Survey of Those Tilling the Fields of Interreligious Leadership and Dialog

In addition to surveying the theoretical literature, there is much to learn from the experience and wisdom of people who work in the field of interreligious leadership. We have heard religious and communal leaders' reflections on leadership in many educational programs. These reflections often cut across cultural, geographical, and religious boundaries. In one recent global leadership summit, for example, which brought together forty-one Jewish communal leaders from nineteen countries and thirty-one communities (speaking eighteen different languages), we identified some key leadership observations—many of which resonate with the notes earlier and many that point to issues that interreligious leaders need to consider and practice.

Though it may seem trite, we have noticed, as other leadership scholars have pointed out, that affective and emotional elements are crucial to leadership and to successful engagement with others, especially in interreligious contexts. So, we begin with an observation from a cohort of Dean's Latin American Jewish communal leaders, namely that music makes everything better (as some neo-Hasidic and renewal movements in Judaism have clearly demonstrated). More deeply, emotion, expression, and engagement are closely related as we seek to learn in different ways from different people.

As will become clear in some of the case studies, there is great value in continuing to find inspiration for ourselves as we seek to inspire others and we need personal growth reflected in developing self-awareness and understanding in a long-term and planned way. Our cross-cultural Jewish leaders taught us the importance of diversity and cross-cultural experiences and sensitivities, but also the value of collaboration, networking, and crafting a community of best practices. While our Jewish leaders evinced different personal, organizational, and cultural sensibilities—many Jews from the former Soviet Union, for example, feel limited by top-down authoritarian notions of communal power and are more focused on bureaucratic management than creative leadership—there is a good deal of difference between leadership in different contexts. In our case, the idea that there is something we could identify as *Jewish* leadership implied a leadership informed by general leadership principles and best practices *along with* Jewish texts, experiences, and contexts. As we will discuss at greater length, we learned from our students that leadership relies on the challenge and importance of being vulnerable and developing agility and resilience. Our students frequently discussed a range of leadership skills and sensibilities, which emerged from their reading of the literature as well as their own experiences. These included building and developing a team; developing relationships; power sharing; humility, strategic planning, thinking, and prioritizing; inspiring others; providing global vision; and a willingness to take risks and fail.

In researching the theme of interreligious leadership, we also surveyed thirty religious leaders involved in interreligious activities in order to learn about their reasons for engaging in interreligious activities, the core issues and challenges they face, the challenges and rewards of interreligious work, as well as particular related experiences they have had and texts and text traditions that they have found helpful in addressing these experiences.

Our respondents were 40 percent Christian (Roman Catholic, Baptist, United Methodist, Pentecostal) and Post-Christian (Unitarian Universalist), 37 percent Jewish (Reform, Conservative, Orthodox), and 23 percent from other religious traditions (Buddhist, Hindu, Muslim, Baha'i, and Zoroastrian). Our respondents were 57 percent male, 40 percent female, 3 percent nonbinary and ranged in age from their thirties to seventies (7 percent thirties; 30 percent forties; 23 percent fifties; 20 percent sixties; and 20 percent seventies).

Core Challenges

Respondents to our survey revealed several general core issues and challenges faced by religious leaders today, including those that relate to the life of religious institutions and those that have a broader global context. We discussed these to some extent in Chapter 2 and earlier in this chapter. Here, the underlying developments and challenges are played out in the context of the specific challenges of religious life and institutions. Religious institutional life is quite complex today, especially as many religious institutions struggle to attract new members, activate current members, and develop plans for long-term sustainability. These, and other, issues cut across all religious traditions and denominations to some extent, reflecting a whole litany of contemporary conditions and concerns—from the voluntary nature of religious affiliation, the distancing of people from institutions (of any kind), the prevalence of technology in social settings, pervasive secularism (though this, like other topics, is the subject of a fair amount of debate), increasingly hybrid identities, and so forth.

While some issues, such as sex abuse scandals, appear on the surface to be particular challenges for some religious denominations—the underpinning issues, related to issues such as morality, ethics, authority, power abuse, culture, and so forth, resonate across all faiths. Many topics and contemporary concerns cut across religious traditions. These include the challenge of finances—funds to support religious institutional activities and physical structures and to pay salaries and cover administrative costs, for example—and financial stewardship of professionals and lay leaders. In part, this underpinning concern is the result of declining affiliation and membership rates, but also of changing expectations and practices related to charity and membership more generally. In addition to finances, other issues of organizational structure and development challenge today's religious leaders.

Another area that resonates across religious groups relates to the experiences of community (or in some traditions, congregational) members generally, including, but not limited to, issues of innovation in worship and convening, the role of women in liturgy and religious life, and models for adult education and engagement. In these and other areas, the relationship (at times tension and conflict) with larger denominational practices and orientations (in addition to the work across denominations) comes up regularly. What happens, for example, when a Conservative Jewish congregation decides to employ liturgy different from that sanctioned by its movement or is open to intermarriages despite the ruling and practices of the central denominational rabbinical council; or when an individual Catholic priest associates with racist or anti-Semitic organizations that his Archdiocese repudiates?

Religious leaders are naturally challenged by contemporary global issues that extend far beyond their own denominations and institutions, even as they may impact them at many levels. Respondents to our survey identified the challenge of fostering unity in a polarized society. We are in an age of supremacies and fundamentalisms, which lead people not only to reject the possibility of other narratives and truths, but at times seem even to incline them less and less to enter into honest, open, and critical discussion. This is a particularly pressing issue in the context of interreligious dialog, which offers rare opportunities for constructive engagement and openness, but is also easily coopted for other purposes, most notably triumphalism and attempts to win others over to a particular cause, religion, or truth.

The divisions that seem so often to plague society and the enmity that pervades many interactions today often lead to bigotry and even, increasingly, to violence. (Inter)Religious leaders, therefore, must grapple with threats and actual violence perpetrated against their coreligionists and, at times, perpetrated by members of their own religion. The number of cases of shootings reported in the press is alarming, but perhaps more so are the acts of violence, often on a massive scale, that occur every day and are rarely reported or discussed. Added to this are the many acts of hatred that, although not violent, create intimidating environments and set the scene for the escalation of other, often more heinous, acts of hatred.

According to a 2012 Pew study, "Religious Hostilities Reach Six-Year High," social hostilities involving religion hit a six-year high in 2012 (and they appear to have returned to those levels after a brief and small decrease in 2014–15 and 2017).[71] Of the 198 countries and territories studied, 33 percent had high religious hostilities (up from 29 percent in 2011 and 20 percent in 2007). Aside from the Americas, hostilities increased in all geographical regions, with the highest increases in the Middle East and North Africa.[72] Similarly, government restrictions on religion were assessed as high or very high in around 29 percent of cases studied (the same as the previous year studied).[73] Seventy-four percent of countries experienced some level of government interference with worship or other religious practices and "governments used force against religious groups or individuals in nearly half (48%) of the world's countries in 2012."[74]

Actions against religious minorities were reported in 47 percent of the countries surveyed in 2012.[75] Violence or threat of violence was used to "compel people to adhere to religious norms in 39% of countries"[76] and mob violence related to religion affected people in 25 percent of countries. By way of example, according to the study,

> In August 2012, for instance, some 500 Sunni hard-liners attacked a Shia community in the city of Sampang, killing two people, burning dozens of homes and displacing hundreds of people. And in Nigeria, hundreds of Muslim youths attacked and burned Christian businesses and places of worship in November 2012 after a Christian was accused of blasphemy. Four Christians were killed.[77]

In 2012, Jews were harassed in 71, Muslims in 109, and Christians in 110 countries.[78] The most recent Pew study on American Judaism (2020) noted that Jewish Americans generally perceive a rise in anti-Semitism in the United

States. More than 90 percent of US Jews surveyed indicated that they believe there is at least some anti-Semitism in America, and three-quarters say that there is more anti-Semitism in the United States today than there was five years ago. Among Jews who think anti-Semitism has increased, more believe that is because people who hold anti-Semitic views now feel freer to express them, rather than that the number of Americans who hold anti-Semitic views has risen; many do think that both of those statements are true. About 60 percent of Jews surveyed report having had a direct, personal experience with anti-Semitism in the past twelve months. Such experiences include seeing anti-Semitic graffiti or vandalism, experiencing online harassment, or hearing someone repeat an anti-Semitic trope. Just over half also indicate that they feel less safe as Jews in America than they did five years ago; very few feel safer now than they did five years ago.[79]

Diverse religious groups and institutions have increasingly been the object of domestic terrorism attacks in the United States[80] and elsewhere. But terrorism can also be religiously motivated, a fusion of religious and racial supremacy played out in political sectarianism and polarization.[81] More generally, terrorist violence related to religion occurred in 20 percent of countries surveyed by Pew in 2012, and a similar percentage witnessed sectarian violence.[82] What is more, the position of minorities (however defined) and issues of vulnerability—discussed throughout this book—have become more and more important. They reveal challenges, but may also provide opportunities for reflection, engagement, and growth.

At the same time, religion has been seen by some as a source for peace and conflict resolution.[83] While not new, the role of religion in social activism is particularly trenchant given these and other concerns and conditions. How do we address the problems facing contemporary societies and religions? How do we anticipate and proactively respond to the future and the conditions that it will bring? We believe that the theories and practices associated with vulnerability, resilience, and systems thinking, along with the valuable prospects of sincere and constructive interreligious dialog and leadership, proffer a way to address these concerns and make a real difference today and for the future.

One of the keys for genuine and effective leadership, and especially interreligious leadership and dialog, as noted in the previous discussion, is openness to other religious traditions as well as knowledge of one's own faith tradition. The state of education is therefore vital in effectuating serious dialog. According to a study of religion and education around the world conducted by Pew in 2016 ("Religion and Education Around the World"), there are widespread and persistent "disparities in average educational levels among religious groups."[84] Levels vary by religious denomination. Jews, for example, have the largest average number of years of formal schooling at 13.4. Christians have 9.3, unaffiliated 8.8, Buddhists 7.9, Muslims and Hindus 5.6.[85] Jews, Christians, and nones (individuals who indicate they have no religion) are likely to have the highest levels of education.[86]

Educational levels vary by religious denomination even within the same region, however. For example, Christians average higher levels of schooling than Muslims in sub-Saharan Africa.[87] In the United States, religious minorities are more likely to have college degrees than Christians: Hindus 96 percent (Hindus have the highest levels of schooling in places where they are a religious minority[88]); Jews 75 percent; Muslims 54 percent; Buddhists 53 percent; unaffiliated 44 percent—Christians at 36 percent (the US average is 39 percent).[89] The gender gaps in terms of average years of schooling can vary—as of the 2016 Pew study, women are equal in schooling among Jews, lag behind by an average of 0.4 years among Christians, and 2.7 years among Hindus, for example.[90] In Europe, among the youngest Christians surveyed, women lead men in higher education.[91] Notwithstanding the current levels, Muslims and Hindus have made the largest gains in average years of formal schooling over the last few decades.[92] There are also generational shifts taking place. Muslims, for example, have gained an average of 3.1 years more of schooling over the past three generations—the youngest Muslims have 6.7 years of schooling. The largest gains have been in the Middle East and North Africa (+4.5 years).[93]

The relationship between religion and education can be complex, however. A 2017 Pew study ("In America, Does More Education Equal Less Religion?") found that adults in the United States with higher levels of education "are linked with lower levels of religious commitment by some measures" (such as belief in God). Only 46 percent of college graduates indicated that religion is very important in their lives, as opposed to 58 percent with no more than a high school degree.[94] On the other hand, those with higher levels of education attend religious services as frequently as Americans with less education.[95] Three-quarters of American college graduates affiliate with some religion.[96] Among religious groups in America, for Christians (the largest population at 71 percent), the level of education does not appear to correlate with the level of religious commitment—in fact, "highly educated Christians are more likely than less-educated Christians to say they are weekly churchgoers."[97] Among highly educated Jews and those who identify with no religion (nones), there appears to be less religious connection.[98] There appears to be "no clear pattern when it comes to the relationship between religion and education for U.S. Muslims."[99]

In terms of education or knowledge about religion—one's own or that of another—there have also been some useful studies.[100] Not surprisingly, among Americans what people know about religion can vary depending on a number of factors. Highly educated individuals and individuals with "religiously diverse networks, show higher levels of religious knowledge." On the other hand, young adults and individuals from racial and ethnic minorities demonstrate somewhat less knowledge about religion.[101] Most Americans can answer basic questions about Christianity, atheism, and (perhaps surprisingly) Islam;[102] fewer seem to know about core beliefs or practices of Judaism, Hinduism, or Buddhism.[103] In our own experience conducting diversity training, those with at least a college education appear to know something about major Jewish holidays and culture, but have little idea of core Jewish beliefs, diversity, population,[104] or differentiation between Israeli and Diaspora Jews.

The same study asked respondents about their views of religious groups on a scale of 0 (most negative) to 100 (most positive).[105] Favorable ratings of other religions were correlated with knowledge about a religion.[106] For example, those with greater knowledge of Buddhism rate themselves on average as sixty-seven, as opposed to those with less knowledge, who rate themselves on average at fifty-three.[107] Those who know more about Hinduism rate themselves eleven points higher than those with less knowledge.[108] Greater overall knowledge of religions generally indicate warmer evaluations of most religious groups.[109] The study notes that "gender, race and ethnicity, age, and marital status also are associated with differing levels of religious knowledge."[110] Men and married people in the United States score higher on levels of religious knowledge; people in the West (14.8 of 32 questions) and Northeast (14.7) score higher than those living in the South (13.6).[111]

It is not only knowledge that makes a difference. Greater familiarity with a religion leads to the expression of "more favorable views of members of that faith ... those who say they personally know someone from a religious group express warmer views of that group."[112] For example, non-Catholics who know Catholics rate themselves at fifty-eight; those who do not know Catholics rate themselves on average at forty-five.[113]

Building on the observation that interreligious dialog and leadership are enhanced when participants have a strong knowledge of other religious traditions and a deep knowledge of, and commitment to, their own religious tradition, it is not surprising that strong religious beliefs can lead either to more closed or more open views. A 2018 Pew study ("The Religious Typology: A New Way to Categorize Americans by Religion"), which identified several groups—Highly Religious: Sunday Stalwarts, God-and-Country Believers, Diversely Devout; Somewhat Religious: Relaxed Religious, Spiritually Awake; and Nonreligious: Religion Resisters, Solidly Secular[114]—indicates that highly religious people say that belief in God is necessary to be moral.[115] Nonreligious individuals, by contrast, largely thought it unnecessary (95 percent for Religion Resisters and 97 percent for Solidly Secular). Highly and somewhat religious groups similarly think that God will judge everyone.[116] On the other hand, "except for Religion Resisters and Solidly Secular [who still say that God loves all people at 57% and 20% respectively], large majorities believe God is all-knowing, all-powerful, and loves all people."[117] This last category has particular resonance and opportunity in the context of interreligious engagement and leadership.

Most Highly Religious groups believe that churches strengthen morality in society—whereas only 14 percent of Religion Resisters and 22 percent of Solidly Secular agree.[118] In the same vein, similar responses correlate with the question of whether religious institutions are unifying.[119] Most Highly Religious groups are "more likely to say it is important to belong to a like-minded community."[120] Not surprisingly, perhaps, Nonreligious groups have the most negative views of organized religion,[121] which is challenging for interreligious discussion, but in some cases means that the focus is more productive outside formal organizational structures.

The connection between education and interreligious leadership is also complex. As we have noted, many studies of interfaith engagement point out that one needs to be well versed in one's own religious tradition and faith to engage actively and productively with another. This requires a spirit of confidence and openness. At the same time, successful interreligious dialog and leadership require an ability to compare traditions in constructive ways, without losing one's own identity. It also requires one to go beyond comparison and to appreciate the diverse manifestation of truths within other faith traditions. Familiarity with other religions, therefore, is necessary but insufficient for genuine interreligious engagement.

As Raimon Panikkar notes, comparison and analogies are always superficial; what is required for serious dialog is "understanding religions from within and discovering their concrete structures."[122] What is more, it is impossible to translate another language. In a stirring metaphor, Panikkar argues that to truly understand another religion one needs to speak its language like a native, as if it were one's own.[123] If debate is about argumentation and trying to convince someone of something, dialog is about inquiry and learning, the unfolding of shared meaning, the integration of multiple perspectives, and the uncovering and examination of assumptions.[124]

Challenges of, and to, Interreligious Leadership

There are many challenges to interreligious dialog and leadership that our survey participants and students have articulated. Some are structural in nature, including internal organizational issues and dynamics as well as intraorganizational and intra-denominational interactions, which can be dictated by organizational as well as religious structures, assumptions, and traditions.

Individual religious institutions often have limited financial and human resources, especially with declining memberships and aging facilities. There are often so many internal challenges that engagement with the outside can seem far beyond the realm of any credible work or remote possibility. Programming is frequently the first thing to be cut and the time, energy, and investment in interreligious work can be quite daunting, especially when other, often internal challenges continually arise. If it is hard enough to attract people to affiliate and participate, engaging the Other seems well beyond the scope of many communities and institutions.

A good deal of interreligious leadership, like leadership more generally, is unsurprisingly related to providing vision and inspiration in the work of the organization that does the work and the people it engages. It also revolves around strategic planning and prioritization. Forward-thinking religious leaders understand that to attract new members, secure funds, and invigorate their institutions and denominations, new and innovative programs and outreach are required. Interreligious work provides this opportunity, but it does not happen on its own. If resilient systems and organizations are ones that continually learn (see Chapter 4), then new ways of engaging laity and developing meaningful adult education programs, as well as other educational experiences and collaborations, are central to success. Such work involves more than the allocation of time and resources—which are often in short supply. It also involves confronting entrenched hierarchies, traditions, and expectations. Often attaining the right level of initial inertia is significant; however, programs and initiatives must also have longer-term staying power and half-life. One-off programs and initiatives will rarely have a long-term impact of any great consequence. At times, interreligious leaders must not only mobilize their constituents—they often have to convince them of the very value of the work, especially in a world increasingly polarized and uncertain. On one hand, they run the risk of preaching to the choir, to those who see the value of such work and who are often at the frontlines of it themselves. On the other hand, they must work to persuade the larger majority of their congregants and communities to take up the work, especially when they are hesitant to do something new or confront the biases that may have plagued them or their denomination now or in the past. What is more, interreligious work requires leaders to work with multiple generations simultaneously. They must inspire the younger generations, which have many competing priorities and interests, while garnering the support of parents, grandparents, and guardians, who may have quite different experiences and perspectives. In part, this challenge requires interreligious leaders to make the work of interreligious dialog part and parcel of regular operations, programs, and mindsets. Such work has to enrich current programs and needs, and it must be ever-present, even when in the background.

It is not only lack of institutional resources that poses a challenge. The very idea of "institutions" is at risk in contemporary society. As Peter Berger writes in *The Many Altars of Modernity: Toward a Paradigm for Religion in a Pluralist Age*,

> De-institutionalization forces individuals to undertake the difficult and anxiety-provoking task of building their own little world. They need help. Modern society has developed an array of agencies to provide such help. Gehlen called them *secondary institutions*; they fill the gap left over from de-institutionalization. They offer an individual different programs to cope with various contingencies. Since they lack the taken-for-granted quality of the old primary institutions, they are more fragile and less reliable. Nevertheless they alleviate the burden of individual world-construction.[125]

As we have noted, the very fabric of religious institutions has changed and the work that was once done through them or under their auspices is now done in more decentralized and more informal ways. Navigating interreligious discussions in changing communal and institutional structures often requires new ways of communicating and engaging people and offers both resource challenges and new opportunities for creative thinking and approaches to big issues that can be helped with an institutional framing but also ossified too.

There are, quite naturally, also what we might term theological-spiritual challenges, as interreligious leaders balance personal and professional or individual and collective needs, approaches, and interests. There are the natural human qualities of cynicism, triumphalism, and intolerance, which research shows are often related to levels of knowledge about other religions as well as one's own religion (see earlier). There is also the question of ambivalence, especially amidst the need to address so many particularistic agendas as well as other large universal concerns—reflecting a wide range of societal trends, from generational perspectives and divides to questions of identity and identity formation and larger cultural and political orientations and discussions (such as globalization, polarization, and competing truth claims).

Beyond structural challenges and conflicts, our survey respondents identified theological and religious impediments to genuine interreligious dialog that leaders must consider and address. The lack of religious literacy among many people can be an impediment to serious interreligious engagement. However, it is not only ignorance of other religious traditions that is a challenge (see earlier). Without a firm understanding of one's own faith tradition, it is quite difficult to engage in discussion with others outside of one's own religion. We have often been surprised that the most lenient rulings related to religious law and practice handed down by religious authorities we have known have come from ostensibly the most learned clergy. Knowledge may not solve all the problems we face, but it does position us to see many more dimensions and it often allows us, when we are open to it, to understand other approaches and considerations; it allows us to see where there are in fact solid boundaries, and where things may be more porous or flexible.

With or without knowledge, the cynicism that people often have or develop—due to many internal reasons as well as past experiences and even projections drawn from the positions of others, media, etc.—can affect the openness of people to dialog and the effectiveness of their efforts. If we are convinced that many Muslims are terrorists or close-minded, for example, it is unlikely that we will enter into a discussion with Muslims with an open spirit and a willingness to look beyond stereotypes. Indeed, embedded prejudices—even when they are socially or culturally constructed or even unconscious—serve as a major inhibitor to engaging with or hearing others when we do engage. At times it is pure and simple ambivalence; we do not care that much about what others think, comfortable in our situation or the way we see the world or simply the reality that we have so many other issues that are front and center in our lives that it is difficult to even think about making room for additional activities or foci. And, after all, we have limited personal, institutional, and communal resources (as noted previously), and these must be distributed according to our priorities and with a good degree of discretion.

A good illustration is the range of moral issues that plague contemporary society. From sex abuse to gender bias, xenophobia, and racism, there are many challenges to true interreligious conversation due to embedded perspectives that often dictate our views of the world and others—sometimes quite consciously, but perhaps more often in unconscious ways. Such inherited perspectives are difficult to confront. They require us to overcome biases, but also to confront ourselves, our communities, our religions, and our pasts. What is more, the challenges facing interreligious dialog are also related to an unwillingness to reflect or change. As a result, much of interreligious dialog gets stuck in platitudes that are not combined with open engagement, present mindedness, and willingness to challenge ourselves while understanding and appreciating others and their contexts.

Core Benefits of Interreligious Engagement

At the same time, interreligious dialog and leadership also offer remarkable opportunities and inherent (and extrinsic) rewards. There are many core opportunities and benefits in engaging in interreligious dialog and in practising interreligious leadership, which our survey respondents and students have shared with us. There are organizational, programmatic, and communal opportunities—from shared spaces to interactions and programs. Interreligious engagement can lead to social change, innovation, experimentation, and renewal. Social action, for example, is regularly connected with interreligious work. As Paul Knitter defines it, social action is "any activity by which human beings seek to resolve what obstructs and promote what advances, human and environmental flourishing."[126] Social action has many benefits in an interreligious setting. As Knitter notes, "By acting together in addressing the needs of those who suffer, religious people who are strangers to each other can lay the *hermeneutical groundwork* for getting to know each other and understanding each other's differences. They form a *community of solidarity* with those suffering oppression which becomes a *community of conversation* with each other."[127]

Recognizing that religion has moral, communal, and social components, many interreligious initiatives revolve around and benefit from social justice and reconciliation activities. And they also address local, regional, national, and increasingly global issues and concerns as well. Action and advocacy are often helpful in making interreligious dialog manifest.[128] Many interreligious dialogs and leadership initiatives focus on collaboration on social projects or the exchange of views on common religious or theological issues. Interreligious dialogs range in nature from daily interactions to formalized programs and can involve a wide range of participants and goals.[129] Indeed, while dialog in the modern sense is a recent development, there have been many engagements—some constructive—between religions throughout history.[130]

Respondents to our interreligious leadership survey noted that interreligious dialog allows us to build trust and collegiality, create a safe environment for discussion, encourage toleration, and set an example for how to engage with others constructively. At the same time, interreligious dialog forces us to confront past events and biases. It also forces us to overcome violence, by developing solidarity with abused, marginalized, and minority populations and by challenging extant ideologies and power centers when they perpetuate violence or inequity. Interreligious dialog offers a powerful means for coming together to tackle and correct fundamental sociocultural evils.

There are also theological opportunities and benefits. Among the benefits of interreligious dialog identified by our survey respondents are those related to facilitating conversations that allow us to learn about others and ourselves. In an age of polarizing views, encouraging dialog cannot be underestimated. It allows us to engage with similarities and differences in respectful and constructive ways—at times leading to overcoming inherent opposition and at other times simply allowing us to hear and understand, even when we do not accept, other views and concerns. Interreligious dialog helps us to establish core values and a common platform for discussion, incorporating the voices and perspectives of others and opening us to new insights. At the same time, interreligious dialog can only be successful when it allows us to maintain our own identity, explain our faith to others, and open us to self-transformation.

The respondents to our survey pointed to the benefits of pluralism (for a more in-depth treatment, see the discussion in Chapter 1), a concept that has useful application in leadership more generally as well. Pluralism has been much discussed in recent scholarship and it is now frequently differentiated from simple openness and diversity. In theory it opens the possibility for significant discussions across religions. Peter Berger argues that "pluralism has the effect of relativizing worldviews by bringing home the fact that the world can be understood differently. In other words, individuals can no longer take for granted the worldview into which they happened to be born."[131] "Pluralism," Berger maintains, "also changes the relations of religious institutions with each other, broadly speaking in the direction of ecumenical and interfaith tolerance."[132]

While pluralism can lead to liberation and choice for some, it provokes in others a lack of certainty—freedom and alienation as two sides of the same coin.[133] The uncertainties some find in pluralism lead to attempts to find truth or certainties. Berger argues that "In the area of religion, as elsewhere, certainties come in two versions: relativism, which makes creed out of the uncertainty, and fundamentalism, which purports to restore the sense of certainty."[134] The former, he believes, leads toward moral nihilism and the latter toward fanaticism,[135] as well as the supremacies we noted in the Introduction.

At its core, interreligious dialog involves engaging with others. As in general leadership, in interreligious leadership, the skills associated with self-awareness, narrative and communications, bringing the outside in, and openness and adaptation, all play a central role in this context. Our survey respondents indicated that among the benefits they found in their work involved getting to know the Other (see Chapter 1), finding common ground, promoting open and meaningful dialog and compassion, and maximizing effectiveness when working together, learning from each other, and building bridges/developing relationships.

Some of our survey respondents, especially those involved in chaplaincy work, pointed to the importance of knowing the faith traditions of those being given pastoral counseling. And yet, as noted previously, interreligious dialog and leadership require comfort with, and knowledge of, one's own traditions and beliefs. In an interesting way, engagement with others helps us to deepen knowledge of our own traditions—as we search for comparisons, try to understand differences, and become open to asking questions of our own faith. David Tracy argues that hopeful interreligious dialog requires three elements: "a self-respect (which includes, of course, a respect for, even a reverence for, one's own tradition or way); a self-exposure to the other as other; and a willingness to risk all in the questioning and inquiry that constitutes the dialog itself."[136]

Interreligious dialog and leadership can involve various relationships of power and hierarchy.[137] As such, they require a common language of understanding— in concepts as well as in a willingness to hear and listen to one another. The act of translation in this case is about literally translating between languages but also translating concepts and vocabulary in ways that help us to understand the experiences and contexts of others and do not simply superimpose ideas onto the cultures, religions, and lives of others in ways that are foreign and can be destructive.[138] Building on the key qualities discussed in contemporary leadership literature, interreligious resilience can help religious leaders with new skills and tools—lead with resilience in ways that help religious leaders and those involved in interreligious engagement understand and engage with diverse and opposing perspectives, communicate across difference, and develop agility and adaptation by learning through social change, crises, and at times even conflict.

Globalization, similarly, has been a key factor in interreligious dialog, opening as it has awareness of other people and other religions and providing opportunities for exchange and acculturation.[139] Globalization has also brought many people into contact with others—through forced and voluntary migrations across traditional national boundaries.[140] In this increasingly globalized world, interreligious work can lead to reducing violence, bigotry, and racism. It simultaneously requires vulnerability, by asking participants to open themselves to examination of their own assumptions and to be open to those of others. At the same time, it embraces the vulnerable—placing minorities and marginalized groups into more direct conversation. Although some would ascribe some violence and conflict, such as in the Israeli and Palestinian conflict, to religious difference, it is quite clear that religion is but one dimension of a much more complex situation. What is more, some have suggested that despite differences, religion may in fact provide opportunities for addressing conflict, rather than merely stirring it.[141] Key to successful interreligious discussions are thoughtful reflections about who represents each religion—in terms of religious and political orientations, and knowledge, but also gender representation.[142]

Interreligious dialog may involve confession. While individuals may not necessarily directly apologize for acts they as individuals did not themselves commit, "participants can confess that they have not tried hard enough to reach out to the other or have blamed the other unjustly."[143] Participants in reconciliation accept individual and collective responsibility for actions in the past.[144] On the other side, dialog involves forgiveness as well—"when individuals of both faiths are able to acknowledge and heal individual and collective wounds," involving "honest storytelling and a willingness to change old ways of being."[145] According to Jeannine Hill Fletcher,

> A Storytelling Model witnesses a rich and complicated approach to interreligious dialogue as it reminds us that "religion" cannot be reduced to doctrines and scriptures, to "what I believe" or "what I do." "Religion" is always "found" embedded in and intertwined with other aspects of our lived condition: economics, gender, social relations, material conditions, life stages, family relationships, and more.[146]

Narratives are powerful leadership tools. In the case of interreligious leadership, they provide valuable and accessible ways to engage across difference and they bring important human dimensions back into our relations with others.

Conclusions

Placing the best practices and emerging considerations of leadership into conversation with our observations from the fields of religious and interreligious leadership leads us to conclude that the challenges and opportunities we face today and for the future are great. We already possess many important tools to develop and sustain meaningful and transformative engagement and leadership and we have a good sense of where many of the possibilities and pitfalls already lay. At the same time, this brief survey leaves us convinced that we need more nuanced and ever-evolving approaches to leadership and to interreligious work if we are to be successful in engaging others, in developing a world with less damaging religious supremacies, and a world that is truly and complexly resilient. Interreligious leadership informed by resilience thinking offers the opportunity to extend key insights of classical leadership studies—building on the importance of relationships to think in terms of systems and networks; practice active listening and critical conversations for understanding others as well as ourselves; cultivating intentionality, building trust, and becoming more aware; and also extending humility to a richer form of vulnerability.

In Chapter 4, we merge the contexts and challenges for religion and interreligious engagement and leadership that we discused in the Introduction and first two chapters of this book with the lessons gleaned in this chapter from a scan of the theory and practice of leadership and religious and interreligious leadership. This merger of insights provides a foundation for our notion of interreligious resilience, which we believe can help us to develop, practice, and sustain interreligious leadership and interreligious engagement for the future and provide tools for other areas of civic, communal, and organizational leadership as well.

4

Interreligious Resilience

Introduction

This chapter advances a way of imagining religion and interreligious leadership through the concepts of resilience and vulnerability. In previous chapters we outlined the history and exemplary models of interreligious engagement, identified and explored the most pressing contemporary concerns that impact interreligious work (and life more generally), and reviewed important concepts and foci of leadership studies (in general and in religious and interreligious contexts) to frame our core concept of interreligious resilience and the VITA (Vulnerability, Intentionality, Trust, and Awareness) pathway. While we have signaled aspects of our resilience and vulnerability approach to religion in earlier chapters, this chapter develops these ideas more fully.

We begin by contextualizing this approach to religion in relation to classic functionalist and contemporary phenomenological theories of religion. Along the way, we discuss some of the long-standing methodological conundrums in religious studies. Although functionalist and phenomenological theories of religion are often seen to be in opposition, in this chapter we assert that they have important connections, made possible by a resilience and vulnerability (as part of interreligious leadership) theory of religion, which can significantly deepen the ways that we think about religion and engage with interreligious work. In doing this, we discuss how a resilience and vulnerability interpretation of religion circumvents some of the methodological problems in religious studies. Our purpose in presenting this interpretation of religion is not to advance scholarship in religious studies or to offer a theory of religion that resolves the limitations of other theories. Although we believe it has value for historical, comparative, and philosophical studies of religion, it is beyond the scope of this book to make that argument. Rather, our purpose is to shift interreligious leadership toward a way of imagining religious similarities and differences that is relevant to the cultivation of interreligious resilience. Our discussion of how this resilience and vulnerability theory can shift the way we understand religious difference lays the groundwork for an elaboration of the VITA pathway to interreligious resilience in Chapter 5.

Theories of Religion: Classic Functionalism and Contemporary Phenomenology

Interreligious leaders working in a religiously diverse world shaped by globalizing, postsecular, acceleratory, polarizing dynamics are compelled by the social realities of diversity and intercultural and interreligious proximity to engage some of the same thorny theoretical questions faced by religious studies scholars (even if they are not fully aware of the more academic contexts of those questions). As anyone reading this book surely knows, the question of what religion is, what precisely the category "religion" refers to, if anything, and what the different traditions identified through the category "religion" have in common, if anything, and how those commonalities justify the meaningfulness of "religion" as a category, or how they do not provide such justification, are some of the most vexing theoretical questions students and scholars of religion face. Another important question concerns what religious people, as religious, have in common with one another, and where and how they are different from one another. Furthermore, what is the relation between interreligious and intrareligious difference? Are interreligious differences, between people who belong to different traditions, the differences that matter most; or are the differences that matter most, on the level of everyday cross-difference engagement, intrareligious? Is there a type of experience that religious people, affiliated with different traditions, have in common, a generalizable structure or form of trans-religious feeling, being, and knowing? Does a generalizable religious orientation to life shape social, cultural, economic, and political practices similarly? As we engage one another as religious people, as we come into conflict with one another, and as we seek to understand one another and even to work together toward common purposes, do we operate with a common understanding of what religion is, and of which intrareligious and interreligious differences are in play? Do we agree that there is a general thing in the world to which the concept "religion" refers and of which our various practices, institutions, values, pieties, and practices are particularized expressions? How do different views and positions on these issues, even if they are implicit rather than explicit, or in the background rather than foreground, influence our encounters with one another? Are certain views on these issues more conducive to interreligious understanding and collaboration?

Since theoretical questions at play in the study of religion are also at play in interreligious leadership, it will be helpful to look more closely at select classic and contemporary theories of religion, focusing specifically on functionalist and phenomenological theories. Functionalist and phenomenological approaches to religion are oriented respectively by questions about what religion does in the world and what it is like to be religious. Each of these approaches to religion presumes that there is a genus, "religion," and that diverse religious traditions are each distinct "species" of the genus. This is to say that functionalist and phenomenological theoretical families agree in the ontological assumption that the category "religion" points to something objectively real in the world, something generalizable across human experience and culture that can be studied and compared. But these families of theories differ in their methodological approaches to what they take the various religions to have in common as members of the genus religion. Functionalist theories take an etic approach to religion, which is to say that they describe and analyze religion from the outside and focus on what religion does in the world, how it works in human societies and cultures. On the other hand, phenomenological theories take an emic approach and describe and interpret religion from the inside and focus on what it is like to be religious, what it means and feels like to act, think, and orient oneself in the world religiously.

Karl Marx, Emile Durkheim, and Sigmund Freud represent classic functionalist theories of religion. As will become apparent in the ensuing discussion, we draw from specific aspects of Durkheim's work (as well as that of more recent scholars) in developing our theory. We present an overview of Marx and Freud, however, in part because they are central functionalist theorists and in part because they throw into relief some of the core considerations that animate our theory. For Marx, "The wretchedness of religion is at once an expression of and a protest against real wretchedness. Religion is the sigh of the oppressed creature, the sentiment of a heartless world, and the soul of soulless conditions. It is the opium of the people."[1] This well-known account of religion treats religion as something that serves a societal function by way of its psychological effects. Like an opiate, according to Marx, religion calms, numbs, and pacifies people who, due to oppressive social conditions, would otherwise be unhappy, dispirited, and alienated. This psychological function of religion serves a social purpose—to distract from or conceal the real causes of oppression, which, for Marx, are primarily material and economic, having to do with the alienating historical mechanics of capitalism and class hierarchies. Religion impedes justice by mystifying the structural causes of injustice. Historical movement toward social and economic justice, then, entails the ending of religion, or, as Marx puts this: "The abolition of religion as the illusory happiness of [the people] is a demand for their real happiness. The call to abandon illusions about their condition is the call to abandon a condition which requires illusions."[2]

Another classic functionalist account of religion is offered by Freud. Like Marx, Freud offers a critical account of religion and treats religion as an illusion. He focuses especially on religion's psychological function, or how it works within the mental and emotional lives of individual persons. For Freud, "Religion is comparable to a childhood neurosis."[3] To describe religion this way is pejorative in a twofold sense—religion for Freud is associated with developmental immaturity and psychological illness. But this pejorative comparison of religion to a childhood neurosis does not explain how religion functions, or why people are religious—are all religious people developmentally immature and neurotic? In a different context, Freud offers a functional explanation: "Religion is an attempt to get control over the sensory world, in which we are placed, by means of the wish-world, which we have developed inside us as a result of biological and psychological necessities."[4] Thus, religion is fantasy, a deluded psychological attempt to manage or manipulate an external world that is otherwise not subject to our control. This is an elaboration of what Freud means by comparing religion to neurosis. And, connecting the neurotic to the developmental, Freud writes: "If one attempts to assign to religion its place in [human] evolution, it seems not so much to be a lasting acquisition, as a parallel to the neurosis which the civilized individual must pass through on his way from childhood to maturity."[5] Thus, Freud extends his psychological critique of religion into a cultural and evolutionary claim—as the child is developmentally immature in comparison to the adult, and as the neurotic is mentally unhealthy in comparison to the psychologically well adjusted, so religious cultures and primitive societies are in comparison to enlightened and civilized ones.

The last classic functionalist theory we will review is Durkheim's sociological account of religion. For Durkheim, "Religion is a unified system of beliefs and practices relative to sacred things, that is to say, things set apart and forbidden—beliefs and practices which unite into one single moral community called a Church, all those who adhere to them."[6] As with Marx and Freud, Durkheim defines religion in terms of what it does. In contrast to Marx and Freud, however, Durkheim's account of religion is less contemptuous. Rather than narcotically numbing (Marx) or neurotically infantilizing (Freud) the masses, religion's social function, according to Durkheim, is to bind people together into a moral community through their adherence to beliefs and practices that partition the world, and communal moral norms, according to a sacral division between the forbidden and sanctioned. So, religion is what religion does, and for Durkheim, religion creates a binding sense of community and morally orients adherents, through beliefs and practices regarding what is held to be sacred, in relation to one another and to the broader world. Positioning himself in relation to the ontological question, Durkheim suggests that "Religion is only the sentiment inspired by the group in its members, but projected outside of the consciousness that experiences them, and objectified."[7] Religion is what religion does, which is to generate communal sentiment and social belonging, and this is all that religion is—but what authorizes, grounds, legitimates, and gives credence to religion's social function is the extension of sentiment into a sense of objective reality. Methodologically, religion is what religion does, and given what religion does, religion is social projection—ontologically, then, religion is not what many religious people think.

Much more could be, and of course has been, said about Marx's, Freud's, and Durkheim's interpretations of religion, but this brief discussion is only sufficient for illustrating three classic functionalist approaches to religion—historical materialist, psychological, and sociological. Although they differ in how they evaluate the way religion works, all three instantiate the methodological claim that the best way to understand what religion is, is to explain what religion does, and the best way to explain what religion does, is critically, from the outside of religion. As a result of these methodological claims and positions, the theorists present views of religion as something other than what many religious people think religion is. For Marx and Freud, religion is socially and psychologically mal-formative—it forms people and societies in detrimental ways. For Durkheim, religion is socially and morally formative—it binds people into moral communities. These moral communities are bound together, in large part, by a sense of their difference from other moral communities, a sense of difference produced by distinct beliefs and practices relative to the sacred. In each of these cases, religion is real—the category "religion" points to something existing in the world and in human experience; but in none of these cases do religious people themselves have an accurate account of what religion really is.

As will be evident soon, our resilience and vulnerability theory of religion does not reject a functionalist approach to religion. It is important for interreligious leaders to have a sense of how religion works in the world, for good and ill, in addition to having a feel for what it is like to be religious, from the inside of a religious tradition. So, we will carry some of the functionalist impulses forward. Although we do not subscribe to Marx's and Freud's accounts of religion as psycho-social pathology, our theory of religion is oriented around varieties of human vulnerability. And although our theory is attuned, along with Durkheim, to the role of religion in community formation, interreligious resilience and the VITA pathway are especially concerned with the role of interreligious leaders across different religious communities.

We now turn to a review of select phenomenological theories of religion that interpret religion through different accounts of religious experience, or what it is like to be religious. While we reviewed classic functional theorists, we will look at two contemporary phenomenological theorists. We have selected these thinkers, in part, because the uniquely intersectional standpoints through which they interpret religion help to illuminate the fecund challenges of phenomenological generalization. They interpret what religion is about, in general, from particular personal and religious standpoints. The fecundity of this results from a combination of critical and sympathetic sensibilities. Critically, their phenomenologies are counterintuitive, insofar as they are organized around different accounts of cultural agency and moral creativity, rather than around experiential accounts of the sacred, holy, or divine. At the same time, their phenomenologies of creative agency sympathetically show how religious experience can be personally and socially salutary.

Philosopher of religion Sharon Welch describes religious experience from a standpoint of intersecting feminist, liberationist, and humanistic religious commitments. For Welch, "religious experience is profoundly meaningful, central to a community's and an individual's sense of identity, and, at the same time, intrinsically amoral."[8] The first part of this claim resonates with Durkheim's concept of religion as a social sentiment that binds people together into a community. But, in direct contrast to Durkheim, for whom the religious sentiment is morally constitutive, Welch describes religious experience as "intrinsically amoral." By "amoral" Welch does not mean "immoral," or morally bad or wrong. She means that religious experience is not inherently charged in a moral way—which is to say that religious experience is "nonmoral." Continuing, she writes that she does not see the religious "in terms of right beliefs and sure foundations, but as responses to amoral powers that can be given self-critically moral purposes."[9] Thus, religious experience is not only "amoral" or "nonmoral," without a moral charge, telos, or ground, but it is noncognitive, something beyond, beneath, or other than thought. As both nonmoral and noncognitive, irreducible to either right behavior or right belief, the religious is rather a structure of feeling or an affective field—a mode of felt experience, which, insofar as it is without intrinsic meaning or inherent moral value, is something to which we give meaning and moral value or, as she puts it, "self-critical moral purposes." This is to say that the religious is a fecund field of moral and cultural creativity, a special *quality* of experience, rather than a special, set-apart *kind* of experience—a quality that, rather than being imbued with its own preexisting meaning and value, demands the making of meaning and naming and claiming of value.

The implications of this view are that conflicts regarding religious truths and values are not conflicts regarding the true nature and right names of ultimate reality, or whether what is really and finally real should be imagined as personal or nonpersonal. Rather than being about the differences or similarities among objects of religious belief or groundings of religious value, interreligious conflict and interreligious collaboration, in Welch's view, are shaped by differences and similarities in modes of belief and belonging. Though she does not explicitly name a fractal logic for interpreting religious difference and similarity, it is implicit.

Still, "What, then, is the religious?" Welch asks. And she answers, "This is the name we give to those encounters, those energies, which are constitutive, but amoral; those encounters, those energies, which are vivid, compelling and meaningful, but fragile."[10] It may be that a community construes those encounters as encounters with the truth of things, with Dharma, or as release and liberation, as moksha or enlightenment, or as encounters with the causal creator of all things, with God. Or it may be, as Welch might say, that those encounters are fully and entirely and unambiguously human, historical, and natural, and nonetheless, soulfully profound. But regardless of how those encounters or energies are named, they are, for Welch, real rather than imagined, they are vivid even though difficult to describe in any definitive way, and they are fragile, or vulnerable, rather than impassable. And, precisely insofar as they are real, vivid, and vulnerable, they are constitutive of human community—diverse communities are forged through the mode of their encounter with the religious and the manner in which they cultivate its moral meaning. We will return to some of these same themes when we elaborate on our resilience and vulnerability approach to religion.

We now turn to another phenomenological theory, this time from the perspective of African American religious humanist Anthony Pinn. For Pinn, "Religion's basic structure embedded in history, is a general quest for complex subjectivity in the face of the terror and dread associated with life within a historical context marked by dehumanization, objectification, abuse, [and] intolerance."[11] Rather than theorizing about formal religious institutions, beliefs, and rituals, Pinn's view of religion is rooted in what can be described as an elemental, expressive, and embodied sense of religion, especially as this is manifest in the varieties of African American religious experience. At the center of this elemental phenomenology of religion is Pinn's concept of "complex subjectivity." Complex subjectivity is "a desired movement from life as corporeal object, controlled by oppressive and essentializing forces to a complex conveyer of cultural meaning, with a detailed and creative identity. This subjectivity is understood as complex in that it seeks to hold in tension many possibilities of being, a way of existing in numerous spaces of identification."[12] The oppressive and essentializing forces Pinn has in mind are simultaneously racial and religious. These are the forces of the history and ongoing forms of white supremacy in the United States and globally, and thus the personal and systemic forces of exploitation, marginalization, and violence toward Black bodies and minds.

Complex subjectivity is thus about claiming historical and moral agency and embodying personhood in resistance to oppressive and dehumanizing forces of racial subjugation. But, for Pinn, complex subjectivity is also about enacting cultural creativity and making meaning in the face of what he and other African American humanists experience as the limitations of formal religious structures, and especially theistic modes of religious life and thought. Against racial subjugation and what he takes to be the limiting forms and modes of theistic religion, Pinn writes, "Complex subjectivity stands for . . . the creative struggle in history for increased agency, for a fullness of life. Religious experience hence entails a human response to a crisis of identity, and it is the crisis of identity that constitutes the dilemma of ultimacy and meaning."[13] In contrast to Marx, for whom religion narcotically neutralized the agency of the economically oppressed, the complex subjectivity of religious experience, for Pinn, enables a sobering embrace of moral agency and cultural resistance to the oppressive forces of racism. And in contrast to Freud, for whom religion was the manifesting of a neurotically immature will to control an uncontrollable exterior world, for Pinn, the complex subjectivity of religious experience inspires a lucidly resolute claim of cultural creativity beyond the bounds of traditional religion. Thus, the religious experience of complex subjectivity, for Pinn, is the event and process through which the fullness of one's personhood is forged against whatever forces in the world seek to constrain us, including, sometimes, the forces of religion, and especially racially essentializing modes of belief and belonging.

Much more could be said about Welch's and Pinn's phenomenologies of religious experience, but we want to take note of how some of their ideas inform our resilience and vulnerability interpretation of religion and the practice of interreligious resilience. For both Welch and Pinn, religion is defined as a structure or field of experience, feeling, and thought, rather than a reified system of beliefs, rituals, myths. This does not mean that Welch and Pinn are anti-institutional, or indifferent to formal religious belief or practice. Rather, it implies, first, that traditional religious forms and institutions do not have a monopoly on religious experience, and second, that the boundaries between traditions are perforated by profound tradition-internal differences of racial, sexual, gender, and class identities. With respect to interreligious resilience, this means that religious experience need not be bounded within the constraints of individual religious traditions but can arise through interreligious encounter—as Panikkar would put this, intrareligious learning and wisdom can be a gift of interreligious engagement.

Another relevant insight from Welch and Pinn is the view that the meaning and value of religious experience is neither inherent to it nor unambiguous, but instead is forged, examined, clarified, and revised through life in community and relationship, in solidarity and through conflict, with religious others, those within our traditions as well as from other traditions. The subject of religious experience is an embodied, enfleshed, historical, and political being, a person-in-relation with other embodied, enfleshed, historical, and political selves, and not an atomistic, disembodied, ahistorical, apolitical individual. This entails that the meaning and value of religious experience emerges relationally through diversely gendered, racial, and socioeconomic standpoints, and through intrareligious as well as interreligious difference. If religious experience is not bounded by traditional religious forms and institutions, and if the subject of religious experience is not an isolable, ahistorical, disembodied individual, then religious experience can be understood as intrinsically and intractably intersubjective and cross-difference. Thus, against someone like Durkheim, Welch and Pinn see religious experience emerging not through encounter with something "set apart" but as arising through the ambiguous textures of the wholeness of human life, across and through varieties of difference within and between culturally and racially diverse religious communities.

The challenge for interreligious resilience, then, is how creatively to work with these differences, the multitude of human and religious contrasts, in ways that honor their reality while simultaneously resisting the many psychological, social, and political impulses to reify those differences into oppositions and hierarchies (the supremacy impulse). In the remainder of this chapter, these insights about religious experience will be integrated into the interreligious resilience counter-fractal to religious supremacy.

Methodological Questions: Fractals and Systems, Resilience and Vulnerability

Recall that the religious supremacy fractal is organized around a logic of belief and belonging defined by a monopolistic approach to religious truth, oppositional identity, and exclusionary belonging. The supremacy fractal presumes that the meaning and value of religious experience is contained within singular traditions, the identity of religious persons is forged against religious others, and religious community is defined by the exclusion of religious difference. The counter-fractal of interreligious resilience, on the other hand, enlivens modes of belief and belonging that are plural, relational, and inclusive—a way of being religious according to which the meaning and value of religious experience can evolve through interreligious engagement, in which the identities of religious persons can be enriched through dialogical contrast with diverse religious others, and in which religious community can be animated by a spirit of invitation, welcome, and hospitality. Let us now turn to a discussion of how this fractal logic relates to methodological questions in religious studies and interreligious leadership.

Beyond the questions of what religion is and what religious experience is like, questions addressed by functional and phenomenological theories, a related methodological question pivots around issues of similarity and difference—do the religions share some generalizable essence or purpose that makes comparison possible, or are the religions incommensurable, so different from one another that they cannot really be compared? On one side of the question is the view that the religious traditions are so distinct from one another, and structure human experience in such unique ways, that there is little-to-no basis for comparison or dialog. Let us call this position the incommensurability view. On the other side of the question is the view that the religions, despite their different narrative, textual, ritual, and institutional elements, are fundamentally all about the same thing; what this thing is—structure, experience, function—varies according to the theorist. Let us call this position the essentialist view.

If we were to think about these methodological differences in terms of translation, the essentialist view would be that the different religions are like different languages situated in a common world of experience. They use different vocabularies, concepts, and grammatical structures to articulate a shared world—the world described, evoked, interpreted, and articulated by the different languages is essentially the same. The incommensurability view, on the other hand, posits that the different religious traditions are not just like different languages, but that they are also fundamentally different worlds of experience. If the religions are different languages in a shared world of experience, then translation and comparison are possible. But if they are not only different languages but also different experiential worlds, there are no shared points of reference by way of which to communicate, let alone to translate or compare religious differences.

Different ways of thinking about translation reflect different understandings of the relationship between languages and the world. For instance, in Yiddish there are two different words for "translation." "Ibersetsung" (over + placing) is possible when a word or concept in an original source text can be lifted and replaced with a nearly identical word or concept from another language. According to Yaakov Herskovitz, translation in this sense is "a mode of equivalence."[14] In contrast to this mode of translation, a different Yiddish word, "fartayshung," focuses more on "destination" in the new text than on the original textual source. Put otherwise, the translational emphasis of "fartayshung" is on reader reception rather than authorial intention. As a result, "fartayshung" suggests a hermeneutic understanding of translation as a "mode of interpretation."[15] Where "ibersetsung" is possible when different languages have equivalent words or concepts that can be easily substituted for one another, "fartayshung" entails an interpretive quest for nonequivalent, or nonidentical, but mutually resonant meanings.

But in addition to the linguistic complexities that account for the differences between translation in a "mode of equivalence" and "mode of interpretation," these modes also reflect different ways of negotiating broader questions about cultural difference and similarity, including differences of social power. In other words, translation is never just an innocent rendering into a different language or a means to interpret. In the context of a discussion of the European colonial encounter with indigenous people and traditions in the Americas, Willie James Jennings describes translation as "the unrelenting submission to another people's voices for the sake of speaking with them."[16] In the context of interreligious encounter generally, and colonial interreligious encounter specifically, "the act of translating creates a theological relativism" according to which "concepts bound to one language system give way to alteration or eradication when drawn toward another language." As Jennings summarizes, "translation necessitates a form of alienation from the original."[17] Thus, translation, especially across power differentials, includes some degree of distortion, and in the historical contexts Jennings examines, the distortion is not simply linguistic or hermeneutical, but political.

Like everything we do, translation is shaped by the intentions or purposes we bring to it, and can have impacts, for good and ill, that are not determined by our intentions or purposes. Good translation aims not only to carry over linguistic meaning from one context to another (whether via the mode of equivalence or interpretation) but also to honor the original linguistic, textual, communal, and cultural source, and this requires empathic understanding of the original. We need to think deeply about how we are reading and interpreting things and how we are sharing them. At the same time, the tension between translating something "as it is" to a different context, on the one hand, and translation as interpretive meaning making, on the other, is a tension that we find in many aspects of interreligious engagement and leadership. While many things can be "lost in translation," translation need not, in all cases, be alienating and distorting, but can afford us the opportunity to apply ideas and concepts in different places and new ways and allow us to create new, constructive, mutually edifying, community-building narratives.

Now, let us return from the topic of translation to the methodological issues discussed previously. Practically speaking, the problem with incommensurability, especially with respect to interreligious leadership, is that through its extreme account of religious difference, it eliminates the possibility of shared reasons, experiences, and values through which to build interreligious relationships. In short, interreligious incommensurability in practice tends to exclude a common world and shared relational context—it renders translation impossible. But the answer to interreligious incommensurability need not be interreligious essentialism. For the problems with the essentialist view are that the presumption of religious sameness reduces, and thereby distorts, the meaningfulness of religious differences that matter to many religious people. It makes translation meaningless. Furthermore, and along the lines that Jennings observed earlier, the positing of essential sameness across the traditions is done from a position of power over different traditions—in other words, the presumption of essential sameness is a universalized projection from a dominant religious, cultural, and intellectual standpoint. As comparative theologian John Thatamanil has argued, the result of the essentialist view "is a hegemonic imposition of sameness upon divergent religious communities."[18] Religious essentialism tends in practice to exclude religious difference. While religious incommensurability honors religious difference, it marginalizes shared experience; while religious essentialism honors shared experience, it marginalizes religious difference. Thatamanil helpfully synthesizes these ideas about difference and similarity as follows:

> Religious traditions are not communities of consensus so much as they are sites of internal contestation. One knows that one belongs to tradition X if one is

claimed by the arguments that consume tradition X and not by some supposed agreement shared by all. . . . Comparison [and, in our case, interreligious resilience] shows that religious traditions are marked by neither simple difference nor flat sameness. . . . If simple sameness obtained across traditions, comparison [and interreligious engagement] would prove uninteresting and unproductive. If simple difference obtained, comparison [and interreligious engagement] would be impossible and learning forestalled. Hence, any definition of the religious that is empirically credible and normatively fecund must interrupt reifications of religious traditions as bounded homogeneities.[19]

Now, what do fractals have to do with any of this? The fractal logic of religious diversity, especially when organized around resilience and vulnerability, interrupts homogenizing reification (and translational distortion and alienation) in unique ways. Recall that, as Schmidt-Leukel defines this, "The nucleus of the [fractal interpretation of religious diversity] is that the diversity that we observe among the religions globally is mirrored in the diversity that we find within each of the major religious traditions."[20] So the methodological questions of similarity and difference are simultaneously intrareligious and interreligious. Another way to put this is to say that the patterns of difference within traditions are similar across the traditions, or that religious traditions are similar, and thus comparable and relatable, because of the patterns of differences within them. As Schmidt-Leukel explains:

> a fractal interpretation of religious diversity assumes that religions are actually comparable precisely in—and because of—their internal diversity. Religions are internally so diverse that the other religion always contains some familiar features or elements. The other religion is therefore always different but, to quote Jerusa Tanner Lamptey, "never wholly other."[21]

Difference and similarity, then, are not opposed to one another, but co-constitutive. The recognition of co-constitutive differences interrupts the power dynamics in encounters with difference by reminding us that we, and our traditions, are similar because of and not despite the patterns of similarity and differences in our traditions. As Thatamanil puts this, "every community [and religious tradition] is striated by patterns of similarity and difference that makes any facile opposition between us and them unsustainable [and] interrupts reification."[22] Differences within religious traditions are constitutive of similarities across the traditions; similarities across the traditions are constituted by the differences within them. The fractal striation of similarities and differences short-circuits the false dichotomies of us and them, right and wrong, and true and false that channel distortion and alienation and feed into logics of domination and supremacy.

The fractal logic of religious diversity thus aligns with the process philosophical and postmodernist sensibilities we described in our introduction, according to which identity and difference, self and otherness are understood relationally. A fractal logic illuminates these ideas: it is a way of thinking about and seeing how difference can be constitutive of identity, and how identity always includes at least traces of alterity. The logic of the fractal, then, along with process and postmodernist sensibilities in general, have ontological implications. To say that identity and difference, self and otherness are relational, is to say something about the nature or being-ness of things, persons, and even, per above, religions. The relational ontology implicit in the logic of the fractal, however, does not mean that identity and difference, self and other, are relationally co-implicated without friction. Difference may be constitutive of identity, and alterity may be traced in the self in different ways. The supremacy and resilience fractals represent very distinct modes of relationship. In the supremacy fractal, religious identity is embodied through a relation of mastery over and exclusion of the difference of the other; for the resilience fractal, religious identity is embodied through a relation of humility toward the other and emerges through empathic mutual learning with and from the other.

Approaching Interreligious Engagement through Dialogs of Head, Hands, and Heart

Because interreligious interactions occur in such different ways, from informal interpersonal encounters to organized, formal interreligious dialogs, and everything in between, it is essential for the interreligious leader to be aware of the type and the salient dimensions of the engagement. Interreligious leadership unfolds in diverse settings, in relation to various issues, and with diverse people. As a result of this, some interreligious thinkers have developed typologies for thinking through the variety and diversity of interreligious engagements. We discussed some of these previously in relation to the work of Jeanne Hill Fletcher, Catherine Cornille, and Eboo Patel. The interreligious thinker Leonard Swidler articulates a helpful account of types and dimensions of interreligious engagement organized around "head, hands, and heart."[23]

"Dialogue of the Head," for Swidler, refers to interreligious engagements oriented by a concern for truth. Such engagements tend to be philosophically or theologically motivated and structured. "In the Dialogue of the Head," Swidler writes, "we reach out to those who think differently from us to understand how they see the world and why they act as they do. The world is too complicated for anyone to grasp alone increasingly, we can understand reality only with the help of the other, in dialogue. This is important, because how we understand the world determines how we act in the world."[24] Dialog of the Head, then, refers to a theological or philosophical challenge: How to respond to the diversity of religious claims to truth, the claims of our own tradition in relation to the claims of others? Not surprisingly, this can be especially challenging for adherents of missionary traditions such as Christianity, Islam, and Buddhism, each of which includes universalizing claims about the truth or rightness of their religious paths. The case of Judaism is somewhat different, as Judaism offers a tradition of witness in contrast to mission and distinguishes between particular obligations for Jews through the covenant at Sinai with the Israelites and the universal human duties of the Noahide Laws for non-Jews. But, in general, concerns regarding religious truth claims involve developing a theology or philosophy of religions that negotiates the differences between the normative claims of one's own tradition and the normative claims of other traditions.

The traditional options in theology of religions are exclusivism, inclusivism, and pluralism. An exclusivist theology of religions argues for the exclusive truth of one tradition in contrast to the falsity of all others. An inclusivist option argues that one tradition contains the whole truth, while others offer either incomplete truth or are false. The pluralist alternative argues that the different religious traditions each present distinct religious truths, such that there is a multiplicity of religious truths. It is beyond the scope of this book to engage the vast literature in theology of religions, but as one would expect, the options just briefly described all have strengths and challenges. The exclusivist option, for example, rightly takes seriously the normative claims of the traditions, and thereby honors religious adherents' reasons for their affiliations with their traditions. Of course, the exclusivist option easily reinforces a monopolistic claim to truth, which is one of the elements of the supremacy fractal. The inclusivist option has a higher regard for the normative claims of other traditions—they are not all false, after all. But the view that other traditions are at best partially or incompletely true, relative to the all-inclusive truth of one's own tradition, smacks of hubris and folds into the patronizing, ethnocentric tendencies of tolerance. Although we are inclined toward the pluralist option, this option is not without its challenges either. For one thing, if the traditions present distinct religious truths, each with their own epistemic protocols for adjudicating evidence and reasons, then it would seem difficult, at the very least, to develop shared, trans-traditional criteria for deliberating about the truth or falsity of anything. A further challenge with the pluralist option is that it can appear to be internally contradictory—after all, what can it mean to say that there are multiple truths, given a common conception of truth as unitary? But in the context of this book on interreligious leadership, we advocate pluralism as a social ideal primarily, for the reasons we advanced earlier. Whether or not the social ideal of pluralism presumes or entails a pluralistic theology of religions is a larger discussion.

Nevertheless, what Swidler refers to as a "Dialogue of the Head" surfaces important elements in interreligious leadership. Even when an interreligious engagement or encounter is not exclusively focused on the philosophical and theological project of adjudicating the differing normative claims of traditions, the normative epistemic questions are at the very least lurking. Although we affirm that questions of truth are implicit in most interreligious engagements, we disagree with Swidler's idealist view that understanding, belief, and the intellectual aspects of religious commitment are determinative of action. Instead, we believe that action, practice, habit, narrative, institutional formation, and ritual shape understanding—what we do and how we live in the world, and what and how we think and believe, are mutually formative of one another. Rather than being unidirectional, there is more of a back-and-forth or to-and-fro interplay between thinking and doing than Swidler suggests. It is still important, however, for religious leaders to recognize and anticipate how questions about truth, or, relatedly, concerns about meaning are inevitably at play in the varieties of interreligious engagement.

"Dialogue of the Hands" is motivated by a concern for what is good and right. Swidler writes:

> In the Dialogue of the Hands we join together with others to work to make the world a better place in which we all must live together. Since we can no longer live separately in this "one world," we must work jointly to make it not just a house for a home for all of us to live in. . . . The world within us and all around us is always in need of healing and our deepest wounds can be healed together with the other, only in dialogue.[25]

Dialog of the Hands thus refers to the ethical challenge of responding to diverse religious values and forms of life. Doing this at interpersonal (moral questions) and societal (political questions) scales may entail different approaches and considerations. There are a range of options, including the ethical correlates to exclusivism, inclusivism, pluralism: ethical absolutism, ethical universalism, ethical contextualism. But, again, how, given one's own tradition-shaped moral views, can one make sense of and learn from the values and virtues, ideals and aims, and moral cosmologies of other religious traditions? Dialog of the Hands thus includes pragmatic considerations about how communally, interpersonally, societally to do what needs doing when what needs doing requires working with people from diverse religious traditions with diverse truths and values.

"Dialogue of the Heart," according to Swidler, is where and when

> we open ourselves to receive the beauty of the other. Because we humans are body and spirit—or, rather, body-spirit—we give bodily-spiritual expression . . . to our multifarious responses to life: joy, sorrow, gratitude, anger, and most of all, love. We try to express our inner feelings, which grasp reality in far deeper and higher ways that we are able to put into rational concepts and words.[26]

Thus, Dialog of the Heart is foundational to the Dialogs of Head and Hands. It is the motivating impulse that leads us into curiosity about others, to concern for their well-being, to the collaborative work required of building a more compassionate, just, and pluralist world. It is the emotional and intuitive space in which empathic imagination is honed, in which we learn, as Panikkar encourages us, to hear what others are seeing through their windows (see the discussion of Panikkar's "window analogy" later in this chapter).

Swidler's mention of "beauty" in the context of the Dialog of Heart is noteworthy. For beauty has a different valence than the truth that concerns Dialog of the Head or the good that concerns Dialog of the Hands. A concern to recognize and honor the beauty of religious others—other religious texts, traditions, persons, symbols, and rituals—recalibrates the Dialogs of Head and Heart. It shifts them onto a different plane and into a different dimension. This is not the plane of competing truths or the dimension of conflicting values. It is instead the plane in which we most fully hear ourselves in the other, and likewise see the other in ourselves. And this leads us into the deepest, most profound dimension of mutual learning and care for one another—interreligious resilience.

Systems Thinking, Resilience, and Vulnerability

In addition to reflecting process and postmodernist sensibilities, fractal logic is shaped by systems thinking, which is a core element of the practice of a resilience and vulnerability approach to interreligious leadership. A system is made of diverse parts that are integrated in ways that allow information or energy to pass through them in support of the function or purpose of the system. Systems exist at many scales, from the atomic and cellular to the civilizational and planetary. Thus, systems thinking pervades many fields and disciplines, from biology to sociology to metaphysics. And yet, as far as we are aware, systems thinking is not often applied to interreligious leadership, even though religious and interreligious life can be interpreted systemically at many levels, from systems of spiritual discipline to systems of interreligious dialog, from collaborations and frictions within and between religious communal systems to systematic approaches to interreligious civic endeavors. Religious traditions themselves can also be interpreted as complex cultural systems, as dynamic historical wholes that are greater than the sum of their symbolic, ritual, ethical, mythic, social, and institutional parts.

One of the benefits of a resilience and vulnerability approach to interreligious leadership is that it enables us to think systemically about interreligious engagement at multiple levels. The salient systems in interreligious engagement, especially when interpreted through a fractal (and process postmodernist) approach to identity and difference, are open rather than closed. An open system is a permeably bounded whole made of functionally or purposively integrated parts. The permeable boundaries of open systems are especially obvious with living systems, such as forest systems or family systems, which are sustained by supporting environments that are themselves made up of various interdependent systems. Open and complex systems lead to the de-emphasis on fixed boundaries and rigid dichotomies. As David Chandler notes, when one thinks in terms of complex systems and resilience, "there is no problematic of the universal and the particular: there are neither fixed universals nor isolated particular subjects. There is no reductionist divide between subject and object, between culture and environment, between agent and structure, between public and private . . .: resilience works on a different and very distinct ontological basis."[27] For this reason, a resilience or systems ontology obviates the methodological conflict between incommensurability and essentialism in religious studies and interreligious leadership.

The concept of a system, however, is an abstraction, whereas religious people, communities, and traditions are particularly embodied, enacted, organic, cultural, and historical realities. To refer to the idea of system as an abstraction does not mean that it is difficult to understand, or that it is unreal, but that it is a way of modeling or selectively simplifying genuine complexity to understand it better—and people, communities, and traditions are some of the most complex realities of which we are aware. By advocating for a systems mindset in interreligious leadership, we are certainly not making a case for engaging religious persons, communities, or traditions as abstractions! On the contrary, it is our humble respect for the irreducible complexity of religious persons, communities, and traditions that motivates our argument for systems thinking as a salient practice in the repertoire of interreligious leadership.

Our emphasis on permeable system boundaries draws attention to this complexity by underscoring the inescapably interpretive, or hermeneutical aspect of systems thinking. Boundary questions, especially in relation to social and cultural systems, are often highly fraught and contested. In fact, one of the main differences between religious supremacy and interreligious resilience concerns the way these different interreligious fractals understand the nature and function of boundaries in religious communities and traditions. Exclusionary belonging, which is characteristic of religious supremacy, depends on a rigidly policed boundary between those who belong and those who do not. Boundaries have to do with the maintenance of an inside and an outside. Questions regarding where one religious system ends and another begins, how they influence one another, which religious culture's interpretive norms should be used to make such determinations, and which and whose perspectives on these questions are authoritative (e.g., the religious historian, theologian, lay person, or clergy person), are all deeply charged questions that require interreligious or intercultural skills to negotiate. All this is to say that systems thinking can be a helpful tool for interreligious leadership even as the interreligious application of systems thinking requires interreligious facility. If this sounds circular, we think of it as a virtuous and generative circle rather than a vicious one. It is a circle of interpretive experience through which one gains interreligious facility with systems thinking by integrating systems thinking into the practice of interreligious leadership.

A systems mindset is indispensable to understanding resilience and vulnerability in general, as well as interreligious resilience and vulnerability specifically. In systems thinking, vulnerability refers to a state, condition, or aspect of a system through which the system is susceptible to disruptive change of some kind. For example, if someone's immune system is compromised, they are more vulnerable to illness and infection than someone with a healthier immune system. Or, for another example, if the doors and windows in a house in Chicago, where we live, are old and cracked, then the house will be less energy efficient, and the homeowners will be vulnerable to higher energy bills than if their doors and windows were more insulated. But insofar as the household is an open system, the leaky doors and windows impact more than the homeowner's energy costs, since the household's energy system is tied to larger industrial and planetary systems. The homeowner's increased consumption of energy, assuming the energy grid is primarily fossil-fueled rather than renewably sourced, will contribute to the increased vulnerability of other's lives, distant and near, through anthropogenic climate change.

All this is to say that if we are talking about open organic and human systems, such as religious communities and traditions, vulnerability is unavoidable—there are no invulnerable organic, human, or cultural systems. All such systems have vulnerabilities and are therefore also susceptible to disruptive change—often through encounter with other systems. The disruption in question could be so traumatic that the system is fundamentally compromised. This does not mean that all the parts of the system suddenly disintegrate into nothingness, but that they are degraded to the point that they can no longer support the function or purpose that has organized the system to that point. But not all change is catastrophic. Change in a system, or to it, whether the change arises internally in the system or through encounter with a different system, can create new potential by disrupting the way things were previously done or arranged—for example, the way the parts were organized or the way the processes were coordinated. If the system is sufficiently resilient, the system can learn new ways of doing and arranging things that enable the system to meet ongoing changes with greater facility. The more learning that occurs in response to vulnerability, the more resilience a system develops.

Systems can be more and less vulnerable, and more and less resilient, depending on their capacity to learn through change. Degrees of vulnerability and resilience vary according to the integrity of the components, structures, and processes that internally constitute a system, the exposure of a system to external threats and risks, and the capacities within the system that allow it to learn, or not, in response to change. The degree to which a system can anticipate, identify, integrate, resist, or adaptively learn from change is the degree to which it is vulnerable or resilient. Resilient systems are characterized by internal diversity, redundancy, agility, cohesion, and responsivity, and by way of these capacities can integrate and learn through change. Conversely, vulnerable systems are relatively homogenous, inflexible, internally disconnected, unresponsive, and therefore at risk of disintegration in response to significant internal or external change. Instead of adaptively "bouncing back" from disturbance or resisting, mitigating, or learning through change, vulnerable systems decompose and are prone to collapse.

These ideas illuminate some important insights. The first and most basic is that in a world of overlapping and interpenetrating systems, some cooperative and some countervailing, vulnerability and risk are ontologically basic—*esse qua esse vulnerabilis est*. To be a system in a world of systems is to be vulnerable. Though many systems are resilient, some more than others, all complex, open systems are vulnerable to some degree and at some point, and in different ways. The second truth is that human systems—from individual selves to cultural, social, economic, and ecological systems—are structurally embedded within, functionally dependent upon, and interconnected with many other types and levels of systems. This interconnectedness means that systems mutually influence one another in diverse ways, positively and negatively. The third truth is that systems are dynamic, and the more complex they are, the more nonlinear and unpredictable their behavior will be.

Rather than aiming for invulnerability—which is a supremacist motivation—a systems framework of interreligious resilience assumes that vulnerability is a part of religious life and seeks to learn from and through experiences of vulnerability. This does not mean that all vulnerabilities should be embraced or accepted, or that all vulnerabilities are natural or given. Some vulnerabilities are contingent and created, and many are unevenly distributed and unjust. Though it should go without saying, when we say that resilience thinking assumes vulnerability and seeks to learn through it, we are emphatically not advocating for making ourselves or others more vulnerable in demeaning, degrading, dehumanizing, or destructive ways. Far from producing harm or resigning in the face of suffering and oppression, the creative use of vulnerability in interreligious resilience is a way of activating practices of mutual interreligious learning, which is indispensable to the work of moving beyond polarization, political sectarianism, and the supremacy fractal, and moving toward social and cultural pluralism.

In addition to providing a context for resilience and vulnerability, systems thinking helps us to think about, and relate to, difference and identity in new ways, as mentioned in the earlier discussion of fractals. First, remember that a system is a bounded whole made of purposively or functionally integrated parts. In any system, then, the parts can be thought of as differences within the system. If one has a collection of things that are identical to one another, or are not purposively or functionally integrated, then one is talking about a set rather than a system. In a system, the parts that make up the boundaried whole play different roles, are informationally connected through feedback loops, and are integrated in support of a common function or purpose. The identity of a system—or what makes it one kind of system rather than another (for instance, a living system versus a mechanical system, an individual person versus a community)—depends on the differences internal to it and the way those differences interact in relation to a distinct purpose or function. Just as vulnerability is not the opposite of resilience, identity and difference are not opposed to one another but are mutually constitutive in a systems mindset—there is no system identity apart from system differences.

The co-constitutive relationship between identity and difference in systems thinking parallels the co-constitutive relationship between resilience and vulnerability. Resilience is neither anti-vulnerability nor invulnerability nor a fixed and unchanging essence possessed by some persons or communities or systems and not others. As the identity of a system is constituted in part by the differences among internally integrated parts in a system, as well as by boundary differences from other systems, so also resilience is learned through vulnerability, and not to the exclusion of it. Resilience is not something that is achieved, once and for all, but something that can be learned and takes continuous practice. If it is not fixed and unchanging, and if it is not the opposite of vulnerability, what then is it? Resilience is a learned capacity that enables ongoing learning. Notice the duplication of "learning" in this definition. Resilience, in the interreligious context, is not innate, but learned—no religious person or community is inherently resilient interreligiously. But they can learn resilience. And what is learned through resilience is how to continue to learn, especially from and through our vulnerable encounters with religious others. In an important sense, then, the opposite of this concept of resilience is an unwillingness to continue learning. And an unwillingness to continue learning is one way to summarize the pedagogical, psychological, spiritual, and moral distortion of religious supremacy. Interreligious resilience can be an antidote to religious supremacy because it enables continuous interreligious learning, whereas the fractal of monopolistic truth, oppositional identity, and exclusionary belonging that constitute religious supremacy impede learning from other traditions and communities.

Resilience has truly become ubiquitous as a term. But resilience can take on different meanings in different disciplinary contexts. In the material sciences, for example, resilience refers to the ability of certain materials (rubber is frequently presented in this context) to withstand compression or expansion and return to their original shape or position. In physiology, resilience is related to efforts to maintain adaptive functioning associated with a certain quality of life and in response to specific functional limitations or chronic health conditions. In behavioral sciences and developmental psychology, it is a process of adaptation in response to some trauma, severe stress, or adversity. In ecology, resilience is the capacity of a natural system to recover from environmental stresses such that the system sustainability can be maintained.

But as we intend it, resilience is not merely about adapting to new situations, circumstances, or environments. Nor is it merely about returning to a status quo or equilibrium after some sort of disturbance or trauma. It is not a coping or survival skill. Interreligious resilience is not about coping with religious difference. While coping may be necessary to multireligious tolerance, it is utterly insufficient and even contradictory to interreligious pluralism. Recall that if diversity describes the social fact of religious difference in the world, pluralism names the idea and the ideal of a social world in which diversely religious people have learned how to mutually respect and learn from one another's differences.

It is important to reiterate here the distinction we suggested at the beginning of this book between simple resilience and complex resilience, a distinction that depends on a particular way of interpreting vulnerability. Simple resilience is the ability to withstand external pressure and return to an original shape, form, or position. Simple resilience seeks to maintain stability, equilibrium, or a trajectory. Complex resilience is about learning and growth. It is not about returning to an original state or condition but is about changing through ongoing learning and the possibility of growing through future challenges or stresses.

This way of thinking about resilience is attuned to the complexity of our changing world, and especially to the demands of living, learning, and leading through times of crisis. As uncomfortable as it may be, when the ordinary is disrupted, when plans are frustrated, when everything seems up in the air, change and disruption create potential to see and do things differently. The shift from simple to complex resilience is a shift from passive to active change, from reacting to change to anticipating and responding to change, from simply enduring change to engaging it, from seeking to return to a status quo to enhancing or altering the conditions of our lives. The shift of perspective from simple to complex resilience is rooted in a deeper shift from an individualist, incremental response to a crisis, to a relational-systems framework. Complex resilience is agentic—it's about making change, rather than merely a set of adaptive capacities that enable us to endure change. It is a way of intervening in a dynamic world and giving shape to it through our spheres of influence. So, the point is that, in contrast to simple resilience, complex resilience is about bringing something new to life. Complex resilience is not an innate or inherited capacity, but a learned habit of thinking and acting that requires practice.

Given this, at the heart of complex resilience is a constructive understanding of vulnerability as opportunity, not weakness, as generative and productive, especially as it opens us up to new ways of thinking and makes us aware of, and sensitive to, the vulnerabilities of others as well as ourselves. Christian theologian Kristine Culp has something like this in mind, for example, in the following observation:

> The biblical notion that humans are creatures made of earth and breath . . . suggests vulnerability—but to transformation as well as to devastation. In this perspective . . . human creatures are susceptible to ill and to good. Vulnerability encompasses not only the capacity to suffer harm and to be damaged, but also capacities implied by contrast: to be kept safe and whole, to have integrity and dignity, and to be healed and lifted.[28]

Part of the work of interreligious resilience and leadership is in finding these opportunities for opening and transformation through vulnerability.

As with complex resilience, this view of vulnerability is different from common assumptions about vulnerability. The term "vulnerability" is derived from the Latin word "vulnus," or wound. Vulnerability is defined in various ways, including the ratio of risk to susceptibility; the inadequacy of means or ability to protect oneself against adverse events and to recover from them; or the capacity to be harmed by a stress or perturbation. Vulnerability is often presented as a counterpoint to, or inversion of, resilience. Vulnerability is often equated with weakness and powerlessness. These ways of thinking about vulnerability make us likely to repudiate our own and others' vulnerability. As feminist philosopher Erinn Gilson notes, "a significant part of what enables the exploitation of vulnerability and rejection of responsibility for vulnerable others is the persistence of the idea that vulnerability is to be avoided. This idea is possible because vulnerability is associated with being harmed, passive, and weak, and this is incompatible with ideal notions of mastery, competence, and wellbeing."[29] The flipside of the assumption that vulnerability is weakness is the valorization of dominance and mastery—aspects of the supremacy fractal. If we idealize invulnerable mastery and dominance, we become uninterested in, or incapable of, seeing things differently, and less likely to position ourselves to see the world from different positions or perspectives. As Gilson continues, "by opening oneself up to others and their effects on the self, one is also open to transformation in relation to these others: receptivity, nonclosure, and self-dispossession endow one with a 'gift of changeability.' Openness to experiencing alterity, and altering in relation to it, is the condition of invention."[30] Whereas invulnerability impedes empathy, learning, and transformation, and thus complex resilience, vulnerability as the "gift of changeability" and openness to being altered through encounters with alterity are integral elements of complex resilience.

But not all vulnerability is the same, and thus interreligious leadership entails consideration of the unevenness of vulnerability and types of vulnerability. Vulnerability includes social, economic, environmental, and institutional dimensions. As a result, both resources and networks affect how vulnerable an institution, community, or person may be. There are various kinds of vulnerability—for example, dispositional (potential), occurrent (actual), or pathogenic vulnerability (vulnerabilities that are particularly ethically troubling, and which may exacerbate existing or create new vulnerabilities). In fact, individuals and communities may face multiple vulnerabilities.

A helpful distinction can be made between creatural and contingent vulnerability. Creatural vulnerability is an ontological condition of life—it is universal, given, inherent. To be a living creature, to be a person, is to be woundable, able to cause and to suffer wounds, to harm and be harmed, to eat and be eaten. Contingent vulnerability, on the other hand, names the kind of vulnerability that disproportionately afflicts some people more than others. Contingent vulnerability is determined by any number of factors, such as where and when we are born, the bodies and minds we are born into, the social and class locations we inhabit, and proximity to environmental hazards.

Unlike creatural vulnerability, which is universal, given, and inherent, contingent vulnerability is uneven, constructed, and systemic. For example, some kinds of bodies are more vulnerable than others. Gender, skin color, and sexual orientation all influence a human body's vulnerability. And this is not because being female or transgender or gay or brown or black-skinned is inherently more vulnerable than being male or cis gendered or straight or light or white skinned. It is because social norms and cultural values confer advantages and disadvantages related to gender, race, ethnicity, and sexuality, and these advantages and disadvantages are systemically transmitted, institutionally reinforced, and historically cumulative. By accident of genealogy and geography some of us have been born into contexts of advantage and have consciously and unconsciously consented to systems that reinforce, justify, and exacerbate our disproportionate and unearned advantages. People and groups who are advantaged in these ways suffer all the "slings and arrows" of creatural vulnerability and natural risk. But people and groups who, through accident of genealogy and geography, have been born into socially, economically, and ecologically disadvantageous contexts are contingently vulnerable. The contingently vulnerable are of course creaturally vulnerable as well, but they are disproportionately exposed to socially manufactured risk. Some people, because of who they are and where they live and because of policies and prejudices, have been made more vulnerable than others. This kind of vulnerability is contingent, or caused, an unjust effect of societal dynamics.

But interreligious resilience asks interreligious leaders also to be attuned to a third kind of vulnerability, creative vulnerability. In an interconnected, constantly changing world, social, cultural, and economic systems are entangled, and, as a result, to thrive and flourish, we need one another. We need to build trusting relationships of mutual support. To live well in this world of pervasive creatural vulnerability and uneven contingent vulnerability, we need to build complex resilience, and concomitantly, interreligious leaders seeking to cultivate interreligious resilience need to learn to see and engage crises not merely as circumstances to endure, but as opportunities for transformation, growth, and mutual learning. Thus, in addition to being attuned to the creatural and contingent vulnerabilities that condition interreligious engagement, interreligious resilience entails practising creative vulnerability.

Creative vulnerability enables mutual interreligious learning and is the cornerstone of interreligious resilience and the VITA pathway of interreligious leadership. By making ourselves (and our communities and traditions) creatively vulnerable to learning with and from religious others, it becomes possible to discover that there is meaning, beauty, and goodness in what is genuinely and deeply different, and this discovery can lead us to embody our religious commitments and practise our religious paths in new and even more deeply reverent ways. When we combine creative Vulnerability with Intentionality, Trust, and Awareness (the other VITA practices) and open ourselves to learning through religious difference, we do not become less religious, but religious in a different way, the difference we identify as interreligious resilience. We now integrate these ideas into a resilience and vulnerability theory of religion.

A Resilience and Vulnerability Theory of Religion

Our purpose in what follows is not to offer a total theory of religion that surpasses all others. For one thing, that impulse smacks of the supremacist logic that this book is working against! For another thing, given all that we do not know, and all that we have not experienced, it would be foolish for us to attempt such a venture. We embrace the vulnerability of our unknowing as the creative ground of our efforts in what follows, and indeed, as an integral element of our approach to interreligious leadership. Among the things we do know, however, is that religion and religious life are extraordinarily complex and continuously changing. Thus, for reasons of our own limitations and the dynamic complexity of religion, we do not pretend here to offer a definitive theory or final definition of religion. Instead, we offer a way of imagining religion through the systemic and human lenses of resilience and vulnerability. By bridging functional insight regarding how religion works historically, socially, and culturally, and phenomenological sensitivity to lived religious experience, this way of imagining religion is attuned to the practical challenges of interreligious engagement and leadership.

Keeping in mind all that we said earlier about functionalist and phenomenological theories of religion, and also about fractals, systems, resilience, and vulnerability in the previous section, we first want to offer a compressed working hypothesis: Religions are historically dynamic and socially integrative cultural systems of symbols, rituals, and beliefs that transform vulnerable groups of humans into resilient human communities by binding them together with a common identity, meaning, and purpose. Phenomenologically, then, religions orient individuals and communities amidst the blessings and burdens of life's vulnerabilities through mutually reinforcing networks of ritual practices, stories, values, transcendent ideals, and social institutions. And functionally, they are historically adaptive cultural projects that transform humans who merely happen to be grouped together in space and time into human communities bound together with identities and purposes that transcend space and time.

Now, let us elaborate on the elements of this hypothesis a bit further.

As historically dynamic, religions change over time in response to various internal and external pressures. Religions are formed and defined in large measure by the ways that religious communities and institutions respond to change over time. We outlined some of these ways of responding to change in Chapter 2, when we discussed various postsecular responses to the pressures of globalization, social acceleration, and polarization—responses that varied from reactionary sectarianism on one end of the spectrum, to integrative pluralism on the other.

As socially integrative, religions orient individuals in communities and larger social collectives. Thus, religions are differentiated, embodied, and expressed at individual, communal, and societal levels. They reinforce norms of reciprocity, fairness, and sanctity which simultaneously integrate their adherents socially into worlds of belonging and set them apart, in certain respects, from others. Through story and ritual, religions establish, justify, and regulate the moral norms, behavioral conventions, and social structures necessary to ordering human social groups at various scales.

As cultural systems, religions are organized around diverse repertoires of cultural symbols, rituals, values, aesthetic practices, and institutions—these are the parts or elements through which religious cultural systems function. What holds these elements together, or what integrates and enlivens them, are the existential, moral, and spiritual potency of transcendent ideals. Transcendent ideals, which serve as the integrative purpose of the religious cultural system, have potency insofar as they give life to meanings, values, and desires that empower and sustain resilience in human lives and communities. Whether these ideals are taken to be metaphysically transcendent or not, or expressed in the personae of gods or not, they are functionally and phenomenologically transcendent. They are transcendent in these respects insofar as they provide critical standards that relativize and order other existential and cultural ideals and ultimately orient human individual and communal life in relation to a shared structure or field of meaning.

Given these historical, social, and cultural aspects of religions, religious experience can be interpreted as the qualitative experience of becoming sensitized to the existentially, socially, and morally functional presence of phenomenologically transcendent ideals. Along with Welch and Pinn, then, this rendering of the "religious" is not a special type of experience monopolized by religions but is a quality of experience that exists potentially within and across diverse registers of human life—intellectual, aesthetic, moral, and political. And along with Durkheim, this theory of religion accents the morally and socially formative function of a religious community. With a nod to Alfred North Whitehead's interpretation of religion, religion and the religious express the solidary (social, communal) and solitary (existential, subjective, embodied) aspects of living amidst the creatural and contingent vulnerabilities of life in a complex, processive world.[31]

Religions describe creatural and contingent vulnerabilities in different ways—consider, for example, sin: alienation or disobedience, at individual and structural levels; suffering/dukkha: craving, anger, greed, delusion, again as experienced in the individual mind-body and as manifest socially; samsaric wandering through cycles of lives and times. Religious people take their transcendent ideals to be saving or liberating insofar as they are connected to what they understand to be of utmost importance, which understanding is mediated through cultural symbols and practices. For theists, for example, this is symbolized through the various names and forms of divinity: Elohim, El Shaddai, Jehovah, Ein-Sof, Ha Shem, Allah, Trinity, Brahman. Nontheists symbolize this through concepts such as Tao, Qi, Li, Dharma, Buddha-nature, and dharmakaya. Because the work of aligning with what is of utmost importance is not just intellectual but is an embodied, social, and historical process, religious life and practice are entangled with cultural customs, styles, manners, etiquettes, and ideologies. As African American philosopher of religion Charles Long has put this, "The religion of any people is more than a structure of thought; it is experience, expression, motivations, intentions, behaviors, styles and rhythms."[32] Religious traditions then are constituted by practices, arguments, stories, rituals, and institutional forms that correlate the truth about what is taken to be transcendently real to the goodness and rightness of what is taken to be transcendently important. The way to salvation, liberation, release, righteousness, obedience, or bliss is to align one's life in piety and devotion, thought and practice, with the tradition's transcendent ideal, variously symbolized as personal or nonpersonal, unitary or multiple, substantial or empty.

This way of imagining religion is useful for comparison across traditions and for interpretations of their internal diversity. For example, one could say that for Christians, the transcendent ideal is salvation, and vulnerability can be understood as a cognate of sin, or alienation from God, self, and others. For Buddhists, the transcendent ideal is nirvana, the bliss of the extinction of ego, while the vulnerabilities of delusion, greed, and hatred are both cause and effect of dukkha and of egocentric attachment to the impermanence of things. For Hindus, the transcendent ideal may be moksha, or karmic release, while vulnerability is related to the future-constitutive karmic weight of the moral past on the moral present. For Muslims, the transcendent ideal is the paradise of Allah, while vulnerability is caused by disobedience to Allah. In Judaism, as well as Christianity, vulnerability is a primary condition of all created things—to be human is to be a finite dust creature, a creature made of earth (*adamah*), a creature of the dirt who will return to the dirt. The story of Jacob wrestling the angel in search of the name of God and receiving a wound along with his own name in return can be read as a figure of the enlivening embrace of human vulnerability that comes through spiritual quest. In the Christian New Testament, God's own vulnerability is expressed by images of the natality of Jesus, his birth in a barn, his crucifixion, and the thorn in the flesh of Paul can also be interpreted as a figure of vulnerability. Differences within traditions can be interpreted as internally diverse ways of calibrating the symbols, rituals, and institutions that orient adherents to their transcendent ideals. For example, Roman Catholics and Protestant Evangelicals have different ideas about the proper calibration of salvation, symbol, ritual, and institution, just as Theravadan and Mahayanan Buddhists present different ideas about how to achieve nirvana, and so on. In sum, different religious traditions signify vulnerability as a fundamental condition in diverse ways and various ways of dealing with this vulnerability are central to their historically dynamic, socially integrative nature as complex cultural systems.

But vulnerability is not only a theme across religious traditions; it is also a central theme in the modern sciences. In biology, all living things and living systems are dynamic and perishable. To live is to be subject to decay and interdependent. Vulnerability is the essence of bios—organic life is intractably perilous, to live is to walk the metabolic razor's edge between consuming and being consumed. And in physics, the hardest of the hard sciences, the vulnerability of our theories about the physical world are apparent to the extent that regularities have taken the place of laws and probabilities and relativities have replaced certainties and absolutes. Beyond science and religion, vulnerability is also a prominent literary trope. The pathos of ancient Greek tragedy, for example, pivots around the interplay of human and divine vulnerability. Sophocles's Antigone illustrates moral vulnerability in a world of competing goods and duties, while the Oedipus cycle illustrates the limitations of human insight and the vulnerability of the present and future to the past. These traditions seem to point to vulnerability as fundamental to reality and human existence. Human being, doing, and knowing is a venture in vulnerability. Vulnerability is an ontological, existential, and epistemic condition. To be vulnerable, as the Latin roots *vulnus* and *vulnerare* indicate, is to be liable to wounding, in both senses of the word—to being wounded, and to being a potential cause of others' wounding.

What is clear is that, as postmodern and process thought teach us, we are never completely separated from others. In fact, we can often (always?) only understand ourselves by seeking to understand others and the trace of others in us. As Judith Butler has provocatively written,

> I find that my very formation implicates the other in me, that my own foreignness to myself is, paradoxically, the source of my ethical connection with others. I am not fully known to myself, because part of what I am is the enigmatic traces of others. In this sense, I cannot know myself perfectly or know my "difference" from others in an irreducible way.[33]

That is, the religious self is not fully understandable without reference to the religious other. This is a powerful insight for interreligious leadership, pointing as it does to the essential recognition of others in us, and by extension, ourselves in others. This serves as a foundation for serious and genuine interreligious engagement and dialog.

To further illustrate the interreligious relevance of resilience and vulnerability, let us turn to an analogy developed by Raimon Panikkar (alluded to earlier in the discussion of Swidler). Panikkar likened a person's or a community's religious worldview to a view of a sacred landscape through a window. The person or community identifies the landscape they see through their window as the whole of what is sacred and saving, the ultimately real and highest good, variously conceived as, for instance, Allah, YHWH, Brahman, Tao, Dharma, Nirvana, or God. But what is interesting is that the person or community does not realize that they are seeing through a window until they learn to hear about the different sacred landscapes that others see through different windows. Until a person or community learns to hear from others about what the others see, their own window is invisible, which allows them to continue thinking that what they are seeing is the whole of the sacred and holy, the final and absolute truth of ultimate reality. However, once the person or community learns to hear what others see through their different landscape, then they can begin to see the window that has framed their own view of the sacred—they realize they have been seeing through a window all along.

Until people learn how to share with others about what they see through their religious windows and learn to hear from others what the others are seeing, they do not realize they are seeing through religious windows at all. And yet, even once they learn to listen to what others see and share what they see, they do not cease seeing through their own windows. They cannot see what others see; they can only hear from others about what they see. Although they cannot see what others see, what they hear from others can have an enriching influence on what they see through their window. So, once the person or community learns to hear what others see, they begin not only to recognize that they are seeing through a window but also to notice different things about the sacred landscape that they see through their window. As they learn to hear what others see, they learn to see what they see differently and more profoundly.

Recognizing the unfinality and incompleteness of their sacred landscape can complexify and deepen their relationship to it, as well as open them to continuous learning with and from others.

Panikkar's window analogy is not perfect. Among other things, it depends on sensory metaphors that have limited relevance for people with hearing and vision impairments. It also raises some interesting philosophical and theological questions. For instance, does the analogy assume that on the other side of the windows there is one all-encompassing sacred landscape (the essentialist thesis), of which each of the religions (windows) has a view of certain aspects? In this case, there is one sacred reality, of which each of the religious ways provides a partial glimpse—the different religions provide different phenomenological approaches to a singular transcendent reality, which none of them sees in totality. To mix metaphors, this would imply there is one mountain with one summit, and the different religions are different paths approaching that summit. This interpretation provokes numerous questions. Are some paths superior to others? Are some more direct? Are others more scenic? Similarly, do some religious windows have a more complete view of the sacred landscape than others? But making such judgments presumes a set of evaluative criteria—are these criteria trans-traditional or tradition-internal? If they are trans-traditional criteria, from what or whose vantage point would they be developed, and how would agreement as to their adequacy be decided? If they are tradition-internal, on what basis could they be legitimately applied to other traditions to make judgments about which path, or which window, is superior to the others?

On the other hand, the analogy could be interpreted to mean that each of the windows is looking onto different sacred landscapes entirely, rather than different aspects of one larger reality (the incommensurability thesis). Rather than one sacred reality which each tradition sees in part, this would imply that there are many different sacred realities; or many different mountains and summits; or, since the mountain summit metaphor privileges a height-depth orientation toward the sacred, which is more familiar within theistic traditions, might the sacred landscapes be indexed to entirely different types of landscape—deserts, streams, oceans? If there are multiple sacred realities, how different are they from one another? Are they so different as to be incomparable entirely, such that it would be quite impossible to "hear" what others are seeing through their windows—can someone who has only known rafts and streams make sense of someone else who has only known the descents and ascents of mountain landscapes, and vice versa? And how deep and wide does this analogy extend, anyway? Does it extend only to different religious traditions, or also to differences between communities or denominations within the same tradition, or even to different individuals within the same community?

There is plenty of room to play with Panikkar's analogy. But we bring it up to make three main points: (1) religious people and communities must learn how to hear what others are seeing through their windows to discover that they themselves are seeing through a religious window; (2) by learning to hear what others are seeing, they also learn how to see what they see differently;

and (3) opening oneself to the possibility of change through encounter with religious difference is necessary to learning to hear what others see.

This process describes what we mean by interreligious resilience—the learned ability, through creative vulnerability, to learn from others, and thereby contribute to ongoing mutual learning. Creative vulnerability is thus a vital condition of possibility for interreligious learning, and of the move from monopolistic to plural truth, from oppositional to relational identities, from exclusionary to inclusionary or coalitional belonging, and toward the ideal of social pluralism. In short, the transformation of the supremacy fractal into the fractal of interreligious resilience turns on the practice of creative vulnerability. Furthermore, learning to hear what others see, and thereby learning to see one's own religious landscape differently, is a condition of being able to address some of the philosophical and theological questions raised earlier.

In this way, then, creative vulnerability is the pivotal practice that links intrareligious growth and learning to interreligious engagement and leadership—the combination of which is what we mean by interreligious resilience. But for creative vulnerability to lead to interreligious resilience, it needs to be put into practice. We now turn to a discussion of the VITA pathway as a framework for this practice.

Part 2

Practical Application

5

The VITA Pathway of Interreligious Resilience

In Part I we examined the history and models of interreligious engagement (Chapter 1), from which we learned about the most effective methods of engagement, especially in the context of massive changes in society (Chapter 2). We turned to a review of some key leadership principles that may be helpful in addressing these changes as well as the associated challenges and opportunities that our students, colleagues, and research identified as particularly important now and for the future (Chapter 3). At the end of Part I (Chapter 4), we elaborated a theory of religion developed through placing resilience and vulnerability into conversation with key classical and contemporary theories of and approaches to religion. Throughout we noted the value of resilience and vulnerability in deepening and expanding interreligious engagement and leadership. For example, while many traditional approaches to leadership recognize the importance of relationships, resilience theory emphasizes the significance of networks and systems in ways that help us to see larger systems and the role that we and others play in them. Similarly, while recent leadership studies note the value of humility, notions of vulnerability add a depth of sensitivity to our own vulnerabilities and those of others, sensitizing and opening us to others in profoundly new ways.

In Part II, we now turn to the VITA pathway of interreligious resilience that emerges from our work in Part I. There are many components to interreligious resilience, which we have defined, broadly, as the learned capacity to continue learning through the challenges, crises, conflicts, and changes of interreligious engagement. This definition is informed by an understanding of how systems function and evolve. Recall our account of systems as permeably bounded wholes comprised of functionally or purposively integrated parts. This is what one might describe as a "moving" or "pliable" definition since it can be applied in diverse circumstances and in relation to various issues. We advocate using this definition of systems as a frame or lens. Like Panikkar's "window," this definition of system provides a way of looking at things, and in the case of interreligious leadership, a way of looking at interreligious engagement. More precisely and less metaphorically, a systems approach to interreligious leadership is a methodology—a patterned way of interpreting, analyzing, and strategizing the various tasks of interreligious leadership. But as with any good methodology, the pattern of interpretation, analysis, and strategy is organized around a sequence of practices: one does one thing, and then another, as a way of moving toward some objective or aim. The aim of this methodology is to catalyze interreligious resilience, to learn how to continue learning through interreligious engagement. Interreligious resilience is a form of complex resilience. As we explained previously, complex resilience is not innate, but can be cultivated over time through iterative passages through vulnerability. Insofar as complex resilience is not innate, but is cultivated, it is a way of bringing something new into the world, bringing life to something that didn't previously exist.

VITA is the acronym we use to represent the sequencing of the distinct but interrelated practices of Vulnerability, Intentionality, Trust, and Awareness, which iteratively can lead to the birthing of interreligious resilience. These practices are interpretations of the elements of the adaptive cycle in complex systems. As explained previously, complex systems can acquire or cultivate complex resilience when the elements of the system are integrated with the function or purpose of the system in ways that allow it to learn through change. In the VITA pathway, the practice of Vulnerability acknowledges that disruptions, crises, encounters, and change are intrinsic to the life of any complex interreligious engagement; the practice of Intentionality is attuned to questions of purpose and mindfulness; the practice of Trust recognizes the need for coordinated relational rapport through the learning process; and the practice of Awareness affirms the interpretive, intuitive, analytic, and epistemic elements of learning.

Each of these VITA practices is organized around a stance and a series of questions that can be applied to diverse types and levels of interreligious engagement. As an iterative process that can be applied in diverse interreligious circumstances, the VITA pathway to interreligious resilience has a fractal logic. Thus, while the VITA pathway provides a useful approach to various challenges of interreligious leadership, it is also a way of cultivating the interreligious resilience counter-fractal to religious supremacy and contributing to the social ideal of pluralism.

Vulnerability

As discussed in Chapter 2, the world we live in today is rapidly changing—and at a rate unprecedented in human history. This leads to a great deal of promise and excitement on one hand, but also a fair amount of insecurity and entrenchment on the other. As philosopher Jonathan Lear recently noted:

> We live at a time of a heightened sense that civilizations are themselves vulnerable. Events around the world—terrorist attacks, violent social upheavals, and even natural catastrophes—have left us with an uncanny sense of menace. We seem to be aware of a shared vulnerability that we cannot quite name. I suspect that this feeling has provoked the widespread intolerance that we see around us today—from all points on the political spectrum. It is as though, without our insistence that our outlook is correct, the outlook itself might collapse. Perhaps if we could give a name to our shared sense of vulnerability, we could find better ways to live with it.[1]

The uncertainty of the world and events can lead us to see the vulnerabilities that we share, creatural and contingent. Yet, as we stressed in Chapter 2, it can also produce a reactive tendency to entrench ourselves in the presumed security of our own positions, standpoints, communities, and traditions. This is the "partisan sectarian" seduction. In response to accelerating social change, and to polarizing political and cultural messaging, we can become intolerant of others' views and positions as a way of defending our own—to invert Lear's insight, it is as if we must insist on the wrongness of others' views to keep our own from collapsing. These tendencies are at the root of the supremacy fractal, and recognizing them in ourselves as well as in others makes opening to our vulnerabilities more important today, perhaps, than ever.

Vulnerability is at the core of interreligious resilience. It is the fundamental stance, posture, and orientation to VITA and, as such, is woven through the practices of Intentionality, Trust, and Awareness. Vulnerability asks us to explore the perspectives and concerns of others even as we open ourselves in deep and meaningful ways to our weaknesses, blind spots, ignorance, our unknowing. This can be not only counterintuitive but also uncomfortable, especially for leaders who have been trained to think of leadership as the heroic, invulnerable, mastery of a field and management of others. When we cultivate a stance of creative vulnerability, we open ourselves to new ideas, values, perspectives, and possibilities. In doing so, we also open ourselves to being wounded and, when we engage with others' vulnerabilities, to the possibility of wounding others. Vulnerability, therefore, if it is to be creative, requires the other VITA practices—Intentionality, Trust, and Awareness.

There are many potential questions and considerations for reflection when donning a vulnerability stance. Vulnerability asks us to identify and reflect on our own vulnerabilities and those of others, both creatural and contingent. Vulnerability requires humility, flexibility, and agility, as well as the capacity to hold multiple perspectives and possibilities in mind. Vulnerability encourages us to ask: What shortcoming or problem is this crisis revealing? To address the interreligious issue at hand, what change do I need to open myself to? What is at risk if I don't change? What will be risked by making change? What is my perspective, and how is it shaping how I see or understand the interreligious scenario? If the scenario is one of conflict, how might I be contributing to the conflict? What do I imagine the others involved in the situation are seeing or feeling? How has the context or their own experiences, and their religious formation, shaped their position or response? Though we can never really put ourselves in someone else's shoes, how might we seek in an interculturally empathic way, to cross over into their perspective, assumptions, approach, concerns? On a different plane, what deeper problem or possibility might the surface situation or crisis be revealing? What bigger issues might the situation be highlighting? And, finally, taking all of this into consideration, what possible approaches to the issue might we take—the ones that seemed initial and most obvious, but also the less obvious ones that emerge as we walk through these various considerations?

Intentionality

Core to intentionality—as we heard from many of our own students and colleagues—is purposiveness (in vision as well as strategy), clarity about the aim(s) of engagement, and tying form and strategy to aim(s). Central as well is boundary setting—the forms, durations, types, and levels of engagements. Guiding questions include What realistic change am I aiming for? What plan/method/strategy will help me to realize that aim?

According to the Stanford Encyclopedia of Philosophy, "As indicated by the meaning of the Latin word *tendere*, which is the etymology of 'intentionality,' the relevant idea behind intentionality is that of mental directedness towards (or attending to) objects, as if the mind were construed as a mental bow whose arrows could be properly aimed at different targets."[2] Intentionality may seem rather obvious and easy, but it is one of the things that is most challenging to do in a consistent and deep way, especially under conditions of stress and crisis. To be intentional requires us to be thoughtful and reflective. It means being proactive, strategic, and planful—seeing the bigger picture and understanding that it takes effort and time for real engagement, effective leadership, and sustainable change. Being intentional requires that we think about our thoughts and actions, but also their impact on others. That is, we must consider the goals, objectives, and purposes of our intentional actions. Are they simply to prove our preexisting assumptions and positions? Or are they related to exploring assumptions and differences in an open and honest way? Intent requires attentiveness or attunement to ourselves and others; it requires patience and it requires us to stretch in ways that may feel unusual or uncomfortable. It is easy to start with intentionality and lose focus, especially when things don't go as we would like or as we expected they would. We often speak about entering dialog with good intentions. And that is important. But good intentions don't count for much if the impact that results is destructive or harmful. Intentionality, therefore, assumes that we begin with carefully considered but revisable intentions and a desire for open engagement, learning, and growth. But it also begins with reflection on the impact our speech and actions may have on others as well. There are, as a result, several key questions to consider in developing intentionality. These include What are my goals—the stated and implicit ones? What am I trying to achieve in what I am about to do; that is, what change am I aiming for? How will the conversation, activity, engagement, and so forth, be perceived by and impact others?

Trust

Significant lasting change requires collaboration, and deep and productive relationships. And, as we have learned from recent leadership studies, in a complex world in crisis, no one of us knows all we need to know. Trust is built through active and open feedback and communication, the connectedness that comes from relationships and that helps to create them, and the articulation and practice of shared commitments, values, and practices. Animating questions relating to trust might include: With whom do I need to work to bring about the change I am/we are aiming for? Is there trust that needs to be established, nurtured, repaired? What will it take to build the necessary trust, to sustain the collaboration?

In *The Gardens of Democracy: A New American Story of Citizenship, the Economy, and the Role of Government*,[3] Eric Liu and Nick Hanauer differentiate between what they term "Machinebrain" and "Gardenbrain." Machinebrain, in this model, is, as the name suggests, a mechanistic approach to the world and to democracy. It is "clocks and gears," "balances and counterbalances," and it is "perfectly efficient and automatically self-correcting."[4] It assumes stability and predictability and corrects through regulation.[5] People are trained as cogs and it reflects "a static mindset of control and fixity."[6] Gardenbrain, by contrast, operates from an ecosystems perspective—"sinks and sources of trust and social capital, webs of economic growth, networks of behavioral contagion."[7] This model assumes instability and unpredictability and so a need for tending to ever-changing systems: "Gardenbrain sees people as interdependent creators of a dynamic world: our emotions affect each other; our personal choices cascade into public patterns, which can be shaped but rarely controlled."[8]

Not surprisingly, trust features prominently in the Gardenbrain model, given the emphasis on interdependence and networks. Liu and Hanauer, in fact, assert that "trust is foremost among the social values that make healthy societies."[9] They conclude that "Trust, in short, is the DNA to be found in all the other habits of citizenship. It is what fuels the fractal impact of small acts of leadership. It is what empowers supercarriers to infect others. It is what makes weak ties useful. It is why we need to preserve a human scale for citizenship."[10]

As we saw, building trust is a core leadership competence. It is helpful in successful collaborations and often leads to creativity and innovation. Trust can exist and function at multiple levels. While personal relationships built on trust are important, the trust that is created at organizational and systems levels helps to build in capacity and willingness to experiment and innovate.[11] Trust is also about how we engage with others, how we get to know them, give benefits of the doubt to others—while trying to understand their assumptions and thought processes, understanding how they communicate and prefer to communicate, and their contexts and concerns. Trust is also about open, honest, and consistent communication and action. When asking about trust, we need to consider with whom we need to collaborate, how best to engage them, and the short- and long-term goals of our collaboration or engagement. Trust is a significant piece of cultural and social capital; but it is much more than that. It is a necessary spark for sincere engagement and willingness to take risks, elements that are essential for resilient interreligious leadership.

Awareness

The practice of Awareness includes the work of gaining knowledge and literacy regarding one's own traditions, as well as general knowledge regarding other traditions. It entails learning interreligious etiquette, basic intercultural competency, and gathering as much knowledge about the participants (and their contexts, histories, vulnerabilities) with whom we are engaging. The practice of Awareness, pivoting as with all the other practices around vulnerability, requires us to consider questions such as: What do I know that I don't know? What do I need to learn? How might I learn what I don't even know that I don't know?

Awareness is a skill and a practice that underpins Vulnerability, Intentionality, and Trust. It is also valuable in and of itself. The American Psychological Association defines awareness as "perception or knowledge of something. Accurate reportability of something perceived or known is widely used as a behavioral index of conscious awareness. However, it is possible to be aware of something without being explicitly conscious of it."[12] Awareness can involve knowledge, perception, and intuition, but it is also a specific stance of inquiry and an effort to see larger systems and connections. When we are truly aware, we begin with awareness of ourselves and also develop sensitivity to contexts and issues that surround us and may impact a particular situation. When engaging with awareness, therefore, it is helpful to first interrogate oneself. What do I think and feel about this issue and why? How have I come to this way of thinking or behaving and what are the implications? Moving outward (and iteratively between inside and outside), we may next ask what is going on "out there," or as one of our consulting colleagues reminds us to ask—what is going on, what is really going on, what is supposed to be going on? In becoming aware of a situation or problem, it is helpful to understand the individuals, entities, and dynamics on their own and in their interactions with each other and with us. From there, it is important to ask what we need to learn to better understand what is going on around us. There is situational awareness that helps us to navigate specific situations; but there is also a more general awareness that can help us grow, lead, and navigate changing conditions. At its heart, awareness is about understanding oneself and broader systems, allowing us to predict problems, mitigate challenges, and respond in more efficient and productive ways.

Conclusions

We developed the VITA pathway from a review of the history and models of interreligious engagement, a consideration of the most pressing issues in society today, an examination of core leadership principles, an analysis of diverse theories of religion, and the elaboration of a resilience and vulnerability approach to religion. In addition to a review of related scholarship in each of these areas, we have also drawn from our own personal and professional experience as well as those of our students and colleagues.

In our own work we have utilized the VITA pathway in a range of leadership and educational contexts, which has been especially relevant and useful in the context of the Covid-19 pandemic, which has brought awareness to so many types and dimensions of vulnerability. In all this work we have come to see the value of the concept of interreligious resilience and the VITA pathway for interreligious leadership. Many of the perspectives and tools that underpin and are developed in interreligious resilience and the VITA pathway can help us to navigate many challenges in our professional work as well as in our personal lives. This chapter and the fourteen case studies that follow in Chapter 6, therefore, are an open invitation to experiment with and translate these ideas and principles in the work we all do in our religious communities and traditions and other contexts as well.

6

Case Studies

From Theory to Practice and From Practice to Theory

Introduction

Case Studies have been used in medical training, business education, and scenario planning for many years as a tool to teach critical analysis and problem-solving. They have been broadly adopted in many academic disciplines and fields of education (along with problem-based learning, simulation, and gaming, as well as a variety of experiential, informal, and co-curricular learning). Taking individual or composite situations drawn from experience, cases may be constructed for a wide range of purposes. The context and the scope of cases can vary considerably, but essentially cases ask us to step into the world of the issue being presented and bring to bear a range of critical-thinking skills to understand the core concerns, outline and evaluate possible responses, and, in some cases, suggest recommendations for response. The analysis of cases requires skills such as contextualization, perspective taking, multidimensional interpretation, problem-solving and analysis, and application.

We have used a diversity of cases in our own teaching for many years and have found this methodology particularly helpful in addressing interreligious engagement and leadership, especially given the iterative nature of engaging with a case and the opportunity to construct case scenarios based on contemporary concerns and input from many people working in the field. Each time we have used a case to teach we have been impressed by the range of ways that people see and understand a situation from different perspectives, how they make meaning of the situation being presented in conversation with their own experiences (even if in different fields), and the richness of discussion that inevitably ensues. That has been true regardless of the setting in which we have utilized case studies—including formal graduate education, professional workshops, public programs, Board retreats, and academic conferences.

The case studies that follow are composites (and they do not use real names of individuals or organizations) and identify some of the most pressing concerns that colleagues working in interreligious engagement have shared with us—in person and through a survey. They are also drawn from discussions with our students over the past six years, as well as our own experiences and sense of the field. In each instance, the case has multiple purposes: to present a substantive issue(s); to provide context that is helpful to understand the specific details as well as broad associated issues; to offer a way to engage with and practice critical thinking skills; to provide a forum for practising leadership (albeit in a simulated way); and to give the means to animate the ideas and principles articulated in this book, especially the VITA pathway that we introduced in Chapter 5.

In each of the cases that follow we present a brief context, the actual situation, and a series of guiding questions. Our intention is that readers bring their own experiences and thoughts to bear on understanding and responding to the key issues in each text. We offer the VITA pathway as one method to such case assessment and response that we have found helpful, that draws from the central arguments and discussions in this book, and that provides a clear and consistent approach that can be applied in other settings and to other cases.

We conclude by offering some general reflections on interreligious leadership and its benefits in dealing with these and other challenges that exist now and may emerge in the future and in cultivating new and valuable leadership skills and enhancing old and acquired skills. We offer some suggestions on how to take lessons from all parts of the book to take back to your leadership work—regardless of setting—especially in religious and interreligious contexts.

Applying the VITA Pathway

Case 1 revolves around contract negotiations and the development of the relationship between congregational leadership and the minister. It points to the challenges inherent in this dynamic more generally, but especially when it confronts changes to traditional ways of doing things or addressing particularly sensitive issues, including interreligious engagement. As such, the case surfaces issues of change leadership, the nature and boundaries of authority, and the need to lead from various positions (leadership as behavior rather than position) and bringing people along (consider the highest levels of leadership agility that call for co-creation rather than simply imparting vision and inspiring others). This case uncovers issues related to liturgy and interreligious dialog, and it also raises important considerations for religious leaders in their work with lay leaders, congregants, denominational leaders, people of other faiths, and the broader communities in which they and their work are situated. Interreligious leaders often face the challenge of introducing new perspectives, ideas, and approaches and they can be met with resistance. The skills needed to negotiate the associated challenges of learning, developing, leading, and changing can be difficult, but are essential if we are to make real, positive, and sustainable change.

Here we present Case Study 1 and then we offer a sample of some ways in which the VITA pathway outlined in Chapters 4 and 5 might be applied in order to address the case.

Case Study 1: Lay-Pastoral Relations in an Interreligious Context

Conflict seems to be an inevitable part of life. This seems particularly to be the case when various constituents interact, each with different worldviews, goals, personal styles, and ways of doing things.

Brittany Smith had finished her seminary training and was excited to begin work in her chosen profession. What she learned in seminary had prepared her for the mechanics of negotiating a contract with a congregation. She knew what to expect in terms of compensation, basic freedom of the pulpit, and even the broad outlines of her responsibilities. What she was unprepared for were the on-the-ground realities of hard-nosed negotiation that the hiring committee utilized and the clear message she was receiving that notwithstanding her pastoral role and knowledge of theology and religious texts, she was a paid employee of the congregation.

What is more, although quite dedicated parishioners and long-time supporters of the congregation and the denomination, the lay leaders directing the hiring committee were experienced businesspeople who transferred their acumen and perspectives from the corporate Board room to the congregational Board room. Of course, the transfer was not completely smooth. Many of the members of the hiring committee were accustomed to knock-down and drag-out negotiations with business leaders and most had little direct experience working in the nonprofit world or in a religious setting. It was one thing to attend worship services and to volunteer; quite another to understand or appreciate the perspective of the clergy and other professionals working in the trenches of daily congregational life.

Brittany could have surmised the complications. After all, the congregation had been through three ministers in five years. She did ask about that situation during her interviews but was assured that the prior ministers went on to other work and that their departure had little to do with the congregation or its leadership.

Brittany was excited when the chair of the hiring committee contacted her and offered her the position. She was a bit overwhelmed when she received the official contract. Brittany knew that her central church dictated that congregations use a standard contract form for retaining ministers. She assumed that it was unnecessary to run the contract by an independent legal counsel, particularly as it might cast her as litigious and difficult to her new congregants. What she failed to realize was that these "congregants" were also her bosses.

The contract was indeed adapted from the standard form authorized by the central church. It covered the basics of job responsibilities, salary, benefits, and the like. However, the standard template allowed for more customized language in several key sections and permitted the addition of unique clauses, intended to address specific congregational needs. Two sections stuck out to Brittany—but she assumed that like the rest of the contract they were general and typical of church contracts, and she accepted them all.

First, the contract indicated that the minister made all decisions regarding liturgy and ritual. That power was circumvented by a subsequent clause that indicated that such decisions had to be ratified by the ritual committee, and, moreover, that the recommendations of the ritual committee had to be enforced by the minister. Brittany could not imagine at the time she assumed her post how she might have any conflicts with the ritual committee. In this section of the contract, the minister was also charged to deliver a weekly sermon on an appropriate and relevant topic. Again, such a stipulation did not seem unreasonable to Brittany, who was quite looking forward to the opportunity to share her thoughts with her new congregants. This clause was not further modified, though Brittany did hesitate momentarily to think about the words "appropriate" and "relevant." Of course, she understood what those words meant and at the time could not imagine how they might be differently construed by people from the same denomination.

The second part of the contract that seemed foreign to Brittany was the dismissal clause. Simply stated, the clause indicated that the hiring committee of the Board could terminate the contract with the minister at will and with or without cause. When she asked about this clause, she was assured by the hiring committee chair that such was standard contractual language in the state, which was an employment-at-will state. The language of with or without cause was a useful way to not have to specify all reasons by which a minister might be removed—saving any misbehaving cleric from the embarrassment of enumerating his or her shortcomings.

Brittany began her tenure at the congregation and was quite excited. The congregants were wonderful people and the work quite rewarding. She worked closely with several congregants on personal issues, and she spent late nights planning sermons and classes that were well attended and positively received. Brittany also played an active role in various regional assemblies of the denomination, which she also enjoyed. Several ritual and liturgical reforms were prominent on the agenda of these assembly meetings. While Brittany was not passionate about all of them, she was supportive of most and committed to several that related to thinking about and engaging with people outside the denomination and especially non-Christians in the liturgy as well as in outreach beyond the faith tradition, and educational programs about other faiths for community members. As was her custom, Brittany brought the substance of these reform discussions into her classes and work from the pulpit.

Not everyone was pleased that Brittany was sharing these developments in either formal presentations or informal conversations. Some objected to the appearance of changing traditions. Some simply felt that Brittany was overstepping her authority. Several members of the congregational Board held strong objections to the attention being given to what they perceived as exceedingly positive language used to describe non-Christians and the increased outreach to the local Black Muslim community. These individuals at first approached Brittany individually and asked her to stop addressing the topic and pushing these initiatives. Although Brittany replied in as courteous and sensitive of a manner as she could and as she felt appropriate, she saw her role as minister to lead the discussion of liturgy, engage in larger outreach and social justice, and provide insights into the larger denominational discussions. What is more, Brittany herself subscribed to several of the changes being discussed. She therefore accepted the feedback graciously but continued along as she had before. This approach further irked several key lay leaders, who soon approached Brittany together, claiming to represent the Board. They reminded Brittany that as a paid employee of the church, whose authority (and limits of authority) were clearly stipulated in her contract, she should accede to their demands or face the threat of release.

It would be easy to demonize the lay leaders that Brittany sparred with in her early career. There is much to suggest that these lay leaders misused their power. However, in confronting her vulnerabilities and developing the resilience to lead change, Brittany must find ways to lead from various positions and she must find ways to identify and move beyond her own limits and weaknesses. To be a communal and religious leader, especially one committed to interreligious engagement, requires creative vulnerability, intentionality, trust-building, and awareness across many dimensions of life.

Suggested Guiding Questions

- What problems does this case reveal?
- How might Brittany and the Board open themselves to deeply understand their own positions, and those of others?
- How might they facilitate constructive conversations?
- What intentions do Brittany and the Board signal by their behavior?
- How might they clarify their intentions or even re-examine them?
- How might Brittany and the Board develop trust—at various points and over the course of their relationship?
- What kinds of communication and behavior might be most helpful to build trust?
- What are the key things of which Brittany and the Board members should be aware—in their own beliefs and behavior, in that of the others, and in the context of larger congregational, denominational, and societal settings?
- Are there ways for Brittany to introduce the changes and activities she has in a way that helps them build on each other and, along the way garner buy-in and support from her lay leaders, congregants, and broader community?
- What steps should both Brittany and the Board consider to prepare for the next round of contract negotiations, assuming they get to that point?

Analysis

In each of the cases that follow we have raised some of the most pressing issues of interreligious work today and, along the way, have signaled more general concerns in religious life and leadership. In Chapter 5 we introduced the VITA pathway. As you turn to the cases—to add texture to the previous chapters and as a tool for your own work and conversations—we provide a sample of how the VITA pathway highlights some best practices in interreligious leadership, but also how it may add to those practices in significant ways. By way of example, let's consider Case 1, just presented.

Brittany has trained extensively for her work. She did well enough to secure a position, implying that she had the requisite knowledge and interpersonal skills to do well in a series of interviews. As is often the case—especially in a first position—there are on-the-ground contexts and realities that are difficult, if not impossible, for which to prepare. Many seminarians have little experience with dealing with the complexities of a congregation—even though many programs now include internships, mentoring, simulations, and even related practical course work. The same can be said of congregational lay leaders (as well as the broader congregation). Oftentimes, lay leaders have significant experience (and successes) in their own professions. They frequently have a good deal of experience with the congregation—that is why they are in the positions they are! Yet, professional insights in one area of work do not always translate precisely or well to another. What is more, despite generally significant immersion in the work of the congregation, lay leaders usually lack the full knowledge, or appreciation, of the work of the clergy and staff. They also have their own specific personal, religious, institutional, and denominational perspectives and proclivities. This is especially the case—and can be quite challenging—when they see themselves as defenders of status quo or as individuals with the best perspective on the institution because of their work and longevity in serving the institution.

Brittany was fresh from seminary, where many current issues get discussed, but she also displayed energy and new perspectives, which the hiring committee may have found attractive, given previous failed hires. Brittany herself sensed some potential red flags, not least around contract negotiations and especially the clauses related to liturgy/ritual, sermon topics, and dismissal. Both Brittany and the lay leadership were excited to move forward, yet there were missteps and concerns on both sides. Throughout the process Brittany and the lay leadership would have benefitted from a VITA approach.

Vulnerability asks us to explore the perspectives and concerns of others even as we open ourselves in deep and meaningful ways to self-examination. It may be uncomfortable to ask clarifying questions or seek to understand the underlying assumptions and guiding motivations of others; however, engaging in such conversations is essential to avoid (or at least mitigate to some extent) disagreements down the road. While the result of such conversations may lead us to the conclusion that we do not and may not see things the same way, they may also help us to navigate differences and perhaps even adjust ourselves as a result. Brittany might have considered a quick internal audit—what kinds of things was she seeing as problems and, importantly, what might be her own contributions to the problems?

When we see difficulties or feel friction, we can find it easy to look for the root of the problem with others—and since we know our side of things and give ourselves the benefit of the doubt, we enter a self-confirming cycle of perception. Vulnerability, however, asks us to step back a bit and consider our own position and behaviors. It also requires that we explore the positions and assumptions of others. That can be challenging to do. After all, we do not always have all the facts and it is hard to know what others have experienced or their unique contexts that might allow them to see or feel certain things and not others.

Taking a vulnerability stance also requires us to be attuned to larger contexts and systems. As such, vulnerability in leadership rehearses many of the core characteristics hailed by traditional leadership best practices—learning, contextualization, communication, empathy, humility, and balancing internal and external (including individual and organizational) dynamics. But vulnerability is simultaneously about these and other characteristics. Vulnerability opens opportunities for a deeper set of conversations, signaling a willingness to consider the positions of others and ourselves and to be changed as a result of them. It is therefore the foundation of change, adaptation, and generative ideas. Vulnerability requires us to take a systems perspective and it keeps the focus on relationships, at multiple levels. When we recognize our own vulnerability, we are more likely to see and take into consideration the vulnerabilities of others, allowing for something more than humility of self and empathy for others, but actually a completely transforming and transformative stance.

Brittany may have felt her vulnerabilities—self-doubt, given her lack of professional experience, intimidation by lay leaders with strong opinions, lots of congregational social capital, and extensive financial resources. In a vulnerability stance, she may have nonetheless tried to understand their perspectives (for understanding but also to modulate her own ideas and practices, perhaps to confirm them, but perhaps also to adjust or scale them). When confronted with challenges (as frequently occurs in interreligious engagements), our first inclination is to fight or set up walls—to posture or become invulnerable. But invulnerability can be counter-productive to complex resilience. In becoming vulnerable, Brittany may also have asked herself about her values, goals, the ways she had interacted with others, and how she might be perceived. Of course, the lay leaders—who have been the driving force through a period of failed clerical leadership (from their perspective)—have become ever more entrenched and convinced that they "know better than others." Adopting a position of vulnerability might have encouraged them to understand Brittany's situation but also her values, goals, and concerns. This is not to suggest that airing differences elides them; rather, when we understand in a deeper way the perspectives, assumptions, and experiences of others, we have the chance for more constructive conversation and potential paths forward. When we do not fully explore these issues, we are more likely to make assumptions and draw conclusions that may not be completely accurate or that, if accurate, could lead to other considerations.

Intentionality is the second component of VITA. While intentionality seems like a common-sense characteristic of good leadership, and a part of many aspects of effective leadership, it is less practised than one might expect. That is because we become accustomed to think and behave in certain ways, and the longer we lead the more prone we are to "trust our instincts." And while great leaders do develop great instincts, intentionality demands that we are always thoughtful and reflective—in the normal course of our work as well as in times of crisis. Intentionality draws from good leadership principles such as strategic planning, proactivity, and seeing the bigger picture. Being intentional also requires that we think about our thoughts and actions, as well as their impact on others, and the thoughts and actions of others. As such, we must focus on our goals—short- as well as long-term—and how they are connected. We cannot—and perhaps should not—think or act the same all the time; but intentionality does not mean that we are consistent for the sake of consistency, but that we are thoughtful about what we say and do relative to particular situations and with an eye toward bigger considerations and goals as well.

In our case, Brittany could have been more intentional in her actions and interactions with the Board. At times she seems to have hunkered down for no good reason, just to push through her ideas and agendas. Rather than think about a comprehensive method to engage and bring her key constituents along, she became reactive and divisive. The Board helped to create and feed this dynamic and does not appear to have provided a great deal of substantive feedback or explanations that could have led to more fruitful discussions. It is unclear that either party gave enough thought to the most important goals of the relationship. And even when the messages were clear, there seems to have been a dearth of giving the benefit of the doubt or assuming good intentions. As we will see further, that was in part because there was a lack of trust developed and awareness cultivated.

Perhaps Brittany could have laid out her vision and goals (that would require her to develop those, rather than respond to developments she heard about) and the Board could have clarified their key concerns for the future. It is likely that they would have disagreed in some ways—but a frank and intentional discussion might have convinced Brittany that change is an iterative process that requires bringing key constituents along. She might have learned where fissures in the congregation might exist and the reasons for them. The Board may have determined that some of what Brittany was suggesting would position the congregation for re-birth and growth in the future.

Without being vulnerable or intentional, neither Brittany nor the Board had built up the trust necessary for a constructive relationship. Trust is necessary at times of crisis or challenge; it is also a key ingredient for day-to-day work. Trust is a central component of healthy relationships, systems, and organizations. It has impact in small decisions and actions, as well as large ones. It gives us the capital to make important decisions and to innovate and try new things. Trust is built over time and through experiences and open dialog.

Brittany had not been at the congregation for long before she shared controversial positions and proposed the introduction of significant changes. She had not yet become a full part of the congregational ecosystem and she was not aware of the concerns of some congregants nor of her own blind spots. Through open discussion, follow-through, and check-in she could have begun to develop trust that would have afforded her, probably further down the road, opportunities to suggest and then initiate changes. The Board members may not have considered that they needed to build trust with Brittany. After all, they ran the congregation, hired, and paid her salary, and were likely to be around much longer than any minister. Nonetheless, trust is not a one-way street.

Even much of the most thoughtful leadership literature seems rather hierarchical—leading by co-opting others. In contrast, resilient leadership demands that we see the bigger system and the range of relationships that make it work. It is avowedly not hierarchical and so the notion of trust is more about the richness and supportiveness of relationships rather than a mechanism for a leader or leadership to leverage in order to get what they want.

Finally, let's consider awareness, the final component of VITA. Awareness is related to vulnerability, intentionality, and trust. It is also valuable in and of itself. Awareness is about perceptions of what is going on around you—it is knowledge as well as a broader sensibility. Awareness is animated by inquiry and sensitivity to others, contexts, and systems. But awareness often starts with awareness of ourselves. Without understanding what we see or assume and why, it is difficult to truly be aware of what is happening outside of us. Awareness operates at specific and general levels, and it allows us to predict problems, mitigate challenges, and respond in more efficient and productive ways.

Early in her career, Brittany seems to have lacked a certain amount of self-awareness—how she spoke, how others perceived her, how her actions impacted others, and so forth. While Brittany was attuned to the big issues animating the denomination and sensitive to some of the most important contemporary societal concerns, she was also relatively unaware of the broader context in which she was working and the specific concerns of at least some of her lay leadership. Awareness implies recognizing and understanding the context, but also considering and responding to it (not simply responding to certain parts and ignoring other, perhaps less convenient, ones). The Board may have been aware of larger denominational and social issues, but also did not extend awareness into an open reflection and discussion. They may have been unaware of some of what Brittany knew from her training or her own personal experiences and perspectives. There are many ways to develop awareness—inquiry, conversation, active listening, soliciting feedback, considering external or opposing data, and so forth. Awareness alone—as with the other aspects of the VITA pathway—is not sufficient for successful leadership, but it is essential.

Taking a VITA stance allows Brittany and the Board to think and behave differently. Reading a good leadership book or working with a consultant might point each of them in the right direction. However, a resilient leadership approach, based on the VITA pathway, highlights some aspects of the most effective approach to leadership and introduces new elements that are derived from the study and practice of resilience. With this brief example in hand, the case studies that follow provide an opportunity to consider a range of issues and to apply the VITA pathway as part of developing truly resilient leadership in a host of topics and situations related to interreligious work.

Case Studies

Globalization and Social Acceleration

As we have noted throughout the book, globalization and social acceleration are significant characteristics—challenges and opportunities—in the modern and postmodern world. Basic human relations have changed dramatically with technology and the ability to reach and engage (in positive and negative ways) with others. At the same time, this shrinking global world and the speed with which we can meet and learn can lead to new chances to understand and build relationships, but also provides us a wealth of information that can come to us without context, and which surface many important social issues.

As in Case 1 earlier, Case 2 focuses on change, though of a different sort. As many religious communities grapple with diminishing membership numbers, they must find new ways to engage current and new constituencies. In some ways, the use of technology to address the Covid-19 pandemic has introduced tools and new mindsets that have been helpful. In other ways, these have tested the structures and traditions (though in some cases, have had more limited impact) in ways that can be generative and/or problematic. Prior to the pandemic and already as US society begins to reopen as infection and fatality rates drop, many religious institutions are facing serious questions about their long-term viability. In some cases, communities are weighed down by facilities that were constructed under different circumstances and are no longer aligned with their needs and trajectories. This case presents several related themes that emerged in many comments from our survey participants—about changing communal memberships and demographic shifts more broadly, the need for new organizational and financial models to remain sustainable, and the need to rethink the nature and use of physical spaces. We have seen many communities consider their missions and strategies and also evaluate their location and facilities. The result in many cases has been mergers with other organizations; but such mergers can be minefields even when the institutions are aligned, leadership has been involved and brought along, members have been properly prepared, and legal and logistical work have been done thoughtfully. The situation can be even more challenging when the organizations involved in the mergers represent different religious traditions, are evolving in different ways, or take on new directions or leadership during or after the merger. Increasingly we have heard about cases of communities from different faith traditions sharing facilities or campuses. And while such sharing offers remarkable opportunities for interreligious engagement and learning, they can also lead to or exacerbate latent tensions. Given the need for new financial and infrastructure models in the years ahead, we suspect that these kinds of conversations will continue to be regular and important. An interreligious resilience lens will be helpful in setting up such conversations and mergers for success. In this case, interreligious resilience extends beyond theology and life stances to address a range of practical considerations as well.

Case 3 addresses relations across religious communities in the context of reputation, changing demographics, and education. The case offers a complex range of external and internal considerations—which may affect the community and its relations with individuals inside and outside, other religious communities, and the broader societal and civic context. Internal instabilities—in this case, financial and leadership crises—can have a significant impact on a community but may also negatively affect how and in what ways it can engage with other communities within and beyond its own faith tradition. At the same time, external factors can lead to internal crises and are often catalysts for internal change. In this case, the appointment of an interim minister and the exercise of strategic planning and futuring must consider both internal and external conditions. What is more, such work can benefit from understanding how others have addressed similar issues; that is, learning can occur in the midst of interacting with others of different organizational and religious perspectives. If the community wants to succeed in attracting new members it will need to understand itself and its net comparative position and advantages. Interreligious leadership requires that we identify and understand our own vulnerabilities and that we use them to find ways to improve and innovate.

Violence against, and abuse of, women continues to be a global problem. In some cases, religion is used as a tool to encourage unequal (in some cases degrading, if not violent) treatment of women. Religion and religious ideas or interpretations can be used as foils to condone or cover up such behavior. Like other significant social issues, redressing what has been and in some cases continues to be a systemic problem requires education, advocacy, and leadership. While there is need to respond to issues within individual faith communities and traditions, there is also value in building coalitions and responding across religions. Case 4 explores this topic and the efforts to educate, counsel, and build capacity to utilize positive religious values to combat discrimination. The case points to challenges and opportunities and the need to create and foster initiatives that are successful and sustainable.

Amplifying some issues noted in Case 4, Case 5 turns to another profound contemporary problem—forced migration and the status of refugees, especially religious refugees. Focused on the religious persecution and genocide of Baha'i, the case offers context related to associated economic and climatic issues, while pointing to the power of propaganda and the need for education to redress religiously motivated violence and to encourage serious interreligious understanding and engagement that expands to humanitarian considerations as well. The case tracks the work that is needed to do effective advocacy work, in the context of the settlement of refugees, but along the way it also addresses effective education and interreligious engagement more generally.

Finally, in Case 6 we offer a situation drawn from the Covid-19 pandemic. The Case rehearses the anxiety of the pandemic, including latent political and social tensions that erupted in various ways and food shortages and lack of access to water (especially for some vulnerable populations). These anxieties could lead to religious tensions. In leveraging interreligious coalitions, an interfaith social action group has decided to seize the moment and try to make people aware of these issues (beyond their own groups and communities). They seek to address the challenging behavior of some politicians and corporations, and they seek to activate grassroots lobbying and activism. As in other cases, the activists in this case begin planning their work. This work requires them to consider several factors and conduct their work on multiple levels. The VITA pathway provides some opportunities to think about and advance their initiatives.

Case Study 2: An Interreligious Congregational Merger

Children of Zion Congregation, a Conservative Jewish synagogue, was celebrating its seventieth anniversary. For most of its history, the congregation was in the same building in the same neighborhood. It had become a pillar of that neighborhood, drawing congregants from the immediate area primarily, but occasionally from other more distant parts of the city as well. Over many years the congregation and its leadership interacted with other congregations and faith communities in joint social justice and social service programs and occasional interfaith programming.

Recently, the demography of the neighborhood began to shift. There was also a decline in affiliation within its denominational parent more generally. The congregation's membership began to decrease, as some congregants disaffiliated from the movement, and some moved from the region for personal and economic reasons. As a result, the congregation's base of support has eroded.

For much of its history, 90 percent of the congregation's revenues were drawn from membership dues and special appeals. The facility is in reasonably good shape given its current needs, however major repairs come up regularly—most recently the air conditioning and new carpet for the social hall—and the facility is beginning to show its age. In the past some wealthier members, who served as presidents and Board members, continued heavily to subvent the costs associated with repairs and building projects. Unfortunately, as the membership has declined, so has the wealth of the remaining members.

As a result of these conditions, the congregation went through several changes (some more strategic and some more reactive), and its lay leadership determined that it was necessary to take steps to address this reality. The leadership suggested that the congregation take in a renter (preferably a similar faith-based organization or congregation) to defray some operating costs or sell its aging facility and move to a new location (raising questions of whether it might relocate to a new part of town or simply resize to reflect its economic conditions and membership needs).

Amidst the discussion of various options, a local Christian congregation, facing somewhat similar conditions, approached the congregation leadership.

The lay leaders were familiar with congregational mergers between organizations of the same denominational affiliation—for example, Conservative Jewish synagogues—and even across denominations within the same religious tradition—for example, a smaller Orthodox Jewish prayer group moving into a traditional or Conservative Jewish synagogue. But they were unfamiliar with a model in which different faith organizations shared space on a more regular basis.

The congregation's leadership tried to imagine what some of the challenges to such a collaboration might be—from perception within their denomination and the religion more generally, to local politics and culture beyond the denomination, the areas of strategic alignment and mission focus between the congregations, and the implications of day-to-day operations (facilities usage, shared space, various associated costs, iconography, etc.).

After determining that the potential benefits outweighed the potential risks, a formal agreement was drawn up and agreed to by both parties. The initial transition was smooth, and the congregations even co-hosted a welcoming dinner and program that attracted a majority of both congregations' memberships and was quite friendly and exciting.

In general, given the relatively small sizes of the congregations and different liturgical calendars and needs, the use of space and allocation of facilities resources was quite smooth. Some concerns began to emerge a few months into the relationship, however. The new congregation had a clerical leadership change. The original minister, with whom the deal had been made, suddenly left the congregation, allegedly because of some scandal involving fiscal mismanagement.

The new minister enjoys a positive relationship with her congregants and leadership and has been a good tenant. She appreciates the Jewish faith and the religious practices of the host congregation. But she has a strong, anti-colonial critique of the State of Israel that has informed some of her sermons and several programs. These programs have included some speeches and lectures that veer into anti-Semitic tropes. Although these programs have clearly been publicized as events for the Christian congregation, they have obviously taken place at the shared synagogue facility. The contract made no stipulations about such issues, which never occurred to anyone on the congregation board.

After the first six months, other concerns began to emerge. The tenant was less respectful of space boundaries, with their programs and supplies seeping into areas that were not part of the original lease. Some of their activities also added significantly to the wear and tear of the facility in ways that the congregation had not expected. For example, the tenant held regular Sunday barbecues and was not careful with kitchen implements and not attentive to clean up. Regularly they left doors open by mistake after hours, potentially compromising the security of the facility—an issue of great concern to the Jewish congregation but of less concern to the tenant.

The leadership of the Jewish congregation has had several informal conversations with the new minister to no avail, and then with key Board members of the Christian church, also with little satisfaction. There is no legal wrongdoing, and the contract is good for five years.

Suggested Guiding Questions

- What problems does this case reveal?
- How might the leadership (lay and clerical) openly discuss their concerns and perspectives, while being open to those of the others?
- How might the various stakeholders and constituents be engaged in a productive way to have conversation and develop understanding across differences?
- What has been intentional and what seems to have been less or un-intentional in the interactions between the groups? In what areas might there be opportunity for greater intentionality?
- Are there ways for the congregations and their leaders to build trust? What might you suggest in terms of small and large steps?
- What kinds of communication and behavior might have been most helpful to establish trust?
- What things do you think each party needs to be aware of in moving forward in a productive way?
- How might lay leaders, and not just clergy, also be involved in these discussions?

Case Study 3: Charting a New Congregational Direction in an Interreligious Key

Like many churches in the area, St. Johns has been hit by a series of crises in recent years. The neighborhood in which the church is located has changed dramatically in recent decades. Although the church membership has remained relatively stable, the gentrification of the neighborhood has meant that costs to run the facility have outpaced the revenue from congregants. And yet, at the same time, the neighborhood remains unsafe in some places. The changing neighborhood demographics have also led to the influx of new residents, many of whom are immigrants from parts of Africa and Southeast Asia and who are practising Muslims of varying backgrounds and Christians of different, and seemingly unfamiliar, faith traditions.

There have been many layers of interaction between the St. Johns' congregants and members of the other religious groups and churches. Some have been quite cordial, leading to friendships, various business partnerships and associations, and in some cases romantic relationships and marriages. There have been less positive interactions as well. Some negative comments in the media and on political platforms—some comments reflecting differing economic and political backgrounds, but also different cultural orientation and religious practices, as well as diverse ethnic and racial backgrounds. While there have been some attempts to develop social action programs across churches and religions, the leaders of St. Johns have struggled to deal with associated prejudices on one hand and the integration of new residents on the other. In both cases, interreligious engagement is of great importance in dealing with these situations. And there is clearly a need for more education about these newcomers, their experiences, and their religious beliefs and practices.

Added to these challenges—which have external and internal dimensions—the congregation has been racked by internal instability. The congregation's finances have been compromised through some sketchy financial practices of the congregation's lay treasury and the congregation has not been proactive in long-term strategic or sound fiscal planning. What is more, one minister has recently gone through a very messy and highly public divorce; the other minister has had a breakdown and sought mental health treatment. Both situations have tested congregational cohesion and lay-minister relations specifically. As difficult as these situations have been, the impact they have on the representation of the congregation in the broader community has also been quite negative, leading to deprecating comments, marginalization, and criticism.

Internally, the congregation needs to rebuild trust and relationships. An interim pastor has been appointed. A new finance oversight committee has been created and staffed. A Board and senior staff/clergy retreat on "futuring" has been organized to explore long-term planning, sustainability, and other pressing short- and long-term issues related to the health of the congregation—including how to lead change, bring congregants along, solve current financial problems, craft a compelling vision, and begin a process of healing.

At the same time, there is an interesting opportunity to learn from the organizing (without extensive physical presence and expensive buildings) by the newest members of the neighborhood. Similarly, the congregation needs to better understand its own strengths and challenges as it combats the negative image that some have developed of it and as it seeks to engage with the newcomers (especially those who have married members of the congregation) and to win them over (as friends or congregants).

Suggested Guiding Questions

- What are the most pressing concerns for the congregational leadership and how might the congregational leaders go about assessing their situation, assumptions, traditions, and needs amidst the changing landscape around them and the internal challenges?
- What things do you expect the congregation might have to give up and what are values, ideas, or practices that might be essential to its identity and survival?
- What are some ways to engage the newcomers and the local authorities that would be helpful for the congregation and its leadership?
- How might the congregation position itself to be a valued and trusted organization for individuals outside its current orbit and a trusted partner for other organizations?
- What would be some useful ways for the congregational leadership to become and stay apprised of the developments in the neighborhood and the larger developments across the city that might also impact them?

Case Study 4: Marginalization, Abuse, and Violence against Women in an Interreligious Context

Despite advances in some places and in some professions, women face significant, often systemic, discrimination in the workplace and far beyond. In some, not insignificant number of cases, women also face horrific exploitation in parts of the world. At times this exploitation occurs within the framework of religion. From domestic violence, sexual assault, and human trafficking to murder, women are an extremely vulnerable population.

The World Health Organization in a 2017 report on violence against women[1] noted that:

- Violence against women—particularly intimate partner violence and sexual violence—is a major public health problem and a violation of women's human rights.
- Global estimates published by WHO indicate that about one in three (35 percent) women worldwide have experienced either physical and/or

sexual intimate partner violence or non-partner sexual violence in their lifetime.
- Most of this violence is intimate partner violence. Worldwide, almost one third (30 percent) of women who have been in a relationship report that they have experienced some form of physical and/or sexual violence by their intimate partner in their lifetime.
- Globally, as many as 38 percent of murders of women are committed by a male intimate partner.
- Violence can negatively affect women's physical, mental, sexual, and reproductive health, and may increase the risk of acquiring HIV in some settings.
- Men are more likely to perpetrate violence if they have low education, a history of child maltreatment, exposure to domestic violence against their mothers, harmful use of alcohol, unequal gender norms including attitudes accepting of violence, and a sense of entitlement over women.
- Women are more likely to experience intimate partner violence if they have low education, exposure to mothers being abused by a partner, abuse during childhood, and attitudes accepting violence, male privilege, and women's subordinate status.
- There is evidence that advocacy and empowerment counseling interventions, as well as home visitation, are promising in preventing or reducing intimate partner violence against women.
- Situations of conflict, post conflict and displacement may exacerbate existing violence, such as by intimate partners, as well as non-partner sexual violence, and may also lead to new forms of violence against women.

The results of this study point to factors that help to predict violence against women, the results of that violence, as well as education and counseling work that can be effective in treating victims and hopefully mitigating violence itself. Nevertheless, these are only broad characteristics, and violence and abuse can happen in any setting and even in surprising conditions. While religion can sometimes offer protection for women, women at times face discrimination in religious law (in response to divorce, custody of children, and cases of physical abuse, for example) and women may face harsh conditions in many religious traditions and communities, with little hope for assistance.

In addressing three broad categories of gender discrimination across religious traditions, an international and interreligious organization has been formed to address gender inequality and violence against women in contemporary society. The organization, Interreligious Women's Advocacy (IWA), faces several challenges. The first set of challenges relates to the professional structure and funding of the organization. The second set of challenges relates to research—learning about key issues, conducting research, and developing educational resources and programs. The third set of challenges revolves around advocacy, and as in the second set of challenges, engaging with religious leaders in different faith traditions to address issues within their own religions as well as more global concerns and to effect real change. The three (of many possible) issues the organization formed to address were economic marginalization; domestic abuse; and representation in religious law, especially around issues of divorce.

Creating the organization has been challenging. There are many organizations focused on some of the issues that IWA wants to address. Often such organizations are local or regional; at times they are focused on one specific religious tradition or community. So, getting broader support has been difficult.

The organizers learned quickly as well that although it was relatively easy to mobilize women in the work, it was important to have not only male allies but also male professional and volunteer partners as well. Surprisingly, the women who began the push to create IWA experienced first-hand some of the gender bias and sexism they had heard about in the world of fundraising. The behavior of some potential donors was particularly shocking considering the cause the women were seeking to fund.

The first set of challenges faced by the founders of the organization related to coalition building—across gender and across faith traditions and the identification and leveraging of positive gender values and religious teachings that supported ethical behavior and fairness and equity in dealing with all people. Finally, the organization's leadership had to walk a fine line between pointing to beliefs, practices, and actions that were gender biased in ways that brought religious and lay leaders along without feeling that their entire religious tradition was to be vilified because of some perceptions, positions, or in some cases simply the bad behavior of some individuals associated with the religious tradition.

The second area that IWA had to address was related more to research and programming. There is a good deal of scholarship (as well as popular literature) on the treatment of women in various religious traditions. IWA had to determine how best to gather and evaluate this material, how to draw from religious texts and traditions—winnowing the less positive from the more utilitarian texts, ideas, and initiatives—without being accused of cherry-picking, watering down or changing religions, or favoring particular religious traditions. They expected this might involve some survey research and interviews with religious leaders, in addition to their own research. How, they wondered, could they facilitate challenging conversations across religious and denominational divides in a way that would lead to recognition of areas for improvement and still surface internal strengths and traditions in various religions that would help advance this important work?

Added to this concern was the realization that it was not only religion that was at play in many cases. Poor treatment of women might be institutionalized in organizations or governments that were not religious in and of themselves, but that were set or contextualized within particular religious streams or traditions. In one part of India, for example, IWA was concerned about the economic exploitation of women, who were paid far less for their work, were forced into disadvantageous economic and legal positions, and frequently had little voice or ability to represent themselves in secular or religious legal contexts.

They were concerned about how shedding light on domestic abuse in one Muslim community in Iraq, in which more than 50 percent of women surveyed indicated some level of abuse, might shift attention to similar concerns in other religious communities, make it difficult to secure support from other Muslim communities, or lead to reprisals against the women already subjected to abuses within that community.

Finally, in addressing the issue of *agunah*—or chained women, especially in Orthodox Jewish circles, whose husbands would not grant their wives a religious bill of divorce, effectively keeping them in limbo and unable to remarry—they wondered how to work in a coordinated way with religious leaders already addressing this issue and simultaneously call attention to similar concerns without only featuring challenges within Orthodox Judaism.

Finally, and closely related, IWA had to plan for the work they wanted to do beyond research and education. How could they be effective advocates for change in general—within individual religious traditions and across denominations and faith traditions? How could they create coalitions to build on the best that religion could offer while addressing negative religious ideas and traditions? What would advocacy look like as they engaged religious practice as well as systemic gender bias that lay under the surface and went far beyond religion itself?

Suggested Guiding Questions

- How might the focus on discrimination and poor treatment of women advance and frustrate interreligious conversations?

- In what ways might the leaders of IWA encourage self-reflection among leaders of individual religious traditions independently and together in ways that would be productive and build a sense of trust and common purpose?
- How might the leaders of IWA open discussions so that religious leaders (and others) can see and understand the vulnerable position that many women are in around the globe?
- What are some strategies they might consider to build partnerships and leverage the work of other organizations to expand its impact?
- How might the leaders of IWA prepare for difficult conversations, criticism, or setbacks? What kinds of self-reflection and assessment might they consider building into their own work?

Case Study 5: Religious Persecution and Religious Refugees

Forced migration remains a major global challenge. Nearly seventy-one million people were displaced in 2018. Often such migration is the result of warfare, economic turmoil, political unrest, or environmental degradation and climate change. It regularly affects religious minorities in a particular region—more than a quarter of all people live in a nation in which they are a religious minority. In 2016 approximately 37 percent of refugees who resettled in the United States were religious minorities. Even countries that have been relatively open to receiving such refugees have decreased the number of people they are willing or able to take in, usually for a variety of reasons, some having to do with religious considerations. While the United States assisted more than 12,500 Syrian refugees in 2016, for example, that number plummeted to 62 in 2018. Various vetting procedures, especially through the Department of Homeland Security, play a role in this dramatic decline.

The Baha'i faith is the second-largest religion after Islam in Iran, where much of its early history (from inception in the last half of the nineteenth century) and the birth of several key religious figures took place. One of these figures, Baha'u'llah, was a Babi who claimed to be the figure foretold by the Bab (who claimed to be the Imam Mahdi and on par with Muhammad) and founded what would become known as the Baha'i faith. While around 90 percent of Iranians are adherents of the Twelver branch of Shi'a Islam, the writings of Baha'u'llah challenge some key aspects of Shi'a Islam and Baha'i are viewed by many Iranian leaders as heretics. Added to this is the fact that early Baha'i did not passively submit to persecution.

At key times in the twentieth and twenty-first centuries, Baha'i have suffered various forms of persecution in Iran—from the raiding and closure of schools and other community organizations to the destruction of houses, arrests, fines, torture and punishments, occupational discrimination, and murder (through government actions as well as incited mob violence). The type and frequency of persecution has varied depending on governmental positions and a wide range of factors. In addition to major pogroms in the nineteenth century, discrimination against Baha'i has occurred in various constitutions (such as the 1906 constitution) and legal pronouncements, for example after the political upheavals of the 1950s. In 1955 clerical incitement by a populist preacher against the Baha'i during Ramadan led to collective violence, destruction of property, and desecration of cemeteries. The anti-Shah movement of the late 1970s circulated propaganda that Baha'i were advisors to the Shah; other propaganda has at times associated the Baha'i with Zionists. The 1979 Islamic Revolution led to more persecution and in 1983 the government banned all community activities of the Baha'i, efforts that have returned or increased at various times since then with government sanction or activity. There have been some successful efforts to resettle persecuted Baha'i. One example is in Canada. In the decade after the Iranian Revolution the Canadian government admitted 2,300 Baha'i, who were settled in more than 200 communities across the country.

With the increasing threat of genocide of Baha'i and other religious minorities that has emerged around the globe, Peter Farmington and Jane Schuster, two well-to-do and retired philanthropists in New York, have decided to try to address this pressing issue. Peter subscribes to the Baha'i faith himself—his parents, both doctors, had fled Iran in the 1970s. Jane met Peter through work at her law firm. She is a practising Catholic, with a penchant for advocacy and a belief in the general dignity of humankind.

As Peter and Jane have thought about their work, they see that there are many models (some more successful than others), many different mitigating circumstances (including political and economic ones), challenges in Iran and abroad, and a good deal to learn.

Peter is pretty knowledgeable about the Baha'i faith, but he has only recently learned about some of the tensions and complicated history of the Baha'i faith in Iran. Although he has absorbed a notion of Baha'i faith as open and peaceful, the faith is more complicated and has had its fair share of run-ins with the Muslim majority in Iran and other places. Peter wonders if there are ways that Baha'i faith claims could in fact be more aligned (and less challenging) to Shi'a Muslims. Are there possibilities for actual interreligious discussion among sectarian leaders in Iran itself, regardless of his sense of the oppressive political and religious climate? Peter himself knows little about Islam, and even less about Twelver Shi'a Islam. What can he learn that might help him in his work? Jane is more of an outsider, and she wonders how to acquaint herself with the religion of the people whose cause she intends to champion and how to understand the historical and theological context in which the Baha'i of Iran are living.

In addition to these questions, Peter and Jane have seen a few successful refugee resettlement initiatives related to the Baha'i and other religious groups. At times these efforts have depended upon the intersection of governmental leadership, refugee advocates, and the broader economic and political conditions in the country. So, they realize that the advocacy needed to advance their work has many dimensions and can be, or seem to be, a bit out of their direct control. They are interested to learn how best to develop an advocacy program over a period of time and how to engage and develop support from key constituents and influencers. What is clear is that this will take work in both Iran and the United States, as both governments will need to agree to key aspects of any plan they are able to develop and fund.

Of course, if they are successful in their efforts, once the refugees arrive in the United States there will be a good deal to do to lay the groundwork for success. This may involve a program of community education among the people with whom the refugees will live and work, as well as education for the refugees themselves, so that they can acquire the skills and self-assurance needed to be absorbed and find gainful employment. At the same time, the refugees need to be prepared for social and religious confrontations they will likely have, particularly among people looking to negatively stereotype them on one hand and proselytize them on the other. Then there are the more mundane, but equally important, efforts to find housing, school and tutoring, and work for the refugees. How, Peter and Jane wonder, can they facilitate a sense of connection to Baha'i tradition and community—especially as individual families will likely settle in scattered locations as they noted in the Canadian model—and interact with the vast majority of people of different faiths around them?

Suggested Guiding Questions

- Vulnerability can come in many forms. While it can sometimes be dangerous, as in episodes of religious violence and persecution, examining our vulnerabilities and those of others can also help us to begin to address them. In what ways are the Baha'i vulnerable in Iran and in their potential new settlement areas?

- In what ways are Peter and Jane themselves vulnerable and how might they creatively work with their vulnerabilities?
- While it is easy enough to blame people who practice violent persecution, what vulnerabilities do the Baha'i have, or what vulnerabilities might they be perceived as having, that might make them appear to be a threat?
- Building an initiative like the one Peter and Jane are launching requires significant planning, resources, and dedication. What kinds of things should they consider as they begin their work? Where might they learn about things they have not considered?
- To what degree are their plans culturally ethnocentric, such that they may work in Western democracies but not in other venues?
- The success of the initiative will depend on building support across several different groups. How can Peter and Jane coalesce support, build enthusiasm for the project, and engender trust in their own work and motivations?
- Where might Peter and Jane get pushback or opposition? How should they prepare for that and react to it? How should they inform themselves about the larger religious, political, and cultural considerations that may be at play in what is a long-standing conflict?

Case Study 6: Spiritual Care in Times of Disaster and Crisis Response

As Covid-19 spread around the globe it affected everyone in some way. From health fears to political unrest, economic challenges, and social isolation, the pandemic brought anxiety and fear in some way to everyone, regardless of geographical location or socioeconomic status. Of course, the experience that people had and their own response could be impacted by a variety of factors.

As is often the case when natural disasters occur, latent political and social tensions come to the surface or may be exacerbated. Similarly, crises do not usually arise in a vacuum, and they often occur in conjunction with other crises. In the Covid-19 pandemic, various other crises (including racial injustice, political instability, and ongoing effects of climate change) converged to sharpen the impact and challenges associated with the health crisis.

Early on during the pandemic, food shortages were a real concern for everyone. There was little clarity about the duration of the stay-at-home orders and in the impact on supply chains and delivery of food. Some of the poorest communities also struggled with access to clean and affordable water on one hand and flooding caused by rising lake levels due to climate change on the other. While this crisis of food and water was extensive and threatened the quality of life, even life itself, of a large number of people, the issue received limited news coverage, given everything else that was going on. As was the case in other issues, the most vulnerable and most marginalized populations were most affected by the pandemic—in terms of both health risk, lack of adequate healthcare, and other associated challenges.

An interfaith social action group, known for its work in environmental issues, decided to address the issue of food and water shortage. They faced an uphill battle to make people aware of the issue, since people were understandably preoccupied with their own needs and concerns and those of their own communities. The group, therefore, had to consider how best to make people aware of the issue and understand, in a deeply personal way, the urgency of the matter. The group leaders thought a lot about how to present the issue without feeding into stereotypes about poorer social classes or particular religious groups.

It appeared that some local politicians had been using the situation to funnel funds into their districts, rather than fully releasing the funds to support those most in need. Several corporations have continued to use enormous volumes of water for manufacturing; several others have pumped significant toxins into the local waterways.

How can the integrity of vulnerable populations be protected from predatory individuals and companies that might take advantage of them absent any kind of legal or political protection? How can they invite others to understand their plight in a productive and supportive way?

The leadership of the interfaith social action group decided to address the situation in a multipronged way, through political lobbying, grassroots activism, and a series of media reports and OpEds. They also knew that some direct social services—in the form of financial assistance, food supplies, and counseling—would be essential. Still, their experience led them to believe that activating religious groups might be the best and most effective way to progress on this important and widespread issue. The leaders recognized the value of leveraging congregational networks, volunteer time and expertise, and philanthropy. Some religious groups that reflected the religious affiliation of the people affected had certain reasons to engage with this issue. Other groups, with less proximate concerns or identification, might require different means of engagement. They thought, therefore, about various educational programs on the issue at large and on the issue of food and water in specific faith-based traditions.

The group leadership identified local clergy from the major religious denominations and began to raise the issue with them and assess what might be possible. As they thought about a strategic plan and how to implement it, they decided that organized interreligious engagement was important and might have valuable lessons that could be applied to this situation. They had also heard about interreligious resilience and ideas regarding the challenges and opportunities of vulnerability. They wanted to engage with these concepts and approaches. How might they start their process, initiate their work, and engage with these concepts?

Suggested Guiding Questions

- What are the main issues that the group seeks to address and in what ways (and by what groups) might they expect to be opposed in their work?
- What would you suggest to our group leaders as they embark on their work so that they can most successfully engage and activate people in different ways and from across different faith traditions and worldviews?
- Members of the group have found that some people view them and their work as stirring the pot and are not always open to their efforts. What kinds of messaging and context would be helpful in addressing these kinds of concerns and developing interest in the work and trust of those involved in leading the initiative?
- This case sits at the intersection of many concerns and issues—some long-standing and some more recent; some related to the pandemic (directly or indirectly) and others that exist alongside and outside the context of the pandemic. What kinds of things should the group consider as they assess the current situation and related concerns and developments?
- What problems does this case reveal?

Postsecular Issues

Postsecular religious hybridity, and the allure of both pluralism and fundamentalism, makes it necessary and complicated to engage in interreligious, and intrareligious, discussions. Increasingly we encounter people with different, and often rather idiosyncratic, religious perspectives and practices, such that we are engaging with people "where they are" as well as the broader traditions in which they are situated or turning away from.

Interreligious engagement and leadership can take place in different contexts and at different levels, often simultaneously. Case 7 introduces the experiences of an individual chaplain within a chaplaincy setting. In some ways this is a very personal case, as the chaplain confronts tensions between their own knowledge, beliefs, and positions and the attempt to remain open and nonjudgmental in relation to religious others. In the process, the chaplain, as an interreligious leader, must be familiar with their own traditions and be able to inquire into the beliefs and practices of others. Since we all come with preconceived notions and perspectives, this can be quite difficult. Added to the difficulty is that others also come to conversations with their own ideas and experiences—even those people who are most open to honest exchange of ideas have been shaped in particular ways by their own contexts. At times of great stress, which are common in chaplaincy settings, such perspectives can be sharpened, and it can be even harder to hear, attempt to understand, or even appreciate the religious perspectives of others. In such circumstances we must leverage our knowledge and experiences, but also our best leadership and professional skills. Talking, listening, and learning across denominational differences and faith traditions requires all of the skills and stances of VITA. At times, this seems even more true when talking to people from our own faith tradition (whether of the same denomination or not). The closer we are to one another the more invested we are in the conversation and the greater the stakes when we have different ideas or draw different conclusions. Case 7, therefore, asks us to think about how we understand and engage with others across many different lines. It also surfaces the observation that no religion is a monolith and that even as we "represent" our faith tradition we are more often representing our views rather than the tradition itself or the views of others within our own faith. Research tells us that to be successful in interreligious discussions we need to be knowledgeable about our own religion and religious traditions, but also open to asking questions of our tradition and challenging ourselves. Balancing a sense of self and identity on one hand and the possibility for openness and change on the other can be incredibly uncomfortable. VITA helps to facilitate such conversations and reflections.

In interreligious dialog we are so focused on engaging with leaders of other faith traditions that we often neglect to engage with secularists and nones (people who do not identify with a particular religious tradition, but who may still have some religious sensibilities and behaviors). But there is a large and growing population of people with no formal religious affiliation or with hybrid religious perspectives and practices as detailed in Case 8. In the postmodern, postsecular world, with increasing polarization between fundamentalism on one hand and secularism on the other, and with increasing individualization of religion, we neglect these groups at our peril. In fact, the best practices in interreligious resilience can help us to build understanding and coalitions across religious/nonreligious lines to support a range of projects, including social action programs. One of the core skills that we must constantly cultivate in interreligious leadership is the ability to understand and work with others with different religious views and different worldviews. Case 8 also asks us to think about how to work across significant differences that may also be geographical, as we move from local and regional to national platforms and issues.

Another form and forum of interreligious engagement is intermarriage across religious lines, which is the focus of Case 9. Intermarriage, depending on the religious affiliations (or lack thereof), can surface intra- or interreligious issues. For a long time and frequently still, intermarriage has been seen in a negative light—leading to assimilation, diminished religious engagement, or individual or familial strife. Many campaigns (social events and educational efforts) have been held to stem the tide of intermarriage. Recently, however, perhaps signaling new sensibilities or concessions to what appears to be the inevitable attraction of people across religious lines (especially as religion is only one aspect of self-identity), some religious leaders (and demographers) have seen intermarriage as an opportunity to open the communal tent rather than as a communal liability. This is especially the case as many intermarried couples make significant decisions about how to raise their children in what can end up being micro interreligious conversations. What is more, religious leaders (clergy, communal professionals, and lay leaders) can benefit from training that focuses on how to develop their own intercultural and interreligious competencies and how to make people more comfortable and open (embracing difference and engaging with vulnerability).

The "Other" has been a regular figure in postmodern philosophy, but visions of the Other have informed interreligious engagement throughout history. At some times, the Other represents an actual person or group with which we have had encounters; at other times, the Other is a construction—imaginative or composite—that serves as a strawman against which we hash out our own ideas or identities. As we have noted earlier in this book, identifying that the Other is part of us and vice versa permits us to think differently about others and also about ourselves. In Case 10 we confront this phenomenon directly by considering challenges to pluralism and the need for educating and redirecting others to move beyond stereotypes to more nuanced and complex understandings of others. The case raises questions about the role of others in our self-identity and self-understanding, but it also asks us to reflect on how we construct our views of others and how we can test and refine those views. It is easy to fall into stereotyping and to lump groups of people together, often regardless of how they may view the others with whom we have lumped them. How we lead in this context is important—it begins with how we behave, and it also includes how we help others to see other perspectives in consistent, informed, and truly human ways. These are essential skills in effective interreligious leadership, but they serve as foundational skills in all areas of leadership and education.

Case Study 7: Hospital Chaplaincy in an Interreligious Context

As a hospital chaplain, Susan works on the front lines of interreligious engagement. She serves at the Catholic-affiliated hospital, though she herself is Lutheran. During her seven years working as a chaplain, she has helped a great many people in the throes of serious illness and the death of family members, and all the surrounding complications. Family dynamics are often quite complex, entailing a range of personal relationships (and at times animosities), as well as healthcare, planning, and economic and legal considerations. The faith traditions and practices of these families have also been extremely diverse—at times even within the same denominations, as individual sensibilities, personalities, and realities play out in different situations and as different perspectives surface. These families turn to Susan in many predictable ways; after all, many struggles have quite universal elements and raise many of the same concerns for people of different backgrounds. And yet, each case has unique context and concerns, many of which are the result of the life choices and religious perspectives and practices of the patients and families.

What continues to surprise Susan, even after her many years working in the field, is how much families expect her to understand their religious concerns and how much they expect her to help them navigate faith traditions that are not her own. Susan attended a theological school that required coursework in world religions, has developed close relationships with chaplains of other religious backgrounds, and has a lot of practical experience. But she still often feels unprepared and unqualified to provide the advice that her patients and their families regularly seek. As a way of coping with some of her anxieties and concerns, Susan tries to focus her conversations on patient care and best ways to engage with medical personnel. But, despite her training and credentials, she has generally steered clear from the larger religious discussions.

Two recent experiences have led her to question her vocation. A Lutheran family approached her and asked some questions about hospice and end-of-life considerations. Susan was honored to have this difficult conversation with people from her own faith tradition. The family members were not pleased, however, with what they thought were Susan's more liberal views and they denigrated her knowledge and personal commitments. Susan felt quite wounded by this interaction. She was certainly aware of the more conservative Lutheran denominations, but she had never engaged with them on substantive issues in such a way and in such an emotional context.

A few days later, Susan had a challenging interaction with a Muslim family. The family was understandably distraught. There is currently no Muslim chaplain in the hospital or nearby. The family had phone access to their imam but had no local support, as they had recently moved into the area and had not found or established any kind of community. The family asked her advice about general issues related to navigating the healthcare system but became quite agitated when she tried to provide general pastoral care and support. They quickly intimated that she should leave them alone since she could not possibly know anything about them or their religion. When Susan indicated that she had worked with Muslim patients before and had completed some training on Islam and end-of-life issues, they scoffed at her and dismissed her. While other families had certainly not wanted to engage with her in the past, in this case Susan felt very bad about being so quickly discounted and dismissed.

Susan began to wonder whether anyone would take her seriously within or beyond her own religious tradition, and this led her to begin to question her vocation as a hospital chaplain. She was committed to self-reflection and spiritual growth but struggled to see how she could help people who were not interested in her help.

Suggested Guiding Questions

- In what ways could the practice of vulnerability be helpful to Susan? How might a vulnerability lens help Susan to think and feel differently about her vocation, and even creatively grow into it more fully? For instance, are there ways for Susan to transform her experience of inadequacy into an opportunity for new learning? What would you recommend?
- How could work on the practice of intentionality be helpful for Susan? Are there implicit motivations, aims, or expectations that you would recommend that she should examine? How could the practice of purposiveness help her to think in new ways about the boundaries, aims, and reasons for her work?
- Do you think there are strategies for Susan that could help her build trust with her clients? What might she need to do or do differently? How might

she position herself? What kinds of words or information might she use that would be most constructive?
- Susan clearly feels quite wounded in both these interactions. What advice could you offer to Susan that might help her with reflecting on her awareness?
- How could the practice of awareness be helpful in this situation? Are there new areas of study, practice, or training that you would recommend to Susan?
- What intellectual, emotional, and spiritual work would you recommend to Susan?
- How could the practice of trust-building be helpful in Susan's circumstances? What existing or new relationships could be helpful for her? Are there relationships and accountabilities beyond the professional chaplaincy community that you would encourage her to cultivate?

Case Study 8: Interreligious Leadership in a New Key: Engaging "Nones" in Interreligious Dialog and Initiatives

Over the last several decades there has been a very appreciable increase in the number of people in North America, who, when surveyed about their religious affiliation, indicate "none." What was 5 percent in the United States in 1972 grew to 7 percent in 1980, 8 percent in 1990, 14 percent in 2000, and 22 percent in 2016.

The rates of individuals who do not identify with any religion vary significantly by country (Canada for example tends to be more socially liberal than the United States, which has a stronger and longer-entrenched Evangelical base) and by region (within the United States, there are lower percentages of nones in the Midwest and South than in the West or Northeast). Identification as a "none" can also be related to age, gender, socioeconomic status, family religious upbringing, and geographic origins, among other factors.

In many countries the difference between religious and nonreligious affiliating seems rather dichotomous—that is, one is affiliated with a denomination or not. In North America, as in some other places, the realities are a bit more complicated. A significant and increasing number of individuals who identify as Jewish in Jewish population studies, for example, indicate that they do not affiliate with any denomination.

What is more, recent research indicates that North American nones are an internally diverse group. One recent study identifies five subgroups of self-declared nones: *involved seculars*, who actively engage in atheist, humanistic, or secular communities and organizations; *inactive nonbelievers*, who do not believe in God and have only slight, if any, spiritual inclinations and do not engage in atheist, humanistic, or secular communities and organizations; *inactive believers*, who do believe in God but attend religious services no more than monthly and have only slight, if any spiritual inclinations; *spiritual-but-not-religious*, who consider themselves moderately spiritual persons but attend religious services less than once a month; and *involved believers*, who believe in God and do attend religious services at least monthly.[2] The position of various nones on core social issues—such as abortion, immigration, gender, same-sex marriage, environment, and government social programs—can also be complex. Given such diversity of backgrounds and orientations, it may not be surprising that engaging with nones requires a good deal of context and nuance.

* * *

A nonpartisan, ecumenical Christian organization, Illuminate, in the US Northeast is looking to develop a social action program related to immigration. They have had some success working with several centrist religious organizations across denominations and traditions. They have also had a good deal of success in engaging liberal religious groups and denominations but have had more challenges engaging with more conservative religious groups. The leadership of Illuminate believes that to get the support (and votes) they will need to advance what they see as a nationwide agenda, they will need to turn some within the conservative religious fold to the cause.

Some members of the senior leadership believe that an outreach to religiously unaffiliated could be quite successful. In the Northeast "nones" tend to share more liberal social sentiments that align with centrist and liberal religious movements. From that standpoint, they seem to be a natural ally in this important initiative.

There are some challenges, however. John Small, the president of Illuminate, has tried outreach to circles of nones in the organization's home region. The nones who are most community engaged tend to be of a very strong atheistic, secularist, or humanist orientation, and while they agree on certain social and political issues, they are highly critical about and cautious in working with any religious groups. The less "affiliated" nones are hard to reach, as they are less socially and civically engaged and have no formal structures.

John has met with leaders of the former, but the sessions have been tense, with the secularist nones quite skeptical about any partnerships that involve religion or the articulation of "religious values" as part of the initiative. In fact, some of the meetings were quite destructive, with John losing his patience and struggling to find a way to build coalitions with people so fundamentally opposed to much of what he believes and stands for.

The challenges are different, but no less complicated, when it comes to the less staunchly secular, but still none-identifying crowd. John has tried to meet with individuals, but the network of these people is appreciably less developed and individual outreach is not making a big difference. What is more, every person John meets with seems quite sui generis, making it difficult to think of how to present a coherent platform that is true to the project and to his and Illuminate's religious orientation and values. John is starting to feel that every conversation is a negotiation that, taken collectively, is eroding the project.

John has met with senior organization leadership (professional and lay), as well as community activists and government officials. He is aware that this issue is not only a "religious issue"; in fact, some might see it as not a religious issue at all, which further complicates John's work. Is he trying to address an ostensibly secular topic by leveraging the power of religious organizations and votes or does he still believe that there is a religious underpinning to this that is essential?

John is no stranger to local challenges of this sort, and he has worked on a number of social justice issues across denominations over the years. But beyond the local challenges, John and his organization are facing another challenge. The dynamics, already complicated in "his own backyard," are even more complex once John looks at other regions and communities across the country. How can John identify partners, build coalitions, and engage the conservatives and/or nones in these areas to move the larger national initiative forward? Every region has its own cultural and religious ecosystem, history, power dynamics, and challenges and opportunities.

While nones are often neglected in questions of interreligious dialog, the large base and very diverse range of people (some of whom do not actively affiliate but do not completely eschew notions of God, the value of religion, or even occasion participation in religious services) makes this a group that must be considered in any kind of dialog and leadership initiative that cuts across religious differences.

Suggested Guiding Questions

- What core problems is John facing?
- Are any of these problems potentially of his own making? How might a vulnerability stance help him to assess his role in the lack of success?

- Are there ways to bridge religious difference through the articulation of, and work toward, other values?
- Are there ways to leverage local, regional, and national concerns and networks that John may not have considered?
- Are there things that John might need to learn about the potential pool of collaborators he is approaching? If so, how might they go about learning them?
- What kind of plan—including articulation of values, goals, timeline, and so forth—would be helpful for John in his conversations?
- Is John trying to superimpose his values upon unwilling and disinterested partners? And is there a potential payoff to that strategy?

Case Study 9: Interreligious Leadership Within and Across Families: Interreligious Marriage—Assumptions, Challenges, and Opportunities for Powerful Dialog

Interreligious marriage was a much-discussed issue in the twentieth century, and it continues to be relevant today, precisely because of the significant number of people involved in marriage across faith traditions and denominations.

For many, interreligious marriage has historically been seen as negative, a form of identity loss and community deterioration. Interreligious marriage was believed to draw people away from active religious engagement on one hand, and potentially cause fissures and confusion within the family on the other.

In some religious traditions, such as Orthodox and even Conservative Judaism, which define Jewishness from a matrilineal perspective, the children of interreligious marriages in which the mother is the non-Jewish partner are not quite Jewish and would need to convert at some point to be accepted as halakhically (legally) Jewish. Even when the mother is Jewish, however, there has often been a stigma associated with the children of interreligious families.

What is more, it was believed (and still is by many people) that many interreligious families would choose not to raise Jewish or non-Jewish children Jewishly when given the choice and that, somehow, their religious observance, commitment, and interest would be less deep and cohesive. Many leaders in these traditions, therefore, worked hard to find ways to stem the tide of interreligious marriage rates, through funded social and educational programs.

But interreligious marriages have not stopped. According to the Pew 2013 Portrait of Jewish Americans, for example, "intermarriage is common among Jews; 44% of all currently married Jewish respondents—and 58% of those who have married since 2005—indicate they are married to a non-Jewish spouse."

Other findings of the survey reveal that:

- Among Jews by religion who are married, 64 percent have a Jewish spouse and 36 percent have a non-Jewish spouse.
- Jews of no religion are much more likely to be in mixed marriages; just 21 percent of married Jews of no religion are married to a Jewish spouse, while 79 percent are married to a non-Jewish spouse.
- Among survey respondents whose current, intact marriage took place in 2005 or later, 58 percent have a non-Jewish spouse. A similar number of those who got married between 2000 and 2004 are also in mixed marriages, as are 55 percent of those who got married in the late 1990s.
- Interreligious marriage rates are lower for those who have been married longer. Of survey respondents who got married in the 1980s, roughly four-in-ten have a non-Jewish spouse. And among those who were wed before 1970, just 17 percent have a non-Jewish spouse.

The rates of interreligious marriage among Jews vary significantly among members of the major Jewish denominations. Ninety-eight percent of Orthodox respondents who are married have a Jewish spouse, as do 73 percent of married Conservative Jews. Around half of married Reform Jews have a Jewish spouse. Among married Jews who have no denominational affiliation, 31 percent have a Jewish spouse.

Recently, some in the Jewish community (primarily among some non-Orthodox populations) have suggested that interreligious marriage may be a positive development, especially as it allows for the increase in Jewish population and as evidence seems to indicate that many interreligious families are in fact choosing to raise their children Jewishly and to engage in Jewish life in some significant, if not always traditional, ways.

In the United States more generally, other Pew Research surveys note that 69 percent of people still marry within their own faith. However, there are indications that "having a spouse of the same religion may be less important to many Americans today than it was decades ago."[3] Since 2010, 39 percent of married Americans have a spouse from a different religious group. That is an increase from the 19 percent married before 1960. Similarly, 15 percent of all new marriages in the United States were between people of different race or ethnicity, up from 6.7 percent in 1980.

The survey revealed that nearly half (49 percent) of unmarried couples are living with someone of a different faith. Still, percentages vary by religion. Ninety-one percent of US Hindus, 82 percent of Mormons, and 79 percent of Muslims, who are married or living with a partner, are with someone of the same religion. The percentage is 65 percent for Jews, 59 percent for mainline Protestants, and 56 percent for unaffiliated people.

* * *

Alan Cabbot runs the ecumenical office of the local Catholic Archdiocese. In his role he works across religious traditions, including across Christian faith traditions. Alan is responsible for training priests, community professionals, and lay leaders. In his experience, many of the individuals with whom he works continue to be concerned by intra-Christian marriage (to spouses who are not Catholic) as well as intermarriage with spouses from other religions. In some ways, they find intra-Christian marriage even more challenging and confusing for the married people they engage with than intermarriage across faith traditions.

Both intra-married and intermarried spouses often feel vulnerable because they lack familiarity with Catholicism, may have grown up with negative attitudes about Catholics, or do not feel particularly welcomed in church or communal settings. On one hand, the leaders Alan trains have an interest in overcoming these challenges; on the other hand, they are often themselves uncomfortable with intra- and intermarriage. They have concern about the religious impact that marriages have on the Catholic spouse and the children in such families. What is more, Alan's constituents come from very diverse backgrounds and the cultural contexts and intercultural competency of some leaders varies significantly.

Alan is developing an educational program for his leaders to help them become more comfortable working with intra- and interreligious families, especially as he knows that the trends in that direction are likely to continue and as he has become familiar with the positive opportunities (even if amidst challenges) that diverse families can bring to faith communities. Alan is especially concerned about the non-Catholic spouses, who often feel very vulnerable, fear the power and judgment of the church and its officials, and may be reticent to share their own stories, experiences, and concerns.

Alan's program builds on some core components. First, he will introduce the concept of intercultural competency and, through various inventories and self-assessments, help participants understand their current intercultural skills and opportunities for development. Within this framework, Alan plans to introduce his leaders to the diversity within Catholicism historically and today.

Next, Alan plans to invite his participants to meet with intermarried families from the Jewish community, so that they can hear their stories—successes and challenges. He will utilize narratives and storytelling to provide his leaders with case studies and simulations to help them work through complex and sensitive issues. Only after he has prepared his leaders with these tools and perspectives, does Alan think he can begin to address what he sees as the more challenging issue of intra- and interfaith families in the Catholic Church.

Suggested Guiding Questions

- How can Alan use discussions of vulnerability, complex resilience, and interreligious resilience to move his program forward in a way that will be sensitive to the complexities of his leaders—their own views and their relationships with congregants and constituents?
- How can Alan be intentional about assuring that the non-Catholic spouses with whom his participants work will feel comfortable being vulnerable and will participate fully (especially without feeling denigrated or proselytized)? What are some strategies in this regard that might help to build trust?
- How might Alan build the awareness he needs to know where to draw boundaries in his work and where he can push the limits of conversation and potential change?
- How can Alan be certain to remain aware of the differences within his own constituency, in terms of religious views, cultural orientations, and individual perspectives?

Case Study 10: Between Relativism and Fundamentalism: Stereotyping the Other in a Faith-based Camp

Working as a camp psychologist for many years, Beth had many experiences at different sleep-away camps—some public and some private and of various religious orientations, including Christian Bible and Jewish summer camps. Most camp sessions were four to six weeks in duration.

In her capacity, Beth was ostensibly charged to assist the campers as they struggled being away from their families, had difficulty integrating, or were dealing with emotional or mental health issues during the long summers. As a religious outsider in relation to most of the groups that attended the camp, Beth also had the opportunity to observe the campers and the broader dynamics of camp life—from the camp leadership and their supervision and training of the counselors to the counselors' work with, and responsiveness to, the campers, as well as the range of campers' interactions and orientations as well.

Beth noticed that in different settings different groups of religious Others (some present and others not present at camp) could be maligned or marginalized in various contexts and for a whole host of reasons. At times, there seemed to be an inverse relationship between the negative perception of some groups—religious and other—and their actual presence at the camp. She also noticed that animosities could flare up, or negative comments could be made about adherents of other traditions even within the same denominations—the denigration of Catholics or evangelicals at some Christian camps for example, or Reform Jews at Orthodox Jewish camps, to take another example.

During one camp season, as tensions between Iran and the United States were reaching a boiling point, Beth had the chance to hear many perspectives on politics. Often the discussions were about foreign policy. But at times the discussions veered into religiously motivated negative comments. "Of course, they are a problem," one counselor said, "all Muslims want to take over the world and they are terrorists. Even when there are some good people, they don't do enough to constrain those who seek to destroy democracy and Christianity. Muslims have always wanted to kill Christians." Beth noticed that the camp director, who overheard the conversation, tried to re-direct the conversation. "Don't you think, Charlie, that is going too far to stereotype everyone in Iran and certainly all Muslims based on the current situation." The counselor clearly had little interest in engaging in reflection and the director was hesitant to push too far. Still, the counselor was not shy about sharing his opinions with other counselors, and from time to time the campers themselves overheard the conversations and chimed in. The camp director decided she needed to take steps to correct what seemed to be widespread ignorance of Islam and religious prejudices among many people in the camp.

At another camp, where Beth worked previously, she noticed that sometimes the most poisonous stereotyping was intrareligious. One summer, Beth worked at an Orthodox Jewish camp. The campers and counselors all came from similar religious households and backgrounds. Most of the camping staff also came from a similar background. While there was not much occasion for the subject of non-Orthodox Jews to come up, Beth recalled an instance in which one camper was talking about another camper's cousin, whose mother was not Jewish. "So, your cousin isn't Jewish either," said another camper. The camper was a bit embarrassed but had to admit that by Orthodox Jewish law the children of a non-Jewish mother were not considered halakhically (legally) Jewish. A counselor and a more senior camp staffer who had been listening in on the conversation took the opportunity to jump in with a few negative comments about Reform Jews, who in their opinion were problematic because they transgressed the laws of the Shabbat and kashrut. The camp director, who shared the same assessment, hardly seemed concerned by the discussion, which quickly devolved into stereotypes of Reform Jews, including questions about their religious commitment more generally, the role of women, ethical standards, and a wide range of negative allegations. Another counselor began to become uncomfortable with the conversation, asserting that we should embrace all Jews and, even if we did not consider some Reform Jews legally Jewish, she had many friends who were Reform and Conservative Jews and who were really good people and, in some cases, very involved in their religious denominations, synagogues, and youth groups.

Suggested Guiding Questions

- In both cases, Beth was an outsider, but also was a member of the senior camping staff. How would you advise Beth, from a stance of vulnerability, to approach these situations? What kind of conversations might she have with camp leadership and what strategies might she employ to get them to engage more openly, and less stereotypically?
- Often, we make off-hand comments without thinking them through. What are some ways Beth might encourage people to be more intentional about what they say in general, as well as under certain circumstances?
- How might Beth build trust with people who only see things in a dichotomous way—as right or wrong, true or false?
- Are there ways for Beth to increase her own and others' interreligious awareness? How might Beth help the campers, counselors, and camp directors to become more aware of the range of religious beliefs and practices and afford them opportunities for open conversation?

Polarization/Sectarianism

Polarization and sectarianism have always existed, but they seem particularly heightened in recent years. People often seem incapable of understanding the assumptions, perspectives, and needs of others (or at least unwilling to understand them) and we struggle to engage in civil and constructive discourse. It seems easy to demonize others who do not look, think, or behave like us—regardless of our own religious or moral perspectives and orientations.

Interreligious encounters at times—today and throughout history—have resulted in or developed in response to violence. Sometimes violence is not directly related to interreligious situations, but it takes on specific meaning or has particular impact because of religious considerations, boundaries, or intersections. Response to violence can, as a result, take a variety of forms—from confronting hatred, bigotry, and violence when perpetrated within our own communities, to engaging with such behavior from other groups (whether one or one's coreligionists are directly impacted), and responding to the broader situation for justice—to make real change for the future. How we reflect on and respond to our own actions and those of our coreligionists and how we do the same with and engage others and other faith traditions is at the core of Case 11. This case is about violence as well as community activism that can and must cross faith traditions and denominational lines. It also points to the importance of understanding the deeper context of the violence and the community dynamics—history, key factors, diversity, changing landscape, and so forth. The case raises questions about how we cooperate with others, leveraging sensitivity toward and knowledge of others and their contexts, and engaging and animating common human and religious values across difference.

The connections binding people of different faith traditions and their formal organizations and congregations can be layered. In some cases, connections are fostered—or tensions escalated—in the context of neighborhood dynamics and concerns. In Case 12 we find individuals from different religious backgrounds engaged in efforts to address issues arising from a cut in local social services. Interreligious leadership is often about action as much as theology (or, ideally, both!). There have been many remarkable examples of the wonderful things that can be accomplished in human and social services when people come together across difference and in fact find significant areas of common concern and shared values. The complication in this case is that the broader initiative was constructed in such a way as to purposefully leave out some community constituents, who have specific religious sensibilities that fly in the face of those of other, more progressive religious people in the neighborhood and who, correspondingly, have not been willing or regular partners on other issues. As the case elucidates, it is difficult to collaborate across fundamental worldview differences. At the same time, the inability to listen and work across difference makes it nearly impossible to develop useful interreligious engagement and cooperation and it makes interreligious leadership more internal and parochial than would be the case if active listening and deep understanding characterized conversations and collaborations. There is a further downside to marginalizing certain groups—a spiraling circle of mistrust and even hatred, which becomes harder to overcome the more sustained and engrained it becomes. Interreligious engagement runs aground when this occurs and, oftentimes, it is impossible to recover from the associated bad feelings that develop.

Case 13 builds on some of the key themes in several other cases. The representation and stereotyping of religious others in media, especially film, is not uncommon. Case 13 considers representation of Muslims in Bollywood films in India to examine the nature and problems associated with anachronism and historical representation (when inaccuracies find their way into a narrative; but even when accurate information is improperly contextualized or used for other, often political or polemical purposes). The case asks us to think about how to engage religious groups that are the ones being marginalized, how to effect change (in the film industry as well as more broadly in other settings), and the most effective ways to organize campaigns and disseminate information to help dispel negative imagery. This is an important component of interreligious resilience, for it is impossible to have serious interreligious engagement when conversations are based on stereotypes and misinformation. Interreligious leaders must become vulnerable to identifying and, as necessary, contesting their own assumptions, even as they remain aware of the broader environments in which they and others operate, and work to build trust through open and nuanced discussions.

Case 14 turns to the thorny issue of interreligious conflict in Israel. Rather than focus on the long-standing and layered situation in the Middle East, however, which is a bit complex for a brief case study, the case instead examines a range of issues from Israel-Diaspora relations, Israel's relations with foreign, non-Jewish groups and states, and initiatives in Israel and Palestine as refracted through discussions and debates on US campuses. Such interactions occur in classes (as in this case), as well as in a range of extramural and co-curricular settings. And as is the case with many interreligious discussions, they often involve issues in addition to religion. The case asks us to engage with the politicization of the situation, to think about how our religious, political, and other identities (and those of others) inform our opinions and interactions with others. It also forces us to take a step back and consider broader historical and theological contexts as well, something that is often difficult to do in heated debates or particularly contested topics.

Case Study 11: Interreligious Dialog and Community Violence

The city had a reputation of being a cultural and educational hub. It had been a major force in regional trade and industry for many years. The city had gone through several economic crises and there have been significant social challenges and political discord in recent years.

In response to a number of issues in one particular neighborhood, especially gun violence, faith leaders in the community have taken to the streets in unity and in attempts to stem the tide of violence through concerted community activism—speeches, church functions, solidarity marches, and the like. They have attempted to work with local law enforcement authorities, although police have been seen as part of the larger problem. They have also attempted to redress social service needs—especially for homeless people and those with drug addictions. The faith leaders have organized a network of supporters on the ground and consulted with experts and professionals from other places and a range of organizations. Through their work, they have realized that they need to provide educational experiences and opportunities to teach about constructive conversation and conflict management. They have also set up a number of community hotlines—for those wanting to report events or concerns, seeking assistance, or simply with questions or suggestions.

The faith leaders do not see everything the same. Their theologies and religious denominational commitments are quite distinct. What has united them is the sense that religion provides an important moral framework that can help to prevent the violence plaguing their community. Joint initiatives on various social issues and events have helped to build solidarity and have provided opportunities for mutual learning about their different faith traditions as well as the broader needs and hopes across the community. But the situation is complicated by the tendency among many residents to explain community problems and mishaps by ascribing blame on other religious groups, some of whom are seen as disloyal to the community or involved with religious initiatives and positions beyond the neighborhood. One local Christian pastor, for example, was castigated for seeking assistance from the neighboring Jewish community—he was accused of pandering to the white Jewish establishment.

On one hand, the community organizing work has attempted to stem the tide of violence and, on the other, to grapple with larger concerns about racism and police violence, which further inflame the local situation. The work of these leaders involves communicating with police and the city council as well as building neighborhood support, especially through the churches. This requires leaders to walk a fine line of criticizing the mayor, city council, and police while also encouraging internal community reflection and self-criticism. The community leaders find themselves simultaneously to be prophets upbraiding their communities, medical and health care advisors, and advocates (even bringing in experts on PTSD), and communal representatives to the larger city.

The religious demographics of the neighborhood are primarily African American Protestant, but there is a significant minority of Muslims in the community as well. The neighborhood shares a boundary with a traditionally

Jewish neighborhood and a large Catholic diocese. Recently there has been something of a resurgence of Jewish life, with the settlement of a small group of Orthodox Jews associated with a local Talmudic academy (yeshiva).

Despite this diversity, historically there were very few crimes committed across neighborhood boundaries, and no record of hate crimes. But recently a member of a white supremacist group in the broader urban area assaulted and killed two African Americans (one Christian and one Muslim) and shortly thereafter entered a Baptist church and killed several African American people attending a bible study. The police arrived quickly, and the gunman died in a shootout at the church.

The mass shooting, which was designated as a hate crime and an act of domestic terrorism, raised many issues—some that had been lurking in the background for years. These involved racist and radical religious stereotypes and a range of cultural, legal, and political impediments to collaboration. Individual clergy had to think about how to address the situation in their own communities and in the media. What is more, people who had been able and willing to participate in interreligious conversations in periods of peace found it much more challenging to continue in this more difficult context.

Divisions within society and the enmity that pervades many interactions today are fuel for violence and bigotry. Religious leaders must grapple with threats and actual violence perpetrated against their coreligionists and, at times, perpetrated by members of their own religious communities. The number of cases of shootings is alarming, but perhaps more so are the acts of violence, often on a massive scale, that occur every day and are rarely reported. Added to this are the many acts of hatred that, although not violent, create intimidating environments and set the scene for the escalation of more heinous acts.

Suggested Guiding Questions

- Assume that you have been invited into this community as an interreligious leader to help the community to move forward and to rebuild trust among themselves. How would you use what you have learned about the psychological, spiritual, and systemic aspects of vulnerability and resilience to develop a plan of action?
- What underlying issues does the case bring to awareness? How might religious concerns play into broader social issues (or not) and how might they serve as a source of strength and improvement of the situation?
- How can one understand the full context and take a broader view of the neighborhood and the dynamics at play, without making assumptions or taking sides?

- Are there ways that trust can be developed within and beyond the differing communities?
- What would be useful responses to the actions outlined in the case from the various religious leaders?

Case Study 12: Liberal Pluralism?

As a result of a recent recession, increasing numbers of people in a midsized city in the Midwest were losing their homes. Making matters worse, social services had been drastically cut in recent years after local and state elections brought in a wave of conservative local and state government representatives.

In response to the rising numbers of homeless people and families, several nonprofit organizations developed initiatives to address the problem, including a number of religious communities. Local religious leaders realized that their individual communal efforts were at times duplicative and that they could be more effective if they could coordinate their resources and efforts.

Pastor Rogers from one of the liberal Christian churches and Rabbi Lefkovitz from the local Reform temple decided to gather religious and civic leaders from across the community to try to galvanize support for a more cohesive and substantive approach to the problem. The city was home to more than a dozen churches, as well as the Reform temple and a mosque. About half of the churches were relatively liberal, mainline Protestant denominations, while the other half were nondenominational evangelical and much more conservative theologically, socially, and politically. Some of the evangelical ministers, for example, were outspoken opponents of abortion, made disparaging comments about Jews and Muslims on social media, and aligned themselves politically with leaders and policies that the liberals considered racist.

The liberal Protestant and Reform Jewish organizers of the homeless initiative decided not to invite the evangelicals to participate in the project. When word reached the evangelical ministers that they had not been invited to participate, they were so upset that they sent an angry letter to the organizers and encouraged their members to write letters to the editor of the local newspaper. The organizers of the initiative, thinking the occasion provided a prophetic opportunity, wrote an OpEd in the local paper denouncing the evangelicals' political support for the elimination of social services, their anti-immigration rhetoric, and their generally exclusionary views of religious truth. Given all of this, they wrote, it was reasonable to assume that the evangelicals would not want to participate in the homeless initiative.

Within a matter of days, members from the different religious communities were denouncing one another on social media and even at local school and sporting events.

Suggested Guiding Questions

- What problems does this case reveal?
- How might the religious leaders organizing the work intentionally engage with their more conservative peers for the benefit of everyone?
- Are there ways for the religious leaders organizing the initiative to adjust their own work and expectations to make an alliance possible?
- Is it possible to disagree about substantive religious and social issues and still build the trust needed to work together on a specific initiative? What specific strategies or actions might help to build (or rebuild) such trust?
- Are there models of collaboration across religious spectrums to consider that could be helpful for the religious leaders in this case?
- How might a vulnerability stance help facilitate shared power and collaboration?
- In this specific case, are there particular incremental steps that might allow for coalition building across the conservative-liberal divide?

Case Study 13: Historical and Cinematic Representation of Religious Others

Bollywood is a mega industry of Hindi cinema, known originally as Bombay cinema—the name being a combination of Bombay and Hollywood. Bollywood is the largest of Indian cinema producers, with more than 360 films in the last couple years and representing more than 40 percent of box-office sales. Indian cinema far outsells Hollywood in terms of tickets, and so the Bollywood phenomenon is massive and influential.

As is the case with Hollywood, Bollywood often produces films with political and social messages, at times built upon contemporary and historical representation of Others, often religious minorities. Bollywood regularly depicts Islam and Muslim characters. Often such depictions reflect political concerns. Muslims are regularly stereotyped as angry, violent, and over the past decades, especially since 9/11 and the Mumbai attacks of 2008, increasingly as terrorists. The cinematography as well as the story lines contribute to negative stereotyping. Both non-Indian and Indian Muslims can be portrayed in a negative light, often as disloyal, criminal, cruel, evil, fundamentalist, and unpatriotic. One recent study suggests that more than 65 percent of Hindi movies represent Muslims unfavorably.[4] At times, these representations carry a religious veneer. At other times, ostensibly secular productions contain similarly disparaging representations of Muslim religious and social life, often focusing on issues of poverty, unemployment, and illiteracy.

Perhaps more troubling are films that place Muslims in historical settings that are more easily anachronistic and subject to all sorts of negative embellishment. One recent example is the 2018 epic drama *Padmaavat* based to some extent on the poem by Malik Muhammad Jayasi (1477–1542), the Sufi poet. Jayasi wrote *Padmaavat* in 1540. It is a poem that depicts the historic siege of Chittor by Alauddin Khalji in 1303. Alauddin is compelled to attack after hearing of the beauty of the Queen Padmavati, the wife of the Hindu king Ratan Singh.

The film producers invested more than US$30 million, though the money expended did not save the film from violent protests that delayed the release. Once released, the film received mixed reviews. The cinematography received positive marks, but the story line was criticized, especially as it represented the evil Muslim king and the righteous Hindu king. Nonetheless, the film was a commercial success, becoming one of the highest-grossing Indian films in history and garnering many film industry awards. According to one study, the film portrays a Muslim ruler awash in pride, lust, and bestial appetite. The film, as such, can be seen to advance Islamophobic sentiment and marginalizes Muslims in contemporary society, feeding on some of the most heinous contemporary stereotypes.

An initiative of religious leaders and activists has formed to address the representation of Muslims in this and other Bollywood films. The group must think about how to engage religious leaders from across faith traditions. It is important to have Hindu and Buddhist leaders as well as Muslim leaders participate. At first it seems quite difficult to bring religious leaders together. Since they disagree about many points of religious observance and theology, and at times harbor negative views of other religions, the group must make an argument for the value of such an initiative.

Getting Muslim leaders to participate has been more challenging than the organizers had anticipated. Many Muslims are suspicious of any attempt to engage with the film industry, which they find impure, indecent, and derogatory—and importantly as a powerful tool by Hindus to marginalize and demonize Muslims. The reticence to participate was also due in part to the range of Muslims but also to the divide in Islamic perspectives and experiences within and outside India.

In overcoming the concerns about, and impediments to, participation, the groups' leaders thought about casting a broader net related to the representation of religious others and minorities in films more generally. They thought that inviting Christian and Jewish leaders to reflect on how Jews have been depicted in Hollywood films might provide a valuable comparative opportunity.

In addition to the participation of Muslim leaders, the initiative has had to grapple with the best approach to making substantive change in the industry and in contemporary society. Should they engage film moguls, producers, actors; should they involve politicians; or should they perhaps reach out to the public. And, they have had to consider what they mean by advocacy. Is it about economic or political pressure or lobbying or does it entail an education agenda?

In any event, the group leaders were convinced that one way to dispel the negative images of Muslims in Indian films was to help produce and circulate films that depicted Muslims positively or at least in an appropriate or neutral context. They also felt that general informational brochures that highlighted key aspects of Islam and featured prominent and patriotic Indian Muslims might also have a positive impact on society more generally.

Suggested Guiding Questions

- What larger systemic problems does this case reveal?
- How should the group identify the individuals and groups to participate in this work? Once they do, how might they cultivate a sense of openness to discussion, which is likely to leave everyone feeling vulnerable and defensive?
- Are there ways, or common concerns, which could help to develop trust across the various groups, especially religious leaders?
- What kinds of short- and long-term goals should the group seek?
- Are there ways you might recommend that they present their findings and recommendations and strategies to make the industry and the broader public aware of the challenges of the representation of Muslims in some films?
- How might the group respond to refusals to participate by groups or specific leaders who may be important and respected voices in their communities?
- Are there other considerations that the group should take into account?

Case Study 14: Interreligious Conflict in the Middle East

The Middle East has been a hotbed for conflict—political as well as religious. Israel has been a major flashpoint but there have been a good number of religious conflicts across the Muslim world and the colonialism that dictated much of the current realities did not alleviate these tensions.

Within Israel, the relations between the State of Israel and a diverse range of Israeli and Jewish groups in Israel and across the Jewish Diaspora have been complex. Equally complex have been relations between the state and other foreign, non-Jewish groups and states, some of which have attempted to broker peace or settlement negotiations. In addition to these various voices, there have been multiple representatives of the Palestinian cause and a number of Arab and Muslim groups and states that have been engaged in more and less productive conversations and, at times, military conflicts as well.

While there are initiatives in place on the ground in Israel and Palestine and while daily life in the region is both harsher and more interactive than many in the West know or believe, the issue of Israeli-Palestinian conflict receives a great deal of attention globally—from the UN, to individual European governments, the media, and a whole host of nonprofit and advocacy organizations (ones that support one group or the other or that still try to find some way to develop and implement a lasting and peaceful solution to the conflict). Frequently, the debates spawned by these groups or between these groups are about political and legal questions. At other times, the debates take on a particularly religious hue, one that has as much to do with the people espousing positions who may have little first-hand experience and certainly do not live in the region. As such, these debates can simultaneously be about many different issues.

This issue is a frequent topic of debate on US college campuses—one of many such debates that have resulted in community lobbying, university action, and sometimes unease among Jewish and Muslim students. In fact, many campuses have become highly political, with BDS movements (which seek to force Israel to make political concessions through pressure exerted from boycotts of and divestments from Israel) on one hand and Israel supporting groups, often backed by local Jewish Federations and organizations, on the other. At some universities, the debates create frustrations and tensions that devolve into more personal attacks and mud-slinging.

At Discordance University, a long-tenured faculty member in the English department, Professor Sarah Fox, has decided to address the Israeli-Palestinian conflict through a course on conflict in English literature. Though the topic is a bit far from her field of research and scholarly writing, she has been an ardent critic of the Israeli government and Israel's treatment of the Palestinians. She is also a supporter of the BDS movement.

Professor Fox has offered the course on Representations of Conflict in English Literature on several occasions. This time she has added several new readings and has opted to be much more direct in her criticism of Israel in the classroom. Some students seem to be aware of Professor Fox's reputation and her views on the issue. As a result, there are several Jewish students enrolled in the class who are critical of Israel and its policies toward Palestinians. There are also several Muslim students enrolled who are anxious to engage with the topic, whatever the alleged focus of the course. At the same time, several Jewish students with strong pro-Israel views have also enrolled in the course. And, of course, there are some students of other religious and political backgrounds who have simply enrolled in the course for the sake of the purported topic, "Conflict in English Literature."

During the first class, the focus of the discussion that is intended to guide the semester becomes clear to everyone. Some students use the opportunity to express their political views. Other students clearly feel quite uncomfortable—a few leave; a few stick around to see what will happen. Pro- and anti-Israel Jewish students square off. They know each other from several other campus debates and other Jewish functions. The Muslim students appear generally to represent an anti-Israel sentiment, though they range in their views as well.

The topics that emerged included accusations of occupation and oppression on one hand and terrorism and hatred on the other. Professor Fox was excited by the energy in the room. She was aware that she had a particular position, and she thought a bit about how to position and guide the discussion in her preparation before the course and during the classes. This was not the first time that she had staged such a course and engaged in this discussion. For the first time that she could remember, however, some of the students who had enrolled ostensibly for the subject of the course (conflict in English literature) stepped into the fray. Perhaps it was because they had been off campus for a while due to the pandemic; maybe it was because they were tired of the highly politicized nature of the discussion; or perhaps they took seriously the idea that the issue of conflict (in the course title) could be addressed, but that it could only be a fruitful conversation with a bit more context and information.

One student asked that the class take one giant step back. "I understand," Samantha said, "that there is a lot of political stuff going on. I imagine that some of that is the product of colonialism, and some is the result of the history of the region and the various wars and politics since the 1920s. It seems to me, though, she added, that there are also some religious issues that are complicating factors." "My family is Jewish," she added, "though we are not very observant or engaged. I'd like to understand why Jews live in Israel, why they want to live in Israel, and why they think it is important for their religion and their personal lives. I'd like to understand the same for the Muslims who live there as well. Why is the land so important? What does it mean for their communities and their theology?"

One pro–Israel Jewish student interrupted—Jews were promised the land by God in the Bible. They have always lived there in some number. A Muslim student recoiled—some of the holiest sites in Islam are in the area and Muslims have lived there continuously for centuries, always in the majority. Jerusalem is central to many Jewish observances and historical identity, a Jewish student who had signed up to read English literature said. That is the case for Muslims too, added a Muslim student.

"Well," Samantha said, "it seems like there are some underlying questions about the land and the connection to the land that go far beyond current politics. If this course is about conflict, shouldn't we explore underlying reasons for conflict. The current politics make me uncomfortable, to be honest, and I feel like I don't really know enough to have a reasoned or reasonable conversation."

Suggested Guiding Questions

- How might a vulnerability stance be used to shape critical, but productive and civil, conversations in this case?
- Are there particular words, concepts, or topics that might trigger a sense of vulnerability in some of the students and how might they be contextualized so that they can be more openly and productively discussed?
- What seem to be the intentions of the various protagonists? Are there ways to set up the course and discussion such that those intentions can be brought to awareness and examined?
- How might Professor Fox use a vulnerability stance to bracket or question her own presuppositions and construct a learning environment that will foster trust and respect for difference?
- How do larger university and societal considerations of these topics impact how they are played out in the classroom?

Notes

Introduction

1. For an interesting discussion of this terminological issue, see Eboo Patel, Jennifer Howe Peace, and Noah Silverman, eds. *Interreligious/Interfaith Studies: Defining a New Field* (Boston: Beacon Press, 2018).
2. For Mike's interpretation of Whitehead, see Chapters 3 and 4 in Michael S. Hogue, *American Immanence: Democracy in an Uncertain World* (New York: Columbia University Press, 2018).
3. Alfred North Whitehead, *Process and Reality: An Essay in Cosmology—Corrected Edition*, ed. David Ray Griffin and Donald W. Sherburne (New York: The Free Press, 1978), 21.
4. Paul F. Knitter, *Introducing Theology of Religions* (Maryknoll: Orbis, 2002), 10.
5. Ibid.
6. Leonard Swidler, "The History of Inter-Religious Dialogue," in *The Wiley-Blackwell Companion to Inter-Religious Dialogue*, ed. Catherine Cornille (Oxford: Wiley-Blackwell, 2013), 3–19, here at 11, 12.
7. Ibid., 13.
8. Ryan C. Urbano, "Levinas and Interfaith Dialogue," *The Heythrop Journal* 53, no. 1 (2012): 148–61, here at 156.
9. Ibid., 157.
10. Ibid., 149.
11. Ibid., 150.
12. Ibid.
13. Ibid.
14. Raimon Panikkar, *The Intra-Religious Dialogue* (New York: Paulist Press, 1999), xvi.
15. Ibid., 34.
16. Ibid., 38.
17. Ibid., 62.
18. Ibid., 82.
19. Ibid., 140.
20. Ibid., 142.
21. Perry Schmidt-Leukel, *Religious Pluralism and Interreligious Theology: The Gifford Lectures-An Extended Edition* (Maryknoll: Orbis, 2017).

22 Perry Schmidt-Leukel, "A Fractal Interpretation of Religious Diversity: An Overview," in *New Paths for Interreligious Theology: Perry Schmidt-Leukel's Fractal Interpretation of Religious Diversity*, ed. Alan Race and Paul Knitter (Maryknoll: Orbis, 2019), 3.

Chapter 1

1. Pope Francis, "Fratelli Tutti," see the opening paragraphs: https://www.vatican.va/content/francesco/en/encyclicals/documents/papa-francesco_20201003_enciclica-fratelli-tutti.html (last accessed July 15, 2021).
2. This "fractal interpretation" of religious supremacy is inspired and informed by the work of Perry Schmidt-Leukel in *Religious Pluralism and Interreligious Theology: The Gifford Lectures—An Extended Version* (Maryknoll: Orbis, 2017). As Schmidt-Leukel defines it, "A fractal interpretation of religious diversity proposes that the differences that can be observed at the *interreligious level* are, to some extent, reflected at an *intrareligious level* in the internal differences discerned within the major religious tradition, and that they can be broken down at the *intrasubjective level* into different religious patterns and structures of the individual mind" (233). Our theses regarding the religious supremacy and interreligious resilience fractals are aimed primarily at the inter- and intrareligious levels. We will discuss this further in Chapter 2.
3. Diana C. Eck, "In the Name of Religions," *The Wilson Quarterly* 17, no. 4 (Autumn 1993): 90–100, here at 91.
4. Ibid.
5. John Hick, "Pluralism Conference," *Buddhist-Christian Studies* 24 (2004): 253–5, here at 253; quoted in Paul Knitter, "Introduction," in *The Myth of Religious Superiority: A Multifaith Exploration*, ed. Paul Knitter (Maryknoll: Orbis Books, 2005), x.
6. Eck, "In the Name of Religions," 92.
7. John J. Thatamanil, *Circling the Elephant: A Comparative Theology of Religious Diversity* (New York: Fordham University Press, 2020), 249.
8. John Hick, *An Interpretation of Religion: Human Responses to the Transcendent*, 2nd edn (Basingstoke: Palgrave Macmillan, 2004), 8.
9. Ibid., 9.
10. Eck, "In the Name of Religions."
11. Versions of this analysis of pluralism can be found throughout Eck's work and is well summarized at the website for Harvard's Pluralism Project: https://pluralism.org/about (last accessed March 2, 2021).
12. Knitter, "Introduction," x; italics in the original. See also Schmidt-Leukel, *Religious Pluralism and Interreligious Theology*.

13 On these distinctions, see Schmidt-Leukel, *Religious Pluralism and Interreligious Theology*, 1–8.
14 Johann Wolfgang von Goethe, *Goethe Werke*, ed. Emil Straiger (Frankfort am Main: Insel Verlag, 1966), vol. 6 (Sprüche), 507; quoted in Paul R. Mendes-Flohr, "Reflections on the Promise and Limitations of Interfaith Dialogue," *European Judaism* 46, no. 1 (Spring 2013): 4.
15 Mendes-Flohr, "Reflections on the Promise and Limitations of Interfaith Dialogue," 6.
16 On civic and social goods, see Mohammed Abu-Nimer and Renáta Katalin Smith, "Interreligious and Intercultural Education for Dialogue, Peace and Social Cohesion," *International Review of Education—Journal of Lifelong Learning* 62 (2016): 393–405; also Mark Waters, "Civic Engagement as an Avenue to Interreligious Cooperation in Religiously Diverse Communities," *Journal of Ecumenical Studies* 53, no. 3 (Summer 2018): 407–20. See also the work of Eboo Patel. And on an international scale, see the articles in the special issue, "Review of Faith and International Affairs," *Journal of Faith and International Affairs*, ed. Jeffrey Haynes and John Fahy 16, no. 3 (2018): 1–18.
17 In addition to sources quoted and cited, this historical review is informed by resources including Katherine Marshall, *Interfaith Journeys: An Exploration of History, Ideas, and Future Directions* (Washington, DC: World Faiths Development Dialogue—Berkley Center for Religion, Peace, and World Affairs, Georgetown University, 2017) and Catherine Cornille, ed., *The Wiley-Blackwell Companion to Inter-Religious Dialogue* (Oxford: Wiley-Blackwell, 2013).
18 Eck, "In the Name of Religions," 93.
19 Quoted in ibid.
20 Ibid.
21 Ibid.
22 Historical documents on WCRP: https://www.swarthmore.edu/library/peace/DG051-099/DG078WCRP.html#:~:text=The%20first%20World%20Conference%20on,in%20the%20fall%20of%201962 (last accessed July 25, 2021).
23 Eck, "In the Name of Religions," 94.
24 Eboo Patel, "Toward a Field of Interfaith Studies," *Liberal Education* 99 (2013): 38. Quoted in *Interreligious/Interfaith Studies: Defining a New Field*, ed. Eboo Patel, Jennifer Howe Peace, and Noah Silverman (Boston: Beacon Press, 2018), xii.
25 Diana C. Eck, *Encountering God: A Spiritual Journey from Bozeman to Banares* (Boston: Beacon Press, 2003), 2.
26 Jeanine Hill Fletcher, "Women in Interreligious Dialogue," in *The Wiley-Blackwell Companion to Inter-Religious Dialogue*, ed. Catherine Cornille (Oxford: Wiley, 2013), 168–83. Fletcher's monographs in the interreligious area include *Motherhood as Metaphor: Engendering Interreligious Dialogue* (New York: Fordham University Press, 2013) and *Monopoly on Salvation? A Feminist Approach to Religious Pluralism* (New York: Continuum, 2005).

27 Fletcher, "Women in Interreligious Dialogue," 170.
28 Ibid., 170-1.
29 Ibid., 172.
30 Ibid., 173.
31 Ibid., 174.
32 Ibid., 175.
33 Ibid., 178.
34 Ibid., 179.
35 Ibid.
36 Ibid.
37 Catherine Cornille, *The Impossibility of Interreligious Dialogue* (New York: The Crossroad Publishing Company, 2008), 2.
38 Ibid., 6.
39 Ibid. 6-7.
40 Ibid. 60.
41 Ibid., 66.
42 Ibid.
43 Ibid., 66-7.
44 Ibid., 95.
45 Ibid., 140.
46 For the concept of "crossing over," John S. Dunne, *The Way of All the Earth: Experiments in Truth and Religion* (New York: Macmillan, 1972).
47 Cornille, *The Impossibility of Interreligious Dialogue*, 151.
48 Ibid., 173.
49 Ibid.
50 Catherine Cornille, "Conditions for Inter-Religious Dialogue," in *The Wiley-Blackwell Companion to Interreligious Dialogue*, ed. Catherine Cornille (Oxford: Wiley-Blackwell, 2013), 28.
51 Ibid.
52 Ibid.
53 Ibid., 29.
54 Ibid.
55 Ibid.
56 Patel prefers the concept "interfaith" to describe the work he and the Interfaith Youth Core engage. Following the work of Wilfred Cantwell Smith, Patel argues that it is the inner relationship between religious adherents and their religious traditions that makes interfaith work important and challenging. As he describes it, the focus of interfaith work is on the interactions between religious persons rather than religious systems, and that the concept of "faith" better describes this personal, inward relationship that religious adherents have to their traditions

than the concept "religious." As we suggest elsewhere, we understand the importance of this inward connection to, and personal investment in, traditions as a crucial element of interreligious work and leadership, and yet favor the concept "interreligious" as more inclusive, since "faith" has roots in theistic and, especially, Christian traditions. For Patel's discussion of this, see his *Interfaith Leadership: A Primer* (Boston: Beacon Press, 2016), 67–86. For Smith's discussion of this, see *Patterns of Faith Around the World* (Oxford: Oneworld Publications, 1962).

57 Patel, *Interfaith Leadership: A Primer*, 92.
58 Ibid., 94.
59 Ibid., 103.
60 Ibid., 130.
61 Ibid., 146.
62 Ibid., 156.
63 Ibid., 158.
64 Ibid., 161.

Chapter 2

1 Jan Nederveen Pieterse, *Globalization and Culture: Global Melange*, 2nd edn (Lanham: Rowman & Littlefield, 2009), 14.
2 Ibid., 3–4.
3 See especially Samuel Huntington, *The Clash of Civilizations and the Remaking of World Order* (New York: Simon and Schuster, 1996).
4 Pieterse, *Globalization and Culture*, 48.
5 Ibid.
6 Ibid., 42.
7 George Ritzer, *The McDonalidization of Society* (London: Sage, 1993), 19, quoted in Pieterse, *Globalization and Culture*, 49.
8 Cees Hamelink, *Cultural Autonomy in Global Communications* (New York: Longman, 1983), 4, quoted in Pieterse, *Globalization and Culture*, 54.
9 Pieterse, *Globalization and Culture*, 25.
10 Ibid.
11 Ibid., 52.
12 Ibid., 55.
13 Ibid., 91–2.
14 Ibid., 56.
15 Ibid., 43.

16 Kristina Stoeckl and Dmitry Uzlaner, "Four Genealogies of Postsecularity," in *Routledge Handbook of Postsecularity*, ed. Justin Beaumont (Milton Park and New York: Routledge, 2018), 269–79.
17 Charles Taylor, *A Secular Age* (Cambridge: Harvard University, 2007).
18 Shmuel N. Eisenstadt, "Multiple Modernities," *Daedalus* 129, no. 1 (Winter 2020): 1–29.
19 On the metaphor of "liquidity" and modernity, see Zygmunt Bauman, *Liquid Modernity* (Cambridge: Polity, 2000).
20 Diana C. Eck, "In the Name of Religions," *The Wilson Quarterly* 17, no. 4 (Autumn 1993): 90–100, here at 92.
21 Benjamin Schewel, *7 Ways of Looking at Religion: The Major Narratives* (New Haven: Yale University Press, 2017), 29.
22 Peter L. Berger, "The Desecularization of the World: A Global Overview," in *The Desecularization of the World*, ed. Peter L. Berger (Grand Rapids: Eerdmans, 1999), 2.
23 American religious historian George Marsden famously wrote that his "unscientific shorthand" for the difference between evangelical and fundamentalist Christians is that a fundamentalist is "an evangelical who is angry about something." See Marsden, *Fundamentalism and American Culture*, 2nd edn (Oxford: Oxford University Press, 2006), 235.
24 Melanie Harris, *Ecowomanism: African American Women and Earth-Honoring Faiths* (Maryknoll: Orbis), 130.
25 Peter Berger, *The Heretical Imperative: Contemporary Possibilities of Religious Affirmation* (New York: Anchor Books, 1980), 28.
26 Pope Francis, *Laudato Si': On Care for Our Common Home*: http://www.vatican.va/content/francesco/en/encyclicals/documents/papa-francesco_20150524_enciclica-laudato-si.html (last accessed July 15, 2021).
27 Hartmut Rosa, *Social Acceleration: A New Theory of Modernity* (New York: Columbia University Press, 2013).
28 Eli Zaretsky and Hartmut Rosa, "The Crisis of Dynamic Stabilization and the Sociology of Resonance: An Interview with Hartmut Rosa," January 18, 2017: https://publicseminar.org/2017/01/the-crisis-of-dynamic-stabilization-and-the-sociology-of-resonance/ (last accessed July 21, 2021).
29 Rosa, *Social Acceleration*, 160–85.
30 Hartmut Rosa, *Alienation and Acceleration: Towards a Critical Theory of Late-Modern Temporality* (Malmö: NSU Press, 2010), 16.
31 Rosa, *Social Acceleration*, 105.
32 Rosa, *Acceleration and Alienation*, 18.
33 Zygmunt Bauman, *Liquid Modernity and Liquid Times* (Cambridge: Polity, 2006).
34 Rosa, *Social Acceleration*, 110–11.
35 Rosa also discusses email as an example of this irony. See *Social Acceleration*, 125–8.
36 Rosa, *Acceleration and Alienation*, 47.

37 Michael Macy, "Opinion Cascades and the Unpredictability of Partisan Polarization," *Science Advances* 5, no. 8 (August 28, 2019), DOI: 10.1126/sciadv.aax0754.
38 Eli J. Finkel, et al., "Political Sectarianism in America," *Science* 370, no. 651 (October 30, 2020): 533–6.
39 Ibid., 534.
40 Ibid.
41 On technologies of gerrymandering, see https://www.theatlantic.com/politics/archive/2017/10/gerrymandering-technology-redmap-2020/543888/ and https://www.wired.com/story/big-data-supercharged-gerrymandering-supreme-court/ (last accessed July 15, 2021).
42 Finkel et al., "Political Sectarianism in America," 534. See also Nolan McCarty, *Polarization: What Everyone Needs to Know* (New York: Oxford University Press, 2019).
43 Two important new books on this topic include Anthea Butler, *White Evangelical Racism: The Politics of Morality in America* (Durham: University of North Carolina Press, 2021) and Robert P. Jones, *White Too Long: The Legacy of White Supremacy in American Christianity* (New York: Simon and Schuster, 2020).
44 See John Gramlich, "What the 2020 electorate looks like by party, race and ethnicity, age, education and religion," (Oct 26, 2020): https://www.pewresearch.org/fact-tank/2020/10/26/what-the-2020-electorate-looks-like-by-party-race-and-ethnicity-age-education-and-religion/ (last accessed January 4, 2022).
45 Finkel et al., "Political Sectarianism in America," 534.
46 Ibid., 533.
47 We will expand on this more fully in Chapter 4.
48 See, for example, Tim Arango, "Hate Crimes in U.S. Rose to Highest Level in More Than a Decade in 2019," *The New York Times* (November 16, 2020): https://www.nytimes.com/2020/11/16/us/hate-crime-rate.html/ (last accessed July 22, 2021). For the FBI source report, see https://ucr.fbi.gov/hate-crime/2019/hate-crime (last accessed July 22, 2021). See also, Michael C. McGarrity and Calvin A. Shivers, "Confronting White Supremacy: Statement for the Record (July 4, 2019)," Statement Before the House Oversight Committee, Subcommittee on Civil Rights and Civil Liberties, Washington: https://www.fbi.gov/news/testimony/confronting-white-supremacy (last accessed July 22, 2021).
49 Jones, *White Too Long*, 54.
50 Eric Tucker and Mary Clare Jalonick, "FBI Chief Warns Violent 'Domestic Terrorism' Growing in US," Associated Press, March 2, 2021: https://apnews.com/article/fbi-chris-wray-testify-capitol-riot-9a5539af34b15338bb5c4923907eeb67 (last accessed July 21, 2021).
51 Jones, *White Too Long*, 54.
52 For instance, see "Who Sees Discrimination? Attitudes on Sexual Orientation, Gender Identity, Race, and Immigration Status: Findings from PRRI's American

Values Atlas," June 2017: https://www.prri.org/research/americans-views-discrimination-immigrants-blacks-lgbt-sex-marriage-immigration-reform/ (last accessed July 15, 2021). See also the data cited in "Summer Unrest Over Racial Injustice Moves the Country, But Not Republicans or White Evangelicals," PRRI Staff, August 2020: https://www.prri.org/research/racial-justice-2020-george-floyd/ (last accessed July 15, 2021).
53 Schmidt-Leukel, *Religious Pluralism and Interreligious Theology*, 223.
54 Eck, *Encountering God*, 10, 11.

Chapter 3

1 Bill Joiner and Stephen Josephs, *Leadership Agility: Five Levels of Mastery for Anticipating and Initiating Change* (San Francisco: Jossey-Bass, 2007), v–vi.
2 Ibid., 6.
3 Ibid., 209–10.
4 Ibid., 8–9.
5 Daniel Goleman, "What Makes a Leader?" in Ronald A. Heifetz, *HBR's 10 must Reads on Leadership* (HBR's 10 must reads (Series)). (Boston: Harvard Business Review Press, 2011), 1–21 (originally, 1996). See also ibidem., *Emotional Intelligence* (New York: Bantam Books, 1995).
6 Peter Drucker wrote many groundbreaking studies and reports. For an overview of some of his key concepts, see Peter F. Drucker, "What Makes an Effective Executive," in *On Leadership*, 23–36.
7 Peter M. Senge, *The Fifth Discipline: The Art and Practice of the Learning Organization*, rev. edn (New York: Currency/Doubleday, 2006 [orig., 1990]), 163ff.
8 Ibid., 13–14.
9 See Ronald A. Heifetz and Donald L. Laurie, "The Work of Leadership," in *On Leadership*, 57–78. Heifetz is well known for other works, especially, Ronald A. Heifetz and Marty Linsky, *Leadership on the Line: Staying Alive Through the Dangers of Leading* (Boston: Harvard Business School Press, 2002) and Ronald A. Heifetz, *Leadership Without Easy Answers* (Cambridge: Belknap Press of Harvard University Press, 1994).
10 Haifetz and Laurie, "The Work of Leadership."
11 Warren G. Bennis and Robert J. Thomas, *Geeks and Geezers: How Era, Values, and Defining Moments Shape Leaders* (Boston: Harvard Business School Press, 2002).
12 Goleman, "What Makes a Leader?"
13 John P. Kotter, "What Leaders Really Do," in *On Leadership*, 37–55.
14 Bennis and Thomas, *Geeks and Geezers*, 93.
15 Ibid.

16 See, for example, Rebecca J. Hester, "Designing 'Smart' Bodies: Molecular Manipulation as a Resilience-Building Strategy," in *The Resilience Machine*, ed. Jim Bohland, Simin Davoudi, and Jeninfer Lawrence (New York and London: Routledge, 2019), 43–61, who argues that "The understanding of life as a network engenders particular kinds of techno-political imaginaries" (47) and that "Arguing against the ideas prevalent in network science that networks are inherently anarchic and anti-authority, and linking biology and cybernetics, they show how protocological control allows networks to emerge and self-organise, albeit in ways guided and directed by protocol, which operates as both form and function" (48).
17 Valerie A. Futch Ehrlich and Brendan P. Newlon, "Designing for Networked Leadership: Shifting from 'What?' to 'How?' A guide to designing and delivering cohort-based leadership and professional development programs for the Jewish social sector" (Center for Creative Leadership, Prepared for the Jim Joseph Foundation, 2021), 4.
18 Ibid.
19 Ibid., 5–6.
20 Ibid., 25.
21 See Jack Zenger and Joseph Folkman, "Research: Women are Better Leaders During a Crisis," *HBR* online. https://hbr.org/2020/12/research-women-are-better-leaders-during-a-crisis (last accessed July 15, 2021).
22 Carol S. Dweck, *Mindest: The New Psychology of Success—How We Can Learn to Fulfill Our Potential*, updated edn (New York: Ballantine Press, 2016), 6–7.
23 See Erica Brown, *Inspired Jewish Leadership: Practical Approaches to Building Strong Communities* (Nashville: Jewish Lights Publishing, 2008), 2ff, for example.
24 Israel Galindo, *The Hidden Lives of Congregations: Discerning Church Dynamics* (Lanham: Rowman & Littlefield, 2004), 1–3.
25 Ibid., 3.
26 Ibid., 57.
27 Ibid., 139.
28 Jeffrey D. Jones, *Heart, Mind, and Strength: Theory and Practice for Congregational Leadership* (Herndon: The Alban Institute, 2008), 29–30.
29 Ibid., 1.
30 Ibid., 20.
31 Ibid., 11.
32 Here the work of Larry Spears, as summarized in Brown, *Inspired Jewish Leadership*, 39.
33 Jones, *Heart, Mind, and Strength*, 24.
34 Ibid., 61.
35 Ibid., 109–11.
36 Ibid., 140.

37 Ibid., 152; see also 159 on the value of inciting stress.
38 Roger Heuser and Norman Shawchuck, *Leading the Congregation: Caring for Yourself While Serving the People* (Nashville: Abingdon Press, 2010), 90; and see Chapter 10, 145ff. See also Brown, *Inspired Jewish Leadership*, 119f.
39 Paul F. Knitter, "Inter-Religious Dialogue and Social Action," in *The Wiley-Blackwell Companion to Inter-Religious Dialogue*, ed. Catherine Cornille (London: Wiley-Blackwell, 2013), 133–48.
40 Catherine Cornille, *The Im-possibility of Interreligious Dialogue* (New York: The Crossroad Publishing Company, 2008), 4.
41 Ibid., 5.
42 Ibid., 9.
43 Jensen H. Shirley, "Congregation Activism: Faith-based Leadership," *NAAAS & Affiliates Conference Monographs* (2010): 1540–75, here at 1544–8.
44 Eboo Patel, *Interfaith Leadership: A Primer* (Boston: Beacon Press, 2016), 11.
45 Ibid., 10.
46 Ibid., 13.
47 Ibid., 93.
48 Ibid., 83.
49 See David Jaffe, *Changing the World from the Inside Out: A Jewish Approach to Personal and Social Change* (Boulder: Shambhala, 2016); Hal M. Lewis, *From Sanctuary to Boardroom: A Jewish Approach to Leadership* (Lanham: Rowman & Littlefield, 2006); and Brown, *Inspired Jewish Leadership*.
50 Patel, *Interfaith Leadership*, 90.
51 Ibid., 63.
52 Ibid., 92–3.
53 Ibid., 98–9.
54 Ibid., 28, 37.
55 Ibid., 139.
56 Ibid., 140.
57 Ibid., 141.
58 Eboo Patel, "Preparing Interfaith Leaders: Knowledge Base and Skill Set for Interfaith Leaders," *New Directions for Student Leadership* 152 (Winter 2016): 75–86, here at 79.
59 See Frank Sesno, *Ask More: The Power of Questions to Open Doors, Uncover Solutions, and Spark Change* (New York: Amacom, 2017).
60 Patel, *Interfaith Leadership*, 84.
61 Ibid., 71.
62 Ibid., 75.
63 Ibid., 130.
64 Ibid., 79.

65 Ibid., 138.
66 Ibid., 112.
67 Ibid., 112, 114.
68 Ibid., 113.
69 In assessing best practices in interreligious work it is important to recognize that the opinions one expresses are one's own and not necessarily those of the entire faith tradition; they are best expressed through personal stories; and a recollection that faith traditions can be quite broad and represent many different perspectives. See Mohammed Abu-Nimer, Amal I. Khoury, and Emily Welty, *Unity in Diversity: Interfaith Dialogue in the Middle East* (Washington: United States Institute of Peace Press, 2007), 37.
70 Beyond this, as work on antiracism has pointed out, we must do more than not behave in racist and demeaning ways, but we must also speak out against others who do and we must actively address hatred or negative discussion of others in religious and civic settings and beyond. See Ibram X. Kendi, *How to be an Antiracist* (New York: One World, 2019).
71 See https://www.pewforum.org/2020/11/10/in-2018-government-restrictions-on-religion-reach-highest-level-globally-in-more-than-a-decade/ (last accessed July 15, 2021).
72 Pew Research Center, "Religious Hostilities Reach Six-Year High," (2014): https://www.pewforum.org/2014/01/14/religious-hostilities-reach-six-year-high/ (last accessed July 13, 2021), 7, 25.
73 Ibid., 7.
74 Ibid., 14.
75 Ibid., 10.
76 Ibid., 11.
77 Ibid., 12.
78 Ibid., 21.
79 https://www.pewforum.org/2021/05/11/jewish-americans-in-2020/ (last accessed July 15, 2021). For regular tracking of anti-Semitism, the Anti-Defamation League provides a range of reports and resources (https://www.adl.org/).
80 https://www.washingtonpost.com/investigations/interactive/2021/domestic-terrorism-data/ (last accessed December 22, 2021).
81 https://www.csis.org/analysis/war-comes-home-evolution-domestic-terrorism-united-states (last accessed December 22, 2021).
82 Pew Research Center, "Religious Hostilities Reach Six-Year High" (2014), 13.
83 Abu-Nimer et al., *Unity in Diversity*, 7.
84 Pew Study, "Religion and Education Around the World" (2016), 5. https://www.pewforum.org/2016/12/13/religion-and-education-around-the-world/.
85 Ibid.

86 Ibid., 11.
87 Ibid., 5, 33.
88 Ibid., 88.
89 Ibid., 19.
90 Ibid., 6.
91 Ibid., 54. An interesting trend is that Jewish men are lagging behind Jewish women in terms of higher education in the United States (114). The Pew study notes that "Although Jews are one of the most highly educated religious groups in the United States, the youngest Jewish men are less likely than the oldest Jewish men to have post-secondary degrees" (114), a 17-point decrease from 81 percent among oldest and 65 percent among youngest generations (114). While there are also decreases among Christian men (3 percent) and men with no religious affiliation (8 percent), the Jewish case is especially high. The Pew study posits that one contributing factor is the large proportion of survey participants identifying as Orthodox, "a group that tends to be less educated than other U.S. Jews" (114). This is a bit misleading, as many Orthodox men continue in higher religious education, even if not in secular universities. What is significant for our study, however, is that Orthodox Jewish men in traditional yeshivot are not likely to learn about other religions or interact with adherents of other religions. The second contributing factor posited by the Pew study is that Jews who identify themselves as "Jews of no religion," and so not included in the Jewish statistics, tend to be highly educated (114).
92 Ibid., 7.
93 Ibid., 28.
94 Pew Research Center, "In America, Does More Education Equal Less Religion?" (2017): https://www.pewforum.org/2017/04/26/in-america-does-more-education-equal-less-religion/ (last accessed July 13, 2021), 4.
95 Ibid., 3.
96 Ibid., 5, 7.
97 Ibid., 3.
98 Ibid., 11.
99 Ibid., 13.
100 Pew Research Center, "What Americans Know about Religion" (2019): https://www.pewforum.org/2019/07/23/what-americans-know-about-religion/ (last accessed July 13, 2021).
101 Ibid., 4.
102 Ibid., 5, 7.
103 Ibid., 5, 8.
104 Ibid., 8.
105 Ibid., 20ff.
106 Ibid., 60–1.

107 Ibid., 20.
108 Ibid.
109 Ibid.
110 Ibid., 47.
111 Ibid.
112 Ibid., 62.
113 Ibid.
114 Pew Research Center, "The Religious Typology: A New Way to Categorize Americans by Religion" (2018): https://www.pewforum.org/2018/08/29/the-religious-typology/ (last accessed July 13, 2021), 5.
115 Ibid., 46.
116 Ibid., 49.
117 Ibid., 47.
118 Ibid., 55.
119 Ibid., 57.
120 Ibid., 68.
121 Ibid., 54.
122 Raimon Panikkar, *The Intra-Religious Dialogue* (New York: Paulist Press, 1999), 18.
123 Ibid., 20–1.
124 Abu-Nimer et al., *Unity in Diversity*, 8.
125 Ibid., 14.
126 Knitter, "Inter-Religious Dialogue and Social Action," 133–48, here at 133.
127 Ibid., 142.
128 Abu-Nimer et al., *Unity in Diversity*, 26.
129 Catherine Cornille, "Introduction," in *The Wiley-Blackwell Companion to Inter-Religious Dialogue*, xii–xvii, here at xii.
130 Ibid., xiii; see Leonard Swidler, "The History of Inter-Religious Dialogue," in *The Wiley-Blackwell Companion to Inter-Religious Dialogue*, ed. Catherine Cornille (New York: Wiley, 2013), 3–19.
131 Peter Berger, *The Many Altars of Modernity: Toward a Paradigm for Religion in a Pluralist Age* (Boston: De Gruyter, 2014), 29.
132 Ibid., 48. Berger suggests replacing secularization theory—the notion that modernity led to a decline in religion—with the concept of pluralism (See Chapter 4 of this book; see also Panikkar, *The Intra-Religious Dialogue*, 23).
133 Berger, *The Many Altars of Modernity*, 37.
134 Ibid., 64.
135 Ibid., 66.
136 David Tracy, *Dialogue with the Other: The Inter-religious Dialogue* (Louvain and Grand Rapids: Peeters Press and W. B. Eerdmans, 1991), 73.
137 See Abu-Nimer et al., *Unity in Diversity*, 39.

138 Ibid., 40.
139 Urbano, "Levinas and Interfaith Dialogue," 148–61, here at 148.
140 Ibid., 149.
141 Abu-Nimer et al., *Unity in Diversity*, 43.
142 Ibid., 48–51.
143 Ibid., 22.
144 Ibid.
145 Ibid., 23.
146 Jeannine Hill Fletcher, "Women in Inter-Religious Dialogue," in *The Wiley-Blackwell Companion to Inter-Religious Dialogue*, 168–83, here at 179.

Chapter 4

1 Karl Marx, "A Contribution *to the* Critique of Hegel's Philosophy of Right: Introduction," *Marx: Early Political Writings*, ed. and trans. Joseph O'Malley (Cambridge: Cambridge University Press, 1994), 57.
2 Ibid., 58.
3 Sigmund Freud, *The Future of an Illusion* (New York: Norton, 1961), 68.
4 Sigmund Freud, *Introductory Lectures on Psychoanalysis* (New York: Norton, 1965), 207.
5 Ibid.
6 Emile Durkheim, *Elementary Forms of Religious Life* (New York: Oxford, 2001), 46.
7 Ibid.
8 Sharon Welch, "Return to Laughter," in *The Religious*, ed. John D. Caputo (Oxford: Blackwell, 2002), 302.
9 Ibid., 305.
10 Ibid., 311.
11 Anthony Pinn, *African American Humanist Principles: Living and Thinking Like the Children of Nimrod* (New York: Palgrave, 2004), 66.
12 Ibid.
13 Anthony Pinn, *Terror and Triumph: The Nature of Black Religion* (Minneapolis: Fortress Press, 2003), 173.
14 Yaakov Herkovitz, "ibersetsung: translation," *Frankel Institute Annual* (Ann Arbor: University of Michigan, 2020).
15 Ibid.
16 Willie James Jennings, *The Christian Imagination: Theology and the Origins of Race* (New Haven: Yale University Press, 2010), 148.
17 Ibid., 156.

18 John J. Thatamanil, *Circling the Elephant: A Comparative Theology of Religious Diversity* (New York: Fordham University Press, 2020), 142.
19 Ibid., 150.
20 Perry Schmidt-Leukel, "A Fractal Interpretation of Religious Diversity: An Overview," in *New Paths for Interreligious Theology: Perry Schmidt-Leukel's Fractal Interpretation of Religious Diversity*, ed. Alan Race and Paul Knitter (Maryknoll: Orbis), 3–24, here at 3.
21 Ibid., 8, 9, 14.
22 Thatamanil, *Circling the Elephant*, 146.
23 Leonard Swidler, "More Than Dialogue: Deep-Dialogue, Critical-Thinking, Competitive-Cooperation," *World Journal of Islamic History and Civilization* 3, no. 1 (2013): 36–41, here at 37.
24 Ibid.
25 Ibid.
26 Ibid.
27 David Chandler, *Resilience: The Governance of Complexity* (London: Routledge, 2014), 50.
28 Kristine Culp, *Vulnerability and Glory: A Theological Account* (Louisville: Westminster John Knox Press, 2010), 3.
29 Erinn C. Gilson, *The Ethics of Vulnerability: A Feminist Analysis of Social Life and Practice* (London: Routledge, 2014), 32.
30 Ibid., 143.
31 Alfred North Whitehead, *Religion in the Making* (New York: Fordham University Press, 1996).
32 Charles H. Long, *Significations: Signs, Symbols, and Images in the Interpretation of Religion* (Philadelphia: Fortress Press, 1986), 7.
33 Judith Butler, *Precarious Life: The powers of Mourning and Violence* (London: Verso, 2006), 46.

Chapter 5

1 Jonathan Lear, *Radical Hope: Ethics in the Face of Cultural Devastation* (Cambridge: Harvard University Press, 2006), 7.
2 Pierre E. Jacob, "Intentionality," *The Stanford Encyclopedia of Philosophy* (Winter 2019 Edition), Edward N. Zalta (ed.): https://plato.stanford.edu/archives/win2019/entries/intentionality/ (last accessed December 3, 2021).
3 Eric Liu and Nick Hanauer, *The Gardens of Democracy: A New American Story of Citizenship, the Economy, and the Role of Government* (Seattle: Sasquatch Books, 2011).

4   Ibid., 10.
5   Ibid., 10, 11.
6   Ibid., 11.
7   Ibid.
8   Ibid.
9   Ibid., 65.
10 Ibid., 66.
11 See also James O'Toole, *Leading Change: Overcoming the Ideology of Comfort and the Tyranny of Custom* (San Francisco: Jossey-Bass Publishers, 1995), 27–9.
12 G. VandenBos and American Psychological Association, *APA Dictionary of Psychology*, 1st ed. (Washington, DC: American Psychological Association, 2007). Here we refer to the online version at: https://dictionary.apa.org/awareness (last accessed December 3, 2021).

Chapter 6

1   https://www.who.int/news-room/fact-sheets/detail/violence-against-women (last accessed December 25, 2021).
2   See Joel Thiessen and Sarah Wilkins-LaFlamme, *None of the Above: Non-religious Identity in the US and Canada* (New York: New York University Press, 2020), 78–9.
3   See Pew Research Center, "America's Changing Religious Landscape," (2015), Chapter 2: https://www.pewforum.org/2015/05/12/americas-changing-religious-landscape/ (last accessed July 25, 2021).
4   https://www.newframe.com/how-bollywood-furthers-indias-nationalism/; (last accessed July 25, 2021).

Bibliography

Abu-Nimer, Mohammed, and Renáta Katalin Smith. "Interreligious and Intercultural Education for Dialogue, Peace and Social Cohesion." *International Review of Education—Journal of Lifelong Learning* 62 (2016): 393–405.

Abu-Nimer, Mohammed, Amal I. Khoury, and Emily Welty. *Unity in Diversity: Interfaith Dialogue in the Middle East*. Washington: United States Institute of Peace Press, 2007.

Arango, Tim. "Hate Crimes in U.S. Rose to Highest Level in More Than a Decade in 2019." *The New York Times* (November 16, 2020): https://www.nytimes.com/2020/11/16/us/hate-crime-rate.html (last accessed July 22, 2021).

Bauman, Zygmunt. *Liquid Modernity*. Cambridge: Polity, 2000.

Bauman, Zygmunt. *Liquid Times*. Cambridge: Polity, 2006.

Bennis, Warren G., and Robert J. Thomas. *Geeks and Geezers: How Era, Values, and Defining Moments Shape Leaders*. Boston: Harvard Business School Press, 2002.

Berger, Peter. *The Heretical Imperative: Contemporary Possibilities of Religious Affirmation*. New York: Anchor Books, 1980.

Berger, Peter, ed. *The Desecularization of the World*. Grand Rapids: Eerdmans, 1999.

Berger, Peter. *The Many Altars of Modernity: Toward a Paradigm for Religion in a Pluralist Age*. Boston: De Gruyter, 2014.

Birkmann, Jörn, ed. *Measuring Vulnerability to Natural Hazards: Towards Disaster Resilient Societies*. 2nd edn. Tokyo: United Nations University Press, 2006.

Brown, Erica. *Inspired Jewish Leadership: Practical Approaches to Building Strong Communities*. Nashville: Jewish Lights Publishing, 2008.

Butler, Anthea White. *Evangelical Racism: The Politics of Morality in America*. Durham: University of North Carolina Press, 2021.

Butler, Judith. *Precarious Life: The Powers of Mourning and Violence*. London: Verso, 2006.

Chandler, David. *Resilience: The Governance of Complexity*. London: Routledge, 2014.

Cornille, Catherine. *The Im-possibility of Interreligious Dialogue*. New York: The Crossroad Publishing Company, 2008.

Cornille, Catherine, ed. *The Wiley-Blackwell Companion to Inter-Religious Dialogue*. Oxford: Wiley-Blackwell, 2013.

Culp, Kristine. *Vulnerability and Glory: A Theological Account*. Louisville: Westminster John Knox Press, 2010.

Drucker, Peter F. "What Makes an Effective Executive." In *On Leadership*, 23–36. Boston: Harvard Business Review, 2011.

Dunne, John S. *The Way of All the Earth: Experiments in Truth and Religion*. New York: Macmillan, 1972.
Durkheim, Emile. *Elementary Forms of Religious Life*. New York: Oxford, 2001.
Dweck, Carol S. *Mindset: The New Psychology of Success—How We Can Learn to Fulfill Our Potential*. Updated edn. New York: Ballantine Press, 2016.
Eck, Diana C. "In the Name of Religions." *The Wilson Quarterly* 17, no. 4 (Autumn 1993): 90–100.
Eck, Diana C. *Encountering God: A Spiritual Journey from Bozeman to Banares*. Boston: Beacon Press, 2003.
Ehrlich, Valerie A. Futch, and Brendan P. Newlon. "Designing for Networked Leadership: Shifting from 'What?' to 'How?' A guide to designing and delivering cohort-based leadership and professional development programs for the Jewish social sector." Center for Creative leadership, Prepared for the Jim Joseph Foundation, 2021.
Eisenstadt, Shmuel N. "Multiple Modernities." *Daedalus* 129, no. 1 (Winter 2020): 1–29.
Fineman, Martha Albertson, and Anna Grear. *Vulnerability: Reflections on a New Ethical Foundation for Law and Politics*. Farnham: Ashgate Publishing, 2013.
Finkel, Eli J. et al. "Political Sectarianism in America." *Science* 370, no. 651 (October 30, 2020): 533–6.
Fletcher, Jeannine Hill. *Monopoly on Salvation? A Feminist Approach to Religious Pluralism*. New York: Continuum, 2005.
Fletcher, Jeannine Hill. *Motherhood as Metaphor: Engendering Interreligious Dialogue*. New York: Fordham University Press, 2013.
Fletcher, Jeannine Hill. "Women in Inter-Religious Dialogue." In *The Wiley-Blackwell Companion to Inter-Religious Dialogue*, edited by Catherine Cornille, 168–83. Oxford: Wiley, 2013.
Freud, Sigmund. *The Future of an Illusion*. New York: Norton, 1961.
Freud, Sigmund. *Introductory Lectures on Psychoanalysis*. New York: Norton, 1965.
Galindo, Israel. *The Hidden Lives of Congregations: Discerning Church Dynamics*. Lanham: Rowman & Littlefield, 2004.
Gilson, Erinn C. *The Ethics of Vulnerability: A Feminist Analysis of Social Life and Practice*. London: Routledge, 2014.
Goleman, Daniel. *Emotional Intelligence*. New York: Bantam Books, 1995.
Goleman, Daniel. "What Makes a Leader?" in *On Leadership*, 1–21. Boston: Harvard Business Review, 2011.
Hamelink, Cees. *Cultural Autonomy in Global Communications*. New York: Longman, 1983.
Harris, Melanie. *Ecowomanism: African American Women and Earth-Honoring Faiths*. Maryknoll and New York: Orbis, 2017.
Harvard Pluralism Project: https://pluralism.org/about (last accessed March 2, 2021).
Haynes, Jeffrey, and John Fahy, eds. "Introduction: Interfaith on the World Stage." *Journal of Faith and International Affairs* 16, no. 3 (2018): 1–8.

Heifetz, Ronald A. *Leadership without Easy Answers*. Cambridge: Belknap Press of Harvard University Press, 1994.

Heifetz, Ronald A., and Donald L. Laurie. "The Work of Leadership." In *On Leadership*, 57–78. Boston: Harvard Business Review, 2011.

Heifetz, Ronald A., and Marty Linsky. *Leadership on the Line: Staying Alive Through the Dangers of Leading*. Boston: Harvard Business School Press, 2002.

Herkovitz, Yaakov. "ibersetsung: Translation." In *Frankel Institute Annual*, edited by Julian Levinson and Justin Camm, 9–11. Ann Arbor: University of Michigan, 2020. Accessible at: https://www.fulcrum.org/epubs/jh343v60k?locale=en#page=1 (last accessed December 14, 2021).

Hester, Rebecca J. "Designing 'Smart' Bodies: Molecular Manipulation as a Resilience-Building Strategy." In *The Resilience Machine*, edited by Jim Bohland, Simin Davoudi, and Jennifer Lawrence, 43–61. New York and London: Routledge, 2019.

Heuser, Roger, and Norman Shawchuck. *Leading the Congregation: Caring for Yourself While Serving the People*. Nashville: Abingdon Press, 2010.

Hick, John. *An Interpretation of Religion: Human Responses to the Transcendent*. 2nd edn. Basingstoke: Palgrave Macmillan, 2004.

Hick, John. "Pluralism Conference." *Buddhist-Christian Studies* 24 (2004): 253–5.

Hogue, Michael S. *American Immanence: Democracy in an Uncertain World*. New York: Columbia University Press, 2018.

Huntington, Samuel. *The Clash of Civilizations and the Remaking of World Order*. New York: Simon and Schuster, 1996.

Jacob, Pierre. "Intentionality." *The Stanford Encyclopedia of Philosophy* (Winter 2019 Edition), Edward N. Zalta (ed.): https://plato.stanford.edu/archives/win2019/entries/intentionality/.

Jaffe, David. *Changing the World from the Inside Out: A Jewish Approach to Personal and Social Change*. Boulder: Shambhala, 2016.

Jennings, Willie James. *The Christian Imagination: Theology and the Origins of Race*. New Haven: Yale University Press, 2010.

Joiner, Bill, and Stephen Josephs. *Leadership Agility: Five Levels of Mastery for Anticipating and Initiating Change*. San Francisco: Jossey-Bass, 2007.

Jones, Jeffrey D. *Heart, Mind, and Strength: Theory and Practice for Congregational Leadership*. Herndon: The Alban Institute, 2008.

Jones, Robert P. *White Too Long: The Legacy of White Supremacy in American Christianity*. New York: Simon and Schuster, 2020.

Kahneman, Daniel. *Thinking Fast and Slow*. New York: Farrar, Straus and Giroux, 2011.

Kendi, Ibram X. *How to be an Antiracist*. New York: One World, 2019.

Knitter, Paul F. *Introducing Theology of Religions*. Maryknoll: Orbis, 2002.

Knitter, Paul F., ed. *The Myth of Religious Superiority: A Multifaith Exploration*. Maryknoll: Orbis, 2005.

Knitter, Paul F. "Inter-Religious Dialogue and Social Action." In *The Wiley-Blackwell Companion to Inter-Religious Dialogue*, edited by Catherine Cornille, 133–48. Oxford: Wiley-Blackwell, 2013.

Kotter, John P. "What Leaders Really Do." In *On Leadership*, 37–55. Boston: Harvard Business Review, 2011.

Lear, Jonathan. *Radical Hope: Ethics in the Face of Cultural Devastation*. Cambridge: Harvard University Press, 2006.

Lewis, Hal M. *From Sanctuary to Boardroom: A Jewish Approach to Leadership*. Lanham: Rowman & Littlefield, 2006.

Long, Charles H. *Significations: Signs, Symbols, and Images in the Interpretation of Religion*. Philadelphia: Fortress Press, 1986.

Mackenzie, Catriona, Wendy Rogers, and Susan Dodds, eds. *Vulnerability: New Essays in Ethics and Feminist Philosophy*. Oxford: Oxford University Press, 2014.

Macy, Michael et al. "Opinion Cascades and the Unpredictability of Partisan Polarization." *Science Advances* 5, no. 8 (August 28, 2019), DOI: 10.1126/sciadv.aax0754

Marsden, George. *Fundamentalism and American Culture*. 2nd edn. Oxford: Oxford University Press, 2006.

Marshall, Katherine. *Interfaith Journeys: An Exploration of History, Ideas, and Future Directions*. Washington: World Faiths Development Dialogue—Berkley Center for Religion, Peace, and World Affairs, Georgetown University, 2017.

Marx, Karl. *Marx: Early Political Writings*. Ed. and Trans. Joseph O'Malley. Cambridge: Cambridge University Press, 1994.

McCarty, Nolan. *Polarization: What Everyone Needs to Know*. New York: Oxford University Press, 2019.

McGarrity, Michael C., and Calvin A. Shivers. "Confronting White Supremacy: Statement for the Record (July 4, 2019)," Statement Before the House Oversight Committee, Subcommittee on Civil Rights and Civil Liberties, Washington: https://www.fbi.gov/news/testimony/confronting-white-supremacy (last accessed July 22, 2021).

Mendes-Flohr, Paul R. "Reflections on the Promise and Limitations of Interfaith Dialogue." *European Judaism* 46, no. 1 (Spring 2013): 4–14.

Nederveen Pieterse, Jan. *Globalization and Culture: Global Melange*. 2nd edn. Lanham: Rowman & Littlefield, 2009.

O'Toole, James. *Leading Change: Overcoming the Ideology of Comfort and the Tyranny of Custom*. San Francisco: Jossey-Bass Publishers, 1995.

Panikkar, Raimon. *The Intra-Religious Dialogue*. New York: Paulist Press, 1999.

Patel, Eboo. "Toward a Field of Interfaith Studies." *Liberal Education* 99, no. 4 (2013): 38.

Patel, Eboo. *Interfaith Leadership: A Primer*. Boston: Beacon Press, 2016.

Patel, Eboo. "Preparing Interfaith Leaders: Knowledge Base and Skill Set for Interfaith Leaders." *New Directions for Student Leadership* 152 (Winter 2016): 75–86.

Patel, Eboo, Jennifer Howe Peace, and Noah Silverman, eds. *Interreligious/Interfaith Studies: Defining a New Field*. Boston: Beacon Press, 2018.

Pew Research Center. "America's Changing Religious Landscape," (2015), Chapter 2: https://www.pewforum.org/2015/05/12/americas-changing-religious-landscape/ (last accessed July 25, 2021).

Pew Research Center. "In America, Does More Education Equal Less Religion?" (2017): https://www.pewforum.org/2017/04/26/in-america-does-more-education-equal-less-religion/ (last accessed July 13, 2021).

Pew Research Center. "Jewish Americans in 2020": https://www.pewforum.org/2021/05/11/jewish-americans-in-2020/ (last accessed July 13, 2021).

Pew Research Center. "In 2018, Government Restrictions on Religion Reach Highest Level Globally in More Than a Decade," (2020): https://www.pewforum.org/2020/11/10/in-2018-government-restrictions-on-religion-reach-highest-level-globally-in-more-than-a-decade/ (last accessed July 13, 2021).

Pew Research Center. "A Portrait of American Jews," (2013): https://www.pewforum.org/2013/10/01/jewish-american-beliefs-attitudes-culture-survey/ (last accessed July 13, 2021).

Pew Research Center. "Religion and Education Around the World," (2016): https://www.pewforum.org/2016/12/13/religion-and-education-around-the-world/ (last accessed July 13, 2021).

Pew Research Center. "Religious Hostilities Reach Six-Year High," (2014): https://www.pewforum.org/2014/01/14/religious-hostilities-reach-six-year-high/ (last accessed July 13, 2021).

Pew Research Center. "The Religious Typology: A New Way to Categorize Americans by Religion," (2018): https://www.pewforum.org/2018/08/29/the-religious-typology/ (last accessed July 13, 2021).

Pew Research Center. "What Americans Know about Religion," (2019): https://www.pewforum.org/2019/07/23/what-americans-know-about-religion/ (last accessed July 13, 2021).

Pew Research Center. "What the 2020 Electorate Looks Like by Party, Race and Ethnicity, Age, Education and Religion," (2020): https://www.pewresearch.org/fact-tank/2020/10/26/what-the-2020-electorate-looks-like-by-party-race-and-ethnicity-age-education-and-religion/ (last accessed July 13, 2021).

Pinn, Anthony. *Terror and Triumph: The Nature of Black Religion*. Minneapolis: Fortress Press, 2003.

Pinn, Anthony. *African American Humanist Principles: Living and Thinking Like the Children of Nimrod*. New York: Palgrave, 2004.

Pope Francis. "Fratelli Tutti." https://www.vatican.va/content/francesco/en/encyclicals/documents/papa-francesco_20201003_enciclica-fratelli-tutti.html (last accessed July 15, 2021).

Pope Francis. *Laudato Si': On Care for Our Common Home*. http://www.vatican.va/content/francesco/en/encyclicals/documents/papa-francesco_20150524_enciclica-laudato-si.html (last accessed July 15, 2021).

Ritzer, George. *The McDonalidization of Society*. London: Sage, 1993.

Rosa, Hartmut. *Alienation and Acceleration: Towards a Critical Theory of Late-Modern Temporality*. Malmö: NSU Press, 2010.

Rosa, Hartmut. *Social Acceleration: A New Theory of Modernity*. New York: Columbia University Press, 2013.

Scharmer, Otto, and Katrin Kaufer. *Leading from the Emerging Future: From Ego-System to Eco-System Economies*. San Francisco: Berrett-Koehler Publishers, Inc., 2013.

Schewel, Benjamin. *7 Ways of Looking at Religion: The Major Narratives*. New Haven: Yale University Press, 2017.

Schmidt-Leukel, Perry. *Religious Pluralism and Interreligious Theology: The Gifford Lectures-An Extended Edition*. Maryknoll: Orbis, 2017.

Schmidt-Leukel, Perry. "A Fractal Interpretation of Religious Diversity: An Overview." In *New Paths for Interreligious Theology: Perry Schmidt-Leukel's Fractal Interpretation of Religious Diversity*, edited by Alan Race and Paul Knitter, 3–24. Maryknoll: Orbis. 2019.

Senge, Peter M. *The Fifth Discipline: The Art and Practice of the Learning Organization*. Rev. edn. New York: Currency/Doubleday, 2006 (orig., 1990).

Sesno, Frank. *Ask More: The Power of Questions to Open Doors, Uncover Solutions, and Spark Change*. New York: Amacom, 2017.

Shirley, Jensen H. "Congregation Activism: Faith-based Leadership." *NAAAS & Affiliates Conference Monographs* (2010): 1540–75.

Smith, Wilfred Cantwell. *Patterns of Faith Around the World*. Oxford: Oneworld Publications, 1962.

Springhart, Heike. *Der verwundbare Mensch: Sterben, Tod und Endlichkeit im Horizont einer realistischen Anthropologie*. Tübingen: Mohr Siebeck, 2016.

Springhart, Heike, and Günter Thomas, eds. *Exploring Vulnerability*. Göttingen: Vandenhoeck & Ruprecht, 2017.

Stoeckl, Kristina, and Dmitry Uzlaner. "Four Genealogies of Postsecularity." In *Routledge Handbook of Postsecularity*, edited by Justin Beaumont, 269–79. London and New York: Routledge, 2018.

Public Religion Research Institute. "Summer Unrest over Racial Injustice Moves the Country, But Not Republicans or White Evangelicals," PRRI Staff, August 2020: https://www.prri.org/research/racial-justice-2020-george-floyd/ (last accessed December 14, 2021).

Swidler, Leonard. "The History of Inter-Religious Dialogue." In *The Wiley-Blackwell Companion to Inter-Religious Dialogue*, edited by Catherine Cornille, 3–19. Oxford: Wiley-Blackwell, 2013.

Swidler, Leonard. "More Than Dialogue: Deep-Dialogue, Critical-Thinking, Competitive-Cooperation." *World Journal of Islamic History and Civilization* 3, no. 1 (2013): 36–41.

Taylor, Charles. *A Secular Age*. Cambridge: Harvard University, 2007.

Thatamanil, John J. *Circling the Elephant: A Comparative Theology of Religious Diversity.* New York: Fordham University Press, 2020.

Thiessen, Joel, and Sarah Wilkins-LaFlamme. *None of the Above: Non-religious Identity in the US and Canada.* New York: New York University Press, 2020.

Tracy, David. *Dialogue with the Other: The Inter-religious Dialogue.* Louvain and Grand Rapids: Peeters Press and W. B. Eerdmans, 1991.

Urbano, Ryan C. "Levinas and Interfaith Dialogue." *The Heythrop Journal* 53, no. 1 (2012): 148–61.

Waters, Mark. "Civic Engagement as an Avenue to Interreligious Cooperation in Religiously Diverse Communities." *Journal of Ecumenical Studies* 53, no. 3 (Summer 2018): 407–20.

Welch, Sharon. "Return to Laughter." In *The Religious*, edited by John D. Caputo, 301–17. Oxford: Blackwell, 2002.

Whitehead, Alfred North. *Religion in the Making.* New York: Fordham University Press, 1996.

Zakour, Michael J., and David F. Gillespie. *Community Disaster Vulnerability: Theory, Research, and Practice.* New York: Springer, 2013.

Zaretsky, Eli, and Hartmut Rosa. "The Crisis of Dynamic Stabilization and the Sociology of Resonance: An Interview with Hartmut Rosa," January 18, 2017: https://publicseminar.org/2017/01/the-crisis-of-dynamic-stabilization-and-the-sociology-of-resonance/ (last accessed December 14, 2021).

Zenger, Jack, and Joseph Folkman. "Research: Women are Better Leaders During a Crisis," *HBR* online: https://hbr.org/2020/12/research-women-are-better-leaders-during-a-crisis (last accessed July 13, 2021).

Index

Page numbers followed with "n" refer to endnotes.

acceleration
   social 60–6, 75–6, 145, 161
   technological 60–6, 75–6
agunah 171
analogical apperception 35
anti-Black racism 68
anti-Semitism 20, 27, 70, 95–6
appreciative knowledge 38, 91
Arinze, Francis Cardinal 11
awareness 37–9, 53–5, 58, 63, 66, 76, 80, 106, 144, 148–9, 159–61
   self- 81, 90, 92, 105

Baha'i faith 172–4
Barber, William 27
Barrows, John Henry 26
Bauman, Zygmunt 55, 64
beauty 124
belief 21, 98–9
Bennis, Warren 82, 84
Berger, Peter 101, 105
   pluralism 104
   postsecularism 57–9
Bollywood films 192, 196–8
boundary fetishism 52, 53
Butler, Judith 137

Cabbot, Alan 187–8
Certeau, Michel de 10
Chandler, David 125
chaplain 177–8
Children of Zion Congregation 164–6
Christendom 26
Christianity 26, 136
Christian New Testament 136
clash-and-conflict model 50–2
Cold War 26–8, 50–1
commitment 33–4, 58, 60, 66, 76
   religious 33–4, 58, 60, 66, 76
common good 37–8

communication 62
   innovations 65
   in leadership 87, 90
community violence 191–4
complex resilience 42, 130–2, 144
complex subjectivity 115
complex systems 125, 128
confession 106
conflict 89
   model 52, 53
congregations 88
consumer capitalism 59–60
contemporary leadership 80–1
contingent vulnerabilities 135
Cornille, Catherine 31–6, 39–41, 89
Covid-19 pandemic, spiritual care and crisis response of 162, 175–7
creative agility 79
creative/creatural vulnerability 85, 132–3, 135, 140, 145
Culp, Kristine 131
cultural commitment 66
cultural difference 63, 76
cultural globalization 49–53, 55, 60
cultural homogenization model 51–3
cultural mixing 52, 53

de-institutionalization 101
diversity 3–4, 9, 13, 22–3, 25, 37–9, 42, 47, 55, 69, 72, 90, 98, 109, 120–1, 130, 136, 151, 183, 187, 191, 194
Drucker, Peter 81, 83
Durkheim, Emile 110–13, 135
Dweck, Carol 86

Eck, Diana 20–2, 26, 28, 29, 37, 73
education 214 n.91
   and interreligious leadership 99
   religion and 96–8
   religious 26–9, 33

effective leadership 91
email 65
emotional intelligence 81
empathy
    empathic imagination 5, 32, 34–5, 41–2, 83, 88, 89, 124, 132, 158
    naïve 35
essentialism 119, 125
exclusivism 122, 123. *See also* inclusivism

faith traditions 178
Farmington, Peter 173–4
feminist model of interreligious dialog 31
The Fifth Discipline (Senge) 81–2
forced migration 163, 172
Fox, Sarah 199–200
fractal 20, 32, 72, 117, 120–2, 124–6, 204 n.2
    of religious diversity 120–1, 204 n.2
    supremacy 13, 69, 117, 121, 122, 128, 131, 140, 145
fragilization of religious belief 54, 63
Francis, Pope 19, 60–1
Freud, Sigmund 110–13, 115
fundamentalism 55, 57, 178, 188–90
furiously religious 57
Futch Ehrlich, Valerie A. 85

Galindo, Israel 88
Ganz, Marshall 39
Gardenbrain model 148
Gardner, Howard 91
gender
    bias 29–30, 170
    discrimination 169
generosity 35–6
Gilbert, Rabbi Arthur 27
Gilson, Erinn 131
globalization 48, 64–75, 106, 161
    cultural 49–55, 60
    recent history of 52
Goethe, Johann Wolfgang von 23
Goleman, Daniel 81, 83
Greenleaf, Robert 88

Hamelink, Cees 52
Hanauer, Nick 147–8
Harris, Melanie L. 59

Hasidic Judaism 48–9
hate crimes 70, 194
Heifetz, Ronald 82, 88
heresy 58–9
heretical imperative 58
Herskovitz, Yaakov 118
Hick, John 21
Hill Fletcher, Jeannine 29–31, 33, 36, 39–41, 106
Hindu chauvinism 71, 197
Hindus 97, 136, 186
history 10
homogenization model 51–3
hospital chaplaincy 180–1
hospitality 35–6
Howe, Julia Ward 30
humility 32–4, 36, 89–90
    epistemic 33
Huntington, Samuel, clash-and-conflict model of 50–1
Husserl's analogical apperception 35
hybridization model 52–3

identities 54, 58, 59, 90, 91
    cultural 55, 63, 66
    and difference 121, 125, 129
    religious 20, 22, 29, 37, 39, 41, 42, 46, 48, 50, 53, 55, 56, 60, 63, 66, 72, 117, 121
    of systems 128–9
Illuminate 183–4
inclusivism 122, 123
incommensurability 119, 125
inspiration 83
intentionality 85, 107, 144, 146–7, 159
    interreligious resilience 146–7
interfaith 3, 37–41, 90, 91
intermarriage 94, 178, 185–8
interreligious 3
interreligious conflict in the Middle East 199–201
interreligious congregational merger 162, 164–6
interreligious context, case study
    hospital chaplaincy in 180–1
    lay-pastoral relations in 153–6
    marginalization, abuse, and violence against women in 168–71
    St. Johns 166–8

interreligious empathy (empathic imagination) 34–5
interreligious engagement 11, 41, 53, 67, 77, 78, 99, 105, 117
  Activist model 30–1
  core opportunities and benefits of 103–6
  history of 25–9
  models of 29–40
  Parliament model 29–31
  Storytelling model 31, 106
  through head, hands, and heart 121–4
interreligious leadership 1–2, 7, 11, 29, 43, 67, 77–8, 82, 83, 89–92, 107, 119, 121, 123, 125, 126, 137, 144, 191. See also religious leadership
  challenges of, and to 100–3
  and dialog 92–103
  dialog and initiatives 182–4
  education and 99
  intermarriage and 185–8
interreligious resilience 1–2, 6, 20, 22, 24–5, 41–2, 71, 77, 78, 81, 105, 107, 116, 117, 120, 121, 126, 128–31, 133, 140, 144
  awareness 144, 148–9
  intentionality 144, 146–7
  trust 144, 147–8
  vulnerability 144–6
Interreligious Women's Advocacy (IWA) 170–1
intra-Christian marriage 187
intrareligious 3
  stereotyping 189–90
Islamophobic 27, 70
Israeli-Palestinian conflict 106, 192, 199–201
IWA. See Interreligious Women's Advocacy (IWA)

Jennings, Willie James 118, 119
Jewish
  Americans 95–6
  Diaspora 199
  education 214 n.91
  intermarriage 185–8
  leadership 92–3
Joiner, Bill 79

Jones, Jeffrey 88
Jones, Robert 70
Josephs, Stephen 79
Judaism 6, 48–9, 95–6, 122, 136, 171, 185

Kaplan, Mordecai 48
Knitter, Paul 8–9, 38, 89, 103
knowledge 81–2, 86, 90, 105
  of interfaith leadership 37–41
  about religion 98
Kotter, John 83

Laurie, Donald 82
lay-pastoral relations 153–6
leadership 29, 43, 67, 76
  adapting and growing from change 84–7
  agility 79, 87
  challenges of 84, 88
  communication in 87, 90
  contemporary approaches to 80–1
  contextualizing and meaning making 82–3
  crucibles of 84
  effective 91
  emotional intelligence 81
  functions 88
  heroic levels 79, 80
  humility 89–90
  inspiring and motivating 83–4
  interreligious (see interreligious leadership)
  interreligious dialog and 96, 98–100, 103, 105
  Jewish 92–3
  knowledge 81–2, 86
  learning 81–2, 86
  and management 83
  modeling values 88
  networked 85
  orientations 85
  post-heroic level 79–80
  religious 77–8, 82, 87–8
    core issues and challenges 93–100
  responsibility 86
  skills 78–80, 82, 85, 89
  strategic direction 87
  systems thinking 81, 87, 96
  traditional approaches to 78–80

vulnerability in 158
   women 85
Lear, Jonathan 145
learning 81–2, 86
Levinas, Emmanuel 11
liberal pluralism 195–6
liquidity 64, 75
Liu, Eric 147–8
Long, Charles 136

McDonalidization 51
Machinebrain model 148
management 83
Marx, Karl 110–13, 115
Matisyahu musical aesthetic 49–50, 52, 55, 57, 58
meaning making, leadership 82–3
Mendes-Flohr, Paul 23
Miller, Matthew Paul 48–9
modernity/modernization 49, 51–60, 75
moral value 114
moral vulnerability 137
motivation 83
multireligious 3
musical genres 49–50, 52
Muslims 17, 97–8, 102, 136, 189
   in historical settings 197
   representation in Bollywood 192, 196–8

naïve empathy 35
national supremacy 70
networked leadership 85
Newlon, Brendan, P. 85, 211n17
nirvana 136, 137
North American nones 182–3

Occidentalism 51
open systems 125, 128
Orientalism 51
"Other" 11, 178
   religious and 188–9
   representation of Muslims in Bollywood 196–8

Padmaavat 197
Panikkar, Raimon 11–12, 99, 116, 124, 138, 139
Parliament of Religions in 1893 27, 29, 30
partisan sectarian seduction 145

Patel, Eboo 28, 44–6, 69, 92
   interfaith 37–41, 90, 91, 206 n.56
persecution 163, 172–4
Pieterse, Jan Nederveen 50–4
Pinn, Anthony 114–16, 135
pluralism 20–4, 31, 37, 38, 40, 42, 54, 55, 60, 90, 104, 122–3, 130
   gendered 30
   liberal 195–6
polarization 81, 128, 178, 190
   elite 68
   political 67–70, 72, 76–7, 96, 145
political sectarianism 67–70, 72–3, 76, 96, 128
postmodernism 10, 55, 64, 76, 77
postsecularism 47, 49, 50, 53–60, 76
power and hierarchy 105

qualities of interfaith leadership 37–41

Rabbinic Judaism 48
racial supremacy 20, 70
racism 115
rapidification 61
Reconstructionism 48–9
Reform Jews 186, 189–90
refugees 163, 172–4
reggae 48–50
relativism 188–90
religion 20–2, 25–34, 36, 47–9, 70, 76, 103–6
   classic functionalist and contemporary phenomenological theories 109–16
   complex subjectivity 115
   creatural and contingent vulnerabilities 135
   cultural systems 135
   different languages 117–18
   Durkheim's theory of 110–13
   and education 96–8
   Freud's theory of 110–13, 115
   knowledge about 98
   Marx's theory of 110–13, 115
   modernity and 56
   Pinn's view of 114–16
   postsecular 55–8, 60
   as quality of experience 135
   resilience and vulnerability theory of 133–40

role in social activism   96
   and science   137
   social hostilities in   95
   theology of   122
   transcendent ideals in   135–6, 139
   and treatment of women   170–1
   violence and   95–6
   Welch's view of   113–16
religious affiliation   178, 182
religious experience   113, 115, 116, 117
religious institutions   93–4, 100–1
religious leadership   77–8, 82, 87–8
   core issues and challenges   93–100
religious others   188–9. See also Muslims
   historical and cinematic representation of   196–8
religious traditions   20–3, 26, 30–4, 36, 50, 58, 72, 91, 117, 119–20, 124, 136, 137
resilience   7, 81, 96, 112, 115, 124–30, 135
   complex   42, 130–2
   defined   1
   interreligious   6, 20, 22, 24–5, 41–2, 71, 77, 78, 81, 105, 107, 116–17, 120–1, 126, 128–31, 133, 140, 144
      awareness   144, 148–9
      intentionality   144, 146–7
      trust   144, 147–8
      vulnerability   144–6
   of religion   133–40
   simple   42, 130
   and vulnerability   126–9
resilient leadership   160, 161
resilient systems   127, 128
responsibility   11
Ritzer, George   51
Rosa, Hartmut   61, 66

sacred   138–9
St. Johns   166–8
salvation   136
Schewel, Benjamin   56, 58
Schmidt-Leukel, Perry   13, 72, 120
Schuster, Jane   173–4
Second World War   26, 28
sectarianism   190
   political   67–70, 72–3, 76, 96, 128
secular   53
secularism/secularization   53, 55–7, 76, 178

self-awareness   81, 90, 92, 105
self-knowledge   92
Senge, Peter
   The Fifth Discipline   81–2
   leadership   83
sexism   170
simple resilience   42, 130. See also complex resilience
skills of interfaith leadership   37–41
Small, John   183–4
Smith, Brittany   153–61
social acceleration   60–6, 75–6, 145, 161
social action   103
social change   63–6
socialization   33
social media   68
Sophocles's Antigone   137
spiritual humility   32–3
Stanton, Elizabeth Cady   30
Stoeckl, Kristina   54
subtractionist narrative   56
supremacy   20–2, 24, 32, 67, 70–3, 107, 117, 120–2, 126, 128, 129
   fractal   13, 69, 117, 121, 122, 128, 131, 140, 145
Swidler, Leonard   27, 121–4
systems   118, 125–30, 132, 133, 144
   complex and open   125, 128
   concept of   125
   identity of   128–9
   interreligious resilience   128
   mindset   126, 129
   resilient   127, 128
   thinking   78, 81, 85, 87, 96, 124–6, 128, 129
   vulnerable   127–8

Taylor, Charles   54
team learning   82
technological acceleration   60–6, 75–6
technological changes   62, 63
technological innovation   62, 65, 66
terrorism   96, 145, 196
Thatamanil, John   21, 119, 120
Theoharris, Liz   27
theology   5
Thomas, Robert   82, 84
tolerance   23–4
Tracy, David   105
traditional leadership   78–80

transcendent ideals   135–6, 139
translation   118–19
transportation innovations   65
transport technologies   62
transsecular theories   58
trust   20, 85, 104, 107, 133, 144, 147–8, 159, 160
truth   10, 11, 21, 23, 24, 33, 36, 72, 114, 122–4, 195

Unitarian Universalism   4
United States
   anti-Semitism in   95–6
   hate crimes   70
   intermarriage   186
   interreligious engagement, history of   25–9
   study of religion   28–9
   terrorism attacks in   96
   white evangelical Christians   70–1
   xenophobic   70–1
unitive pluralism   9
Urbano, Ryan   11
Uzlaner, Dmitry   54

velocity of communication   62
violence   21, 95, 190–1
   community   191–4
   and conflict   106
   against women   163, 168–71
VITA (Vulnerability with Intentionality, Trust, and Awareness)   1, 24, 113, 133, 143–50, 152, 178
   in interreligious leadership   156–61

vulnerability   7, 20, 24, 41, 42, 60, 66, 75, 81, 96, 106, 112, 113, 115, 120, 124–34, 144–6, 157–8. *See also* resilience
   complex resilience   131, 132
   contingent   135
   creative/creatural   85, 132–3, 135, 140, 145
   defined   126, 131
   dimensions   132
   moral   137
   of religion   133–40
   resilience and   126–9
   and science   137
   of systems   127–8

WCRP. *See* World Conference of Religions for Peace (WCRP)
Welch, Sharon   7, 113–16, 135
Westernization   54
white evangelical Christianity   68, 70–1
Whitehead, Alfred North   7–8, 135
women
   abuse   169–71
   economic marginalization   170
   violence against   163, 168–71
   World Health Organization report on   168–9
World Conference of Religions for Peace (WCRP)   26
Wray, Christopher   70

xenophobic   70, 71

www.ingramcontent.com/pod-product-compliance
Lightning Source LLC
Chambersburg PA
CBHW062215300426
44115CB00012BA/2079